Jack Warner

Bertolt Brecht

Joe and Mia May

Fritzi Massary

Ernst Lubitsch

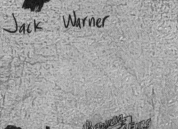

Villa Aurora

Warner Bros. Theatre

Unitarian Church

European Film Fund

Paul Kohner Agency on Sunset Blvd.

Marta and Lion
Feuchtwanger

William Dieterle

Max Reinhardt

Nelly and Heinrich Mann

The Manns as
Public Intellectuals

Thought and Action
Refugees, Supporters, and the New Left

Film Exile in Hollywood

Beginnings of a New Music

Leisure Under Palm Trees

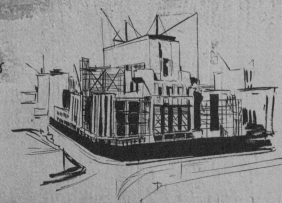

L.A's Literary Radiance

A City in Transition

Thomas Mann's Los Angeles

Stories from Exile 1940–1952

Thomas Mann's Los Angeles

Stories from Exile 1940–1952

EDITED BY **Nikolai Blaumer** · **Benno Herz**

ILLUSTRATIONS BY **Jon Stich**

ANGEL CITY PRESS

Katia and Thomas Mann with grandchildren Frido and Toni Mann in Pacific Palisades, 1945

CONTENTS

AUTHORS' NOTES: **9**

PREFACE: **10**

INTRODUCTION: **18**

PART 1: THE MANNS AS PUBLIC INTELLECTUALS 23
SHRINE AUDITORIUM · *Benno Herz* **28** | NBC STUDIOS · *Nikolai Blaumer* **30**
ELEANOR ROOSEVELT · *Morten Hoi Jensen* **32** | UCLA ROYCE HALL · *Kalani Michell* **34**
ERIKA MANN · *Irmela von der Lühe* **38** | GOLO MANN · *Friederike von Schwerin-High* **40**
UNITARIAN CHURCH · *Heinrich Detering* **42**
HOLLYWOOD MASONIC TEMPLE · *Nikolai Blaumer* **46**
HOLLYWOOD FAIRFAX TEMPLE · *Nikolai Blaumer* **48** | FLORENCE HOMOLKA · *Kaltërina Latifi* **50**

PART 2: THOUGHT AND ACTION: REFUGEES, SUPPORTERS, AND THE NEW LEFT 53
EUROPEAN FILM FUND · *Martin Sauter* **58** | BRUNO & LIESL FRANK · *Friedhelm Marx* **60**
CHARLOTTE DIETERLE · *Diane Sippl* **62** | SALKA VIERTEL · *Donna Rifkind* **64**
MAX HORKHEIMER · *David Jenemann* **66** | LUDWIG MARCUSE · *Nikolai Blaumer* **68**
BERTOLT BRECHT · *Steven Lavine* **70** | KONRAD KELLEN · *Helmut Anheier* **72**

PART 3: FILM IN EXILE IN HOLLYWOOD 75
CARL LAEMMLE · *Jaimey Fisher* **80** | ERNST LUBITSCH · *Kai Sina* **82**
WILLIAM DIETERLE · *Noah Isenberg* **84** | JACK WARNER · *David Wallace* **86**
MAX REINHARDT · *Nikolai Blaumer* **88** | FRITZI MASSARY · *Verena Mund* **90**
FOX VILLAGE THEATRE · *Benno Herz* **92**
WARNER BROS. HOLLYWOOD THEATRE · *Benno Herz* **94**
BLUE DANUBE RESTAURANT · *Jan-Christopher Horak* **96**

PART 4: LOS ANGELES'S LITERARY RADIANCE 99

NELLY & HEINRICH MANN · *Michaela Ullmann* **106** | LION FEUCHTWANGER · *Claudia Gordon* **108**
MARTA FEUCHTWANGER · *Friedel Schmoranzer* **110** | VICKI BAUM · *Alexis Landau* **112**
ALFRED DÖBLIN · *Stefan Keppler-Tasaki* **114** | FRANZ WERFEL · *Adrian Daub* **116**
ALFRED NEUMANN · *Tobias Boes* **118** | LUDWIG HARDT · *Sylvia Asmus* **120**
UPTON SINCLAIR · *Hans Rudolf Vaget* **122** | ALDOUS HUXLEY · *Andreas Platthaus* **124**
SUSAN SONTAG · *David Kim* **126** | CHRISTOPHER ISHERWOOD · *Stefan Schneider* **128**

PART 5: THE BEGINNINGS OF A NEW MUSIC 131

THEODOR W. ADORNO · *Alex Ross* **136** | ARNOLD SCHOENBERG · *Jeff High & Glen Gray* **138**
IGOR STRAVINSKY · *David Kaplan* **140** | HANNS EISLER · *Nikolai Blaumer* **142**
ALMA MAHLER-WERFEL · *Lily Hirsch* **144** | ERNST TOCH · *Lawrence Weschler* **146**
BRUNO WALTER · *William Kinderman* **150** | OTTO KLEMPERER · *Nikolai Blaumer* **152**

PART 6: LEISURE UNDER THE PALM TREES 155

THOMAS MANN & NIKO · *Rembert Hüser* **158**
THOMAS MANN ON THE BEACH · *Benno Herz* **160** | THE HOLLYWOOD BOWL · *Benno Herz* **162**
DOWNTOWN THEATER DISTRICT · *Anthony Caldwell* **164**
THE BROWN DERBY · *Benno Herz* **166** | HOTEL MIRAMAR · *Nikolai Blaumer* **168**
MAX'S SWISS CHALET · *Nikolai Blaumer* **170**

PART 7: A CITY IN TRANSITION 173

LOS ANGELES FREEWAYS · *Josh Widera* **178** | HOUSING CRISIS · *Nikolai Blaumer* **180**
RICHARD NEUTRA · *Heike Mertens* **182** | J.R. DAVIDSON · *Lilian Pfaff* **186**
UNION STATION · *Nikolai Blaumer* **188** | THE AIRPORTS OF LOS ANGELES · *Benno Herz* **190**

ABOUT THE AUTHORS: **194**   BIBLIOGRAPHY: **200**
ABOUT THE CONTRIBUTORS: **195**   IMAGE CREDITS: **207**

AUTHORS' NOTES

Time and again, people come to the Thomas Mann House and tell us stories about Thomas Mann, his family, and the exile community in Los Angeles. They tell us where someone met Mann for schnitzel or ice cream, where they would think about the political dilemmas of the day. They speak of that famous house, a gathering spot for many a filmmaker, author, and intellectual. And they tell us of the beaches and hotels where those irreverent, radical thinkers used to lay about, relax, and dream in the sun.

In speaking with our many interested guests and visitors, as well as with the Fellows of the Thomas Mann House, we found ourselves immersed in these places and stories on a daily basis. We sought a way to materialize the where and who of the exile community and make their stories accessible to more than just those visiting the Thomas Mann House. *Thomas Mann's Los Angeles* reconsiders the map of Los Angeles to accommodate these stories from the past and provide new insights into this highly mediated city.

Back in March 2020, at the start of the COVID-19 pandemic, we had been looking for new ways to work with all the stories we had heard about the exiles on the Pacific coast. We launched a new series on our social media channels with the hashtag #MannsLA. With each new place we explored, ten more stories would emerge. The series became a class, taught in collaboration with the Digital Humanities program at UCLA, highlighting the exciting possibilities of new platforms that could help visualize the exiles' stories and make them available in new ways. At some point, we realized that this series deserved a larger scope, which eventually led to this book.

We are very grateful to every contributor to this book. The impetus for this work stems from, and would have not been possible without, the groundbreaking research on German exiles in California and on the Mann family by scholars and authors including Hans Rudolf Vaget, Ehrhard Bahr, Anthony Heilbut, Irmela von der Lühe, Heinrich Detering, Alex Ross, Tobias Boes, Tilmann Lahme, Lilian Pfaff, Donna Rifkind, David Jenemann, Lawrence Weschler, and Heinrich Wefing, among others. The essays in this book rely on and draw inspiration from their seminal work. A bibliography, including source material and further reading, appears at the back of the book.

We thank Villa Aurora and Thomas Mann House for supporting this publication, especially Markus Klimmer, Heike Catherina Mertens, and Steven Lavine. Many thanks to the archives and archivists who assist us in our work and have allowed us to include many of the images herein: Michaela Ullmann and the USC Special Collections Library, Rolf Bolt and the Thomas Mann Archives at ETH Zürich, Sylvia Asmus and the German Exile Archive 1933–1945 at the German National Library, Tanja Fengler-Veit and the Deutsches Literaturarchiv Marbach, and the Literaturarchiv Monacensia at Hildebrandhaus. Thanks also to Lena Trüper and Julia Welter for their support with acquiring image rights, and to Alaina Dexter for editing the bibliography.

May the legacy of Thomas Mann, the Angeleno, not be forgotten!

—N.B., B.H.

THOMAS MANN HOUSE

PREFACE
The Mann Family and Their Path to California
Nikolai Blaumer

Thomas Mann during his "German Speech," Beethovensaal Berlin, 1930

Goethe in Hollywood," read the headline in the *New Yorker* in December 1941, shortly after the German writer and émigré Thomas Mann had settled with his family in California. In no fewer than twenty-four pages, journalist Janet Flanner painted a picture of a literary grandmaster clinging to the German lifestyle on the Pacific coast: "His face has the ligneous angles of a museum woodcut. Beneath his properly tailored tweeds, he moves with the correct, erect, salon stiffness of an older Teutonic generation." Since then, the notion of the alienated, homesick exile has dominated the memory of Mann's life in America for decades.

But that is not the full story. In Los Angeles, Mann captivated thousands of readers and listeners. He built friendships with American writers, politicians, and formative figures in Hollywood. He found a spiritual home with the Unitarian Church of Los Angeles and fostered connections with the Jewish community in the Fairfax district. In his spare time, his days were filled with the pleasures of everyday life in Los Angeles—parks, beaches, and restaurants that he frequented and loved, many of which are still enjoyed today.

How did Mann come to settle in Los Angeles? Why did the successful, nearly sixty-year-old writer turn his back on his homeland in the early 1930s? What hopes and expectations guided him? What paths did he take to reach the West Coast? And what public role did the author play in his host country, where he would eventually become a citizen?

When Mann's wife, Katia, spoke of her forced exile shortly before her death in Switzerland, her outrage had not abated. She complained to the publicist Inge Jens: "We have been thrown out! And that after an honorable life!" In Germany, when Mann's career was on the rise, he would not have guessed he would soon be facing exile. Yet, in the years before the Nazis seized power, he became one of Hitler's most important public opponents. In his widely acclaimed speech "An Appeal to Reason," he provoked his German audience with the words: "Is there any deep stratum of the German soul where all that fanaticism, that bacchantic frenzy, that orgiastic denial of reason and human dignity is really at home?" Mann made it unmistakably clear that not only were political interests and convictions at stake in confronting the Fascists, but also the question of the essential nature of Germany and its future. Amid the ideological turmoil of the Weimar Republic, he spoke out loudly against inhuman barbarism and declared his support for democracy."

Mann's political engagement led to opposition and slander from nationalist (*völkisch*) forces. Already in 1927, the police department of his hometown, Munich, had begun to compile a carefully maintained dossier on the writer. In addition to press reports, authorities documented his support for Social Democratic workers and references to his novel *The Magic Mountain*, which officials saw as evidence of Mann's pro-Jewish sentiments. These documents played a significant role in his later expatriation.

Katia Mann, née Pringsheim, had another reason for living in exile. She had been born into a respectable, assimilated Jewish family. Even though she was baptized a Christian, the institutionalized anti-Semitism that manifested itself in occupational bans and the boycott of Jewish businesses soon after the Nazis came to power posed an existential threat to her and her family.

Thus, Thomas and Katia Mann left their home country just two weeks after Hitler's appointment as Reich Chancellor. The immediate trigger had been a lecture tour organized for the fiftieth anniversary of the death of the composer Richard Wagner, for which the couple had traveled to Amsterdam. Mann, a self-confessed Wagnerian, had already given the lecture a few days earlier at Munich University. Following the lecture, which contained both tributes and critical passages, conservative representatives from music and the arts published a protest letter accusing him of denigrating Wagner.

Only days later, an official process was set in motion that resulted in a "protective preventive custody" (*Schutzhaftbefehl*) against Mann in July 1933. This was not something to be trifled with and marked the beginning of what Mann would call his "national excommunication." If he had reentered Germany, he could have been incarcerated and sent to a concentration camp. The way back was blocked not only for Thomas and Katia but also for their son Klaus and for Thomas's brother Heinrich. Like Thomas, Heinrich was a widely read author in Germany whose books ended up on Nazi "black lists" and were publicly burned in May 1933.

Through the mediation of a writer friend, René Schickele, the Mann family rented a house on the French Mediterranean coast, where Katia celebrated her fiftieth birthday. Their son Golo was the last to arrive from Germany. He had seen to the liquidation of the parental home and brought Thomas and Katia's savings to safety. In Berlin, he had avoided detection while witnessing the burning of the books of his uncle Heinrich and his brother Klaus.

The fishing village of Sanary-sur-Mer in France had become a center of the German intellectual elite in the early 1930s, a "capital of German literature," as the philosopher Ludwig Marcuse called it. Schickele, the historian Wilhelm Herzog, and others had foreseen the rise of National Socialism early on and had settled there before the seizure of power. They were followed by a who's who of German literature: Marcuse, Franz Werfel, Lion Feuchtwanger, Bruno Frank, Stefan Zweig, and Alfred Neumann, as well as the playwright Bertolt Brecht. Many of these figures would meet again years later in exile on the American West Coast.

Writing from France, Mann noted in his diary on May 23, 1933: "The glorious weather, which I am heartily prepared to admire in spite of much misery, continues." Despite the comfortable conditions of his early exile, he experienced a deep crisis. His notes contained numerous entries such as "woke up in a state of increasing agitation and despondency," "nausea and depression," "profound melancholia," or "There are moments when I fear that my nerves will give away."

Thomas Mann in Sanary-sur-Mer

Though today Mann is known for his passionate struggle against Hitler's Germany, at the time he was initially hesitant to enter into a public confrontation with the regime. Mann was torn between conflicting forces. On the one side, above all, were his children Klaus and Erika, as well as his brother Heinrich. In the year of the National Socialist takeover, they were already working on the creation of an opposition that sought to influence from exile the increasingly homogenized Germany. On the other were the expectations of his Jewish publisher in Berlin, Gottfried Bermann Fischer, who appealed to the writer's responsibility to his homeland and wanted to keep the door open for Mann to publish in his native country.

While Mann's novel *The Tales of Jacob* (*Die Geschichten Jaakobs*) was indeed published in Germany in October 1933, Thomas and Katia decided to move to Küsnacht, in Switzerland, with their two youngest children, Elisabeth and Michael. Reviews of the novel in the Nazi press were scathing, but the first ten thousand copies sold out in just one week. Three subsequent editions continued to sell out at breakneck speed. While the Mann family settled down on Lake Zurich over the next few years, Mann's works continued to be published in Germany until Fischer was forced to immigrate to Vienna.

In May 1934, Thomas and Katia traveled across the Atlantic for the first time for the publication of the American edition of *The Tales of Jacob*. They traveled first class and stayed on the twenty-fourth floor of the posh Savoy-Plaza Hotel in New York. Mann was impressed by the view of the city from the hotel elevator, which ascended so quickly he could feel the pressure in his ears.

Parties were organized for the Manns, including one attended by Mayor Fiorello La Guardia. At Yale, Mann gave a lecture on Goethe. Though flattered by the warm welcome, the Nobel laureate found his struggle with the English language degrading. For example, in publicly praising his American publisher, Alfred Knopf, for his creativity, he said, "He is not only a publisher, he is a creature too." Despite these minor misfortunes, this first trip to America was a great success. The seeds were sown, and after two weeks, the Manns returned to Europe in high spirits.

At the invitation of Harvard University, the Manns returned to the United States in June 1935. Before an audience of six thousand, Mann received an honorary doctorate along with Albert Einstein. It would more than compensate for the revocation of his honorary doctorate by the University of Bonn the following year. The highlight of the trip, however, was dinner at the White House, where the Manns met President Franklin Delano Roosevelt and his wife, Eleanor, for the first time—a defining experience that shaped Mann's time in American exile personally as well as politically.

Roosevelt and his New Deal policies played a central role in Mann's novel *Joseph the Provider*, and for Mann, Roosevelt stood as a kind of messianic counterfigure to the barbarian leader in his homeland. In a speech for Roosevelt's fourth presidential campaign, later published in the German-language magazine *Aufbau*, the author called him a man as clever as serpents and as without falsehood as doves. "Sophisticated and simple as genius; enlightened with intuitive knowledge of the necessity of the times, the will of the world spirit."

Faced with harrowing news of persecution and concentration camps in Germany, Mann broke several years of political silence in February 1936. In an open letter to the *Neue Zürcher Zeitung*, he condemned German anti-Semitism, making clear that it is an attack on the moral foundations of Western civilization: "it is the attempt (symbolized in the withdrawal from the League of Nations) to shake off the ties of civilization, and this is threatening to create a ruinous alienation between Goethe's country and the rest of the world." The statement, Mann noted, was a liberation with which he finally saved his own soul.

In response, Mann's German citizenship was revoked. Geographically and intellectually, he was now cut off from his homeland. But this only encouraged him to throw himself into the fight against Nazism. In the spring of 1938, he was persuaded to embark on a two-month North American lecture tour titled "The Coming Victory of Democracy," which took him to Chicago, Toronto, Washington, D.C., Kansas City, and Los Angeles.

Harvard awards honorary degrees to twelve men on June 12, 1935.
Among them in the front row are Albert Einstein, center, and Thomas Mann, far right.

Within a few months, a writer who had been careful and discreet once again became a public intellectual who made the fight against National Socialism his most important task. In his lectures, Mann espoused a concept of democracy marked by hope and humanity and contrasted it with the Fascism of his native Germany: "Dictators are lordly creatures, they despise the masses, and while they make themselves the mouthpiece of vulgar opinion, they let the masses understand what seems incomprehensible and unjustified—namely, that they have nothing but contempt for them."

Even though Mann publicly left little doubt about the need to crush Fascism, he distrusted his own attitude. In *Esquire* magazine, he self-critically questioned the possible traits he shared with Hitler. Manns called him "A brother—a rather unpleasant and mortifying brother" and described the relationship as "painful to a degree." He made fun of himself for his role as an "itinerant preacher of democracy." But the situation in Germany was growing increasingly hopeless, and his political commitment was carried by a wave of approval and overwhelming public interest, which benefited him both professionally and financially.

The 1938 tour would mark Thomas, Katia, and Erika's first visit to Los Angeles. Mann spoke on April 1 at the Shrine Auditorium—the "colossal amphitheater," in his words—right next to the campus of the University of Southern California. An audience of several thousand filled the hall. Mann's speech was introduced by author and friend from Munich Bruno Frank and none other than the American Nobel laureate Sinclair Lewis.

Princeton University soon made Mann a generous offer of a position as "lecturer in the humanities"—with only six lectures a year and the salary of a full professor. Mann wrote to his friend and patron Agnes E. Meyer, wife of Eugene Meyer, the *Washington Post* publisher, whom he had met the previous year. He told her he was torn between Princeton on the one hand and life on the Pacific on the other: "it may sound a little strange if I add that the promises made to us about California have been fulfilled beyond our expectations, and that the idea of settling here has crept into our thoughts a little during these weeks."

In view of the so-called *Anschluss* of Austria to the National Socialist German Reich, even Switzerland was no longer a safe place to live, and the offer from Princeton became one that Mann could not refuse. The Manns therefore decided to move to New Jersey. At Princeton, Mann spoke about Goethe's *Faust*, Wagner's Ring Cycle,

Comic featuring Erika Mann, 1941

Sigmund Freud, and his own literary work. These two years were also marked by further extensive political lecture tours, which took Mann from Ottawa, Canada, to Houston, Texas.

Meanwhile, the family was celebrated by the American press. *Life* magazine published a multifaceted feature in 1939, richly illustrated with photographs of the smoking intellectual and his relatives; even his medals, walking sticks, and slippers were carefully portrayed. *Vogue* reported on the talents of the Manns and how they read and recited to each other in their New Jersey home. Mann even got excited, the magazine wrote, when the Princeton versus Yale football game was on!

After three semesters, Mann grew tired of teaching at Princeton, and the engagement was amicably terminated in May 1940. That summer, Thomas and Katia rented a large house in Brentwood (441 North Rockingham Avenue), a posh neighborhood on L.A.'s westside, for themselves, Erika, Klaus, and their two housekeepers, Lucy and John. Mann enjoyed the sun and long walks. But life was not without its worries.

From the other side of the Atlantic, disturbing news continued to arrive. In mid-July 1940, for example, a telegram was received from the socialist writer Kurt Kersten and the journalist Robert Breuer. Both were stuck in Casablanca and wanted to reach the United States. Mann noted in his diary on July 14, 1940: "Cable for their sake to the U.S.A. Consul there. Klaus notes the emigrants resemble a nation that considers me its envoy. It seems natural that everyone should turn to me."

At the same time, Mann's son Golo, who had remained in France, was arrested in a raid. He was in an internment camp near the French city of Nîmes. After weeks, he finally gained access to the district commander, who released him, probably because of his last name. In Marseille, he met up with his seventy-year-old uncle Heinrich and his wife, Nelly. With the help of the Emergency Rescue Committee (ERC), all three illegally fled across the Pyrenees to Spain and reached the United States via Lisbon.

In September 1940, an English ship bound for Canada was sunk by a German U-boat. Mann's daughter Monika and her husband, the Hungarian art historian Jenö Lányi, were on board. Monika clung to a piece of debris for hours and survived, but her husband did not. She recovered in a hospital in Scotland before traveling to the United States.

In addition to concerns about family and friends, money worries accrued during those months. Most of the six Mann children were unable to make ends meet in the United States, and the expenses of the family, who were accustomed to upper-class living conditions, were high. Through the mediation and financial support of Agnes Meyer, Mann was appointed a temporary honorary consultant by the Library of Congress, which guaranteed him a monthly income.

Shortly thereafter, the Manns decided to settle permanently in California. They acquired a plot of land in Pacific Palisades, at 1550 San Remo Drive, not far from the homes of friends and acquaintances such as the authors Eva Herrmann, Aldous Huxley, and Bruno Frank, and the philosopher Ludwig Marcuse. Initially, they were in talks with architects such as Paul László and Richard Neutra, but for financial and aesthetic reasons decided to hire the Berlin-born architect Julius Ralph Davidson.

After a nearly ten-year odyssey through France, Switzerland, and the United States, the Manns finally had their own roof over their heads again in February 1942. Happy, Mann wrote to his colleague Hermann Hesse: "You should see the landscape around our house, with its view of the ocean. Cheerful sensory impressions are not few in such times, and the sky is cheerful here almost the whole year, sending an incomparable, all-beautifying light."

Mann's next eleven years in Los Angeles were an intense time in which he interacted with the city and its public in a variety of ways. These included political appearances, such as at the Shrine Auditorium or Hollywood Fairfax Temple, where Mann sought to rouse his American audiences and raise awareness of the urgency of military intervention in the war against Nazism. Starting in 1941, Mann also regularly recorded speeches for the BBC at NBC Studios in Hollywood to "German Listeners!," during which he called his countrymen's attention to the atrocities of Hitler's regime.

In addition to his public speeches, Mann and his family were committed to the needs of persecuted people and refugees. They became part of a network of supporters primarily carried by two institutions. The first was the Emergency Rescue Committee, a refugee aid organization under the patronage of Eleanor Roosevelt to which some four thousand European artists and intellectuals owe their escape from Europe. The second was the European Film Fund, organized by Liesl Frank and Charlotte Dieterle, which helped threatened Jewish European intellectuals enter the United States and supported them after their arrival in Los Angeles.

Part of this humanitarian network were outstanding film directors Ernst Lubitsch, Billy Wilder, Fritz Lang, and William Dieterle, as well as the agent Paul Kohner, the producer Max Reinhardt and his sons, and many more. It was here that Mann forged his connections to Hollywood and the German-Jewish filmmakers who played a significant role in the creation of the film industry as it is known today. Studios like Warner Bros., MGM, and United Artists each made its own contribution to the mobilization against Nazi Germany.

Mann was also surrounded by political thinkers who reflected not only on totalitarianism but also on America's capitalist excesses. These included his neighbors Max Horkheimer and Theodor W. Adorno, who completed their groundbreaking work *Dialectic of Enlightenment* in Los Angeles. Also, in the early years of World War II, visions for a European postwar order and questions of how to deal with German war guilt were already being discussed among the émigrés on the Pacific coast. In this context, the playwright Bertolt Brecht, who lived in Santa Monica, and Mann, in particular, were rivals.

In contrast to Brecht, from the very beginning Mann advocated a clear attribution of historical responsibility to Germany and committed himself to a liberal democracy based on social justice. This attitude was nourished by Mann's experiences in the Weimar Republic and by his long-standing involvement with American literature and religion. Of the Unitarian Church of Los Angeles, Mann said in an editorial from the pulpit in 1951: "Rarely, if ever, have I taken so lively and militantly an interest in any religious group." The connection to that liberal universalist tradition sprang not only from a theological affinity but also from personal friendships with Unitarian reverends in Los Angeles such as Ernest Caldecott and Steven Fritchman.

Mann also maintained contact with other literary figures in Los Angeles, as well as with outstanding musicians. These included friends and acquaintances from his Munich days, among them the writer Lion Feuchtwanger and his wife, Marta,

(From left) Thomas Mann reads to Michael Mann, Katia Mann, Golo Mann, Erika Mann, Klaus Mann, and Elisabeth Mann in his study

the author Alfred Neumann, and the conductor Bruno Walter. Mann was also inspired by American authors such as Upton Sinclair. He met with Susan Sontag, who was only sixteen years old at the time, and exchanged ideas with the musical geniuses Igor Stravinsky and Arnold Schoenberg in order to experience a new era of modern music that was emerging in Southern California.

Mann experienced Los Angeles as a city in transformation. This included interactions with architects Neutra and J.R. Davidson, both of whom participated in the Case Study House Program in the 1940s and redefined modern living in Los Angeles. L.A. embodied the image of a modern, forward-looking city at that time: from the new highways that would make it possible to reach any part of the sprawling metropolis in only twenty minutes, to the international airport that connected the American West Coast with far-flung locales, to the social construction projects that in the postwar period nourished the hope that the racially and economically divided city could be brought together.

In addition to his public work, Mann enjoyed the many rewards of the city during his afternoons and days off from writing. He attended concerts at the Hollywood Bowl, strolled along the picturesque Ocean Promenade in Santa Monica, frequented the theaters in downtown Los Angeles, and dined at his favorite restaurants. Here, under the California sun, he enthused in 1942 in a letter to Hermann Hesse, "I am working under outward conditions for which I cannot be grateful enough—in the most beautiful work room I have ever had. I wish you could see the country around our house and the view of the ocean; the garden with its palm, olive, pepper, lemon and eucalyptus trees, the luxuriant flowers, the grass plots, which were being mowed a few days after the seed was sown. Bright sensory impressions are not to be sneezed at in such times; the sky is bright almost all year long and sheds an incomparable, all-beautifying light."

The happiness was not to last. In 1949, Mann was portrayed in *Life* magazine and later in the *American Mercury* as a Communist-friendly intellectual insensitive to the moral challenges of his time. Worried about the slander and persecution of the McCarthy era, Mann and his family left their paradise on the Pacific in 1952, returning to Switzerland. Despite his departure, he did not want to give the impression that he was turning his back on or condemning America, which had become his home and to which he owed so much. From Switzerland, he wrote to Agnes Meyer: "Please help, if there should be a need, to counter that impression! I'm remaining, of course, an American Citizen."

INTRODUCTION

Thomas Mann House · 1550 North San Remo Drive
Benno Herz

Where are we? In the study! But which one? In the "Tölzhaus," behind which the fir forest darkens and from whose open veranda one has a beautiful view of snowy peaks of the Karwendel mountains? Maybe. In Munich, . . . by the river Isar? But the house in which we grew up and in which you thought you would grow old is no longer. . . . Where are we? In the "Niddenhaus" on the Curonian Spit? The thought would be obvious . . . (We are obviously at home and, it is summer sea air, which comes in through the open window!) . . . No, it is clear, we are where we will stay, at home, in Pacific Palisades.

—ERIKA MANN

It sounds like a scene out of a Hollywood movie: Springtime, the late 1930s. A father and daughter, arriving in Los Angeles by train, promptly fall in love with the city. After many stops and detours, they decide a large, empty lot will soon become their new family home. Formerly an outdoor film set, it's now filled with lemon trees and surrounded by seven palm trees. But it has potential, and it soon brings together a sense of community for which they had been longing since leaving their home in Germany. It's as if it were made just for them. The area had been recently rebranded by a slick California real estate agent who wanted to recreate the Italian Riviera in the hills of Southern California, and this lot, at 1550 San Remo Drive, or "San Remi," as they lovingly dubbed it, would be a gathering spot for many.

On March 23, 1938, when Thomas Mann and his daughter Erika stepped off the train at L.A.'s Union Station, this lot, perched on the western edge of the city, was still overgrown with lemon trees. Mann had embarked on a lecture tour of the United States and was set to speak at the Shrine Auditorium. Mann and his daughter were so impressed by L.A. that they decided to take a break from their exhausting travels—Thomas's appearance at the Shrine was not until April 1—and rented one of the twenty-three well-appointed bungalows at the iconic Beverly Hills Hotel, at 9641 Sunset Boulevard. Mann described their twenty-four-day holiday as his "most favorite layover" of the whole tour. In their rented Ford convertible, they eagerly explored the city under the hot California sun, noting that a "light suit was urgently needed." Mann attended a party at motion picture executive Jack Warner's house and met with the writer Aldous Huxley for lunch.

This first visit and subsequent holiday might have been one of the reasons the family decided, after returning home to Princeton, to make the cross-country move to Los Angeles. In July 1940, Mann again boarded a westbound train, this time with his wife, Katia. On July 5, they rented a house at 441 North Rockingham Avenue in Brentwood, not far from Pacific Palisades, where they would settle two years later. By September, the family had made the decision to stay in Los Angeles permanently. "Much consideration given to the question of settling down here. It would seem reasonable, because a rapid change for the better cannot be expected," Mann noted in his diary.

After a short intermezzo in Princeton in the winter of 1940, on April 8, 1941, Thomas and Katia returned to Los Angeles and leased a house at 740 Amalfi Drive, a five-minute walk from the lot on San Remo. Their new place was much more to Mann's liking: "White, clean, rural house, not impractical, but imperfectly furnished . . . garden patio with a view of the ocean," he wrote on their first day. He resumed his daily walks with Niko, this time up and down Amalfi Drive as he acquainted himself with their new surroundings.

The neighborhood, known as the Riviera, encompasses a stretch of Sunset Boulevard dotted with spacious residences offering expansive ocean views. But back in 1925, when real estate agent and architect Frank L. Meline first started to develop the area, tucked between the Pacific Ocean and the mountains of Santa Monica and Topanga, Sunset was still called Beverly Boulevard. The road connecting Pacific Palisades with Brentwood and Westwood had been paved only recently, making it more accessible to cars. Meline's marketing compared it to the Italian Riviera, thus attracting the wealthy. Just to the west, overlooking the Pacific Ocean, Meline had previously developed the neighborhood of Castellammare, or "castle by the sea," a reference to the port of the same name in Naples, Italy. Even the architecture evoked the Italian coast: the first twelve houses built by the Frank Meline Company were designed in the Italian Renaissance style. The streets of Meline's new development were named after Italian coastal towns, selling the southern European dream to wealthy Americans and exiles driven out of Europe: Amalfi, Capri, Corsica, D'Este, San Remo. Part of Pacific Palisades, including the Riviera, was previously used by the director Thomas Ince as a giant outdoor film set. But neither Ince nor the Meline Company were the first to settle, live, and work there: that distinction belonged to the Tongva and Chumash peoples, who have inhabited the coast from the Los Angeles Basin to the Southern Channel Islands for more than ten thousand years. The Indigenous Tongva named the area Topanga, believed to mean "where the mountain meets the sea," or "a place above." In Tongva, Topaa'nga has the root *topaa'*, which likely derives from the Chumash language.

In September 1940, Thomas and Katia toured various lots in the Riviera with a real estate agent, but it was the one at the corner of Monaco and San Remo Drives that drew their attention. Meline's savvy Tuscany-on-the-Pacific marketing resonated with Mann: "Remarkably like the Tuscan [landscape] . . . I have what I wanted—the light, the dry heat, the ocean promenade," he wrote in a letter to Erich von Kahler. He and Katia promptly bought the property. However, the first cornerstone would not be laid until nearly a year later, on July 7, 1941, when the *Evening Outlook* ran the headline "Thomas Mann Home Started on Riviera. Noted Novelist Plans to Become Californian." In the article, Mann famously stated, "I will become a real Californian now," as he pointed to the scores of lemon trees surrounding his property. Those ten months in between were plagued by financial doubts, second thoughts, and the difficult process of finding the right architect for what would be the family's fourth home. Mann's academic appointment at Princeton had just ended, and the sales of his recent works *The Beloved Returns* (1939) and *The Transposed Heads* (1940) had fallen short of expectations. Even though the Manns were in a significantly better

Thomas Mann House, c. 1942–1952

financial position than many other exiled artists and intellectuals, a steady flow of income could not be taken for granted. Only after his friend and patron the American journalist Agnes E. Meyer arranged comfortable employment for him as a consultant in German literature to the Library of Congress could plans for the house move forward.

The Manns considered three of L.A.'s most sought-after modernist architects: Paul László, Richard Neutra, and Julius Ralph (J. R.) Davidson. The reasons were less likely Mann's own tastes in architecture than the fact that "all three architects came from Europe, spoke German, built a series of residences in Southern California, and frequented émigré circles in Los Angeles," as Heinrich Wefing put it in his key text, *"We Are at Home Wherever the Desk Stands": Thomas Mann's Residence in Pacific Palisades.*

At first Thomas and Katia favored the Hungarian exile László, but the estimated costs for his project soon exceeded their budget. The Austrian Neutra forced himself into the picture: as the most well-known architect on the West Coast at the time, he felt entitled to the job. Mann wasn't fond of Neutra's more radical style of modernism, and seemed to be annoyed by his ambition and persistence. During Mann's first visit to L.A. in 1938, Neutra had taken him on a tour of the architect's hillside modernist homes; the next day, Mann described Neutra's signature style as "unpleasant," "cubist glass box-style." Neutra did not easily take no for an answer, which, according to the now-infamous anecdote, led Mann to exclaim loudly, "Get that Neutra off my back!" during a party hosted by the writer Vicki Baum.

The Manns preferred J.R. Davidson's more moderate approach, influenced by the International Style. Davidson was likely introduced to Mann by their mutual friend the director Ernst Lubitsch. Davidson's design reflected his client's wishes and needs: the stretched L-shaped building with the study facing southeast, away from the living areas, secluded Mann from the hustle and bustle of the rest of the house. A stairway connected the study with the main bedroom on the first floor, which allowed him to move between his private quarters without having to see anyone. The spacious living room was the social center of the house. By incorporating the few pieces of furniture they were able to save from their house in the Poschinger Strasse 1 in Munich, the family wished for an interior design that would re-create their lost German home, comforting them with memories of their previous lives. The gramophone, a Wheelock baby grand piano, and Ludwig von Hofmann's art nouveau painting *The Source* (*Die Quelle*) made the living room a welcoming hangout for the family and their visitors. For the interior design, they hired their old friend from Munich Paul Huldschinsky, to the displeasure of Davidson, who would have preferred to handle it himself. (This might be one of the reasons why Davidson later distanced himself from the house and did not include it in his portfolio.)

Huldschinsky successfully reimagined the look and feel of the former home: traditional wooden furniture, sofas covered with flower-patterned fabrics, and Persian rugs placed over the carpeted floor. The interior was in clear contrast to the modern exterior, symbolizing the divided nature of a family in exile. On the outside, adaptation to California modern; on the inside, memories of their homeland.

Finally, on February 2, 1942, the family moved into their new home, which they soon came to love. "Never lived more beautiful," Mann wrote in a letter to Agnes Meyer. In an interview with the *Los Angeles Times,* Katia snapped, "So we have a modern house. We like it, though." Over the next ten years, the house became a vibrant hub for a who's who of the European émigré community and an important place to network; the "White House of Exile," as Mann expert and scholar Heinrich Detering later called it. Musical evenings around the gramophone and the baby grand piano with friends Bruno and Liselotte Walter, hours of conversation about music theory with the young philosopher Theodor W. Adorno in preparation for Thomas's essential California work *Doctor Faustus,* and political debates with Aldous Huxley and the philosopher Max Horkheimer, both of whom lived right across the street—the list of names, stories, and encounters was endless.

Giving in to the pressures of the McCarthy era and in fear of political persecution, which so many of Mann's contemporaries had already suffered, the family decided to move back to Switzerland in 1952. Though they considered renting out their beloved home to the German Consul for a year, that did not come to pass. With heavy hearts, the Manns decided to sell San Remo and left Los Angeles on June 24, 1952. In March 1953, in their newest place of residence in Erlenbach, Mann opened one of the desk drawers in his study. Inside were photographs from the life they had left behind in the Pacific Palisades. "I can't look at it without my heart clenching," he noted in his diary. Mann continued to dream about the villa in California under seven palms and a lemon tree. He would never see it again. Thomas Mann died on August 12, 1955, in Switzerland.

And the home at 1550 San Remo Drive? As the years progressed, it became overgrown with cacti and surrounded by eucalyptus trees. Only a small plaque reminded relentless searchers of its fabled history. In 2016, when the owners decided to sell, the property was advertised as a teardown in a neighborhood now peppered with multi-million-dollar homes. Davidson's elegant but spatially limited International Style no longer met the needs and standards of interested buyers. But the anticipated demolition did not happen. Voices of many artists, intellectuals, and politicians—first and foremost the Nobel laureate Herta Müller— grew loud, clamoring to save this shining symbol of European exile in Los Angeles and the ongoing cultural exchange between Germany and the United States. With the help of German president Frank-Walter Steinmeier, the Thomas Mann House is now a residency center and, in the spirit of Mann's years in the house, a vibrant space for transatlantic debate. Sometimes, on a hot summer evening in the Riviera, you may hear the muffled voices, piano notes, and gramophone crackles emanating from the former lighthouse of Weimar on the Pacific.

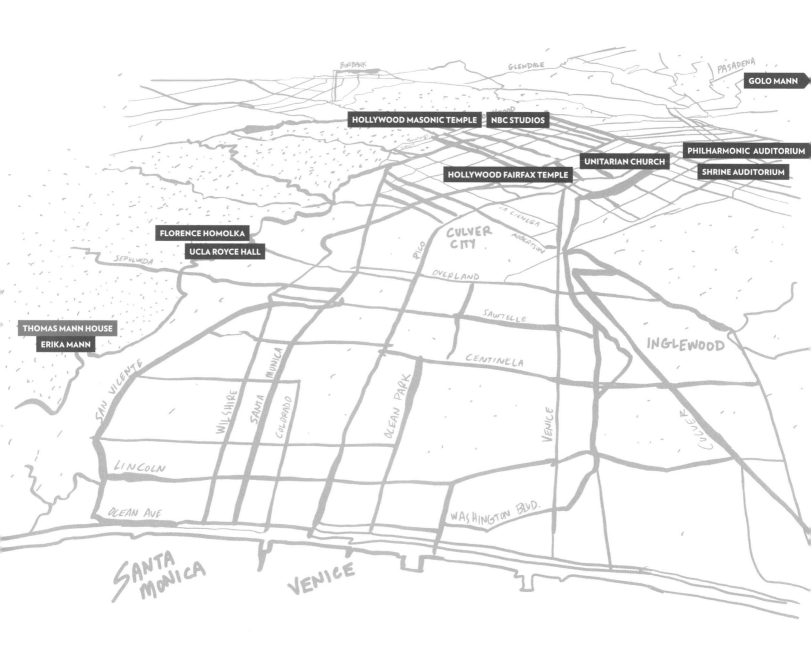

PART 1

BURBANK

GLENDALE

PASADENA

GOLO MANN

HOLLYWOOD MASONIC TEMPLE   **NBC STUDIOS**

PHILHARMONIC AUDITORIUM

UNITARIAN CHURCH

SHRINE AUDITORIUM

HOLLYWOOD FAIRFAX TEMPLE

LA CIENEGA

ROBERTSON

FLORENCE HOMOLKA

UCLA ROYCE HALL

CULVER
CITY

PICO

SEPULVEDA

OVERLAND

SAWTELLE

INGLEWOOD

THOMAS MANN HOUSE

ERIKA MANN

CENTINELA

SAN VICENTE

WILSHIRE

SANTA
MONICA

COLORADO

OCEAN PARK

VENICE

CULVER

LINCOLN

OCEAN AVE

WASHINGTON BLVD.

SANTA
MONICA

VENICE

THE MANNS AS PUBLIC INTELLECTUALS

Nikolai Blaumer

The Mann family's connections to Los Angeles date back to the 1920s. In 1927, Erika and Klaus, Thomas's daughter and son, set out together on a trip around the world that eventually brought them to Los Angeles. Accustomed to European urban cities, they were initially sorely disappointed. Klaus recalled in his autobiography the image of a "hypertrophied jellyfish, a massive polyp stretching its arms in all directions with blind greed." After jumping into the Pacific Ocean and setting foot in Santa Monica, however, the siblings were soon reconciled to the metropolis, marveling at the beautiful colors of the sunset and the promenade lined with swaying palm trees.

Mann's children, who were only in their early twenties, were welcomed everywhere with open arms. They met the director Ernst Lubitsch and actors Ramon Novarro and Emil Jannings, and toasted at parties with Pola Negri and Greta Garbo. Both Erika and Klaus immersed themselves in the life of the metropolis. They attended a football game, a service by the Pentecostal preacher Aimee Semple McPherson, and saw a boxing match at the Olympic Auditorium. When they met the writer Upton Sinclair in Pasadena, they were gravely impressed by his work ethic: "A writer who takes his trade as seriously as a carpenter takes carpentry." Klaus and Erika observed that poets have a very different social standing in the United States. Here, they are critical members of their society, without any nimbus: "They have completely distanced themselves from the poet ideal of our father."

Such words would prove prophetic, for when their father first came to Los Angeles a decade later, he had long since detached himself from the ideal of the genius artist removed from society. Faced with the humanitarian crisis of his time, he had come to believe that to be apolitical was ultimately to be anti-democratic. He had thrown himself into the fight against Hitler and Fascism, putting all his energy into convincing the American public of the need to defend freedom and humanity across the Atlantic, by force if necessary.

The arrival of the Nobel Prize winner in 1938, as part of his lecture tour "The Coming Victory of Democracy," was a major cultural event for Los Angeles. "The intelligentsia of the film colony is on its toes in anticipation of an erudite treat tonight, when Thomas Mann, the celebrated German novelist, will lecture . . . at the Shrine Auditorium," wrote the *Los Angeles Examiner*. Mann was proudly announced as the "Greatest Living Man of Letters." The Shrine was packed with six thousand people. From day one, Mann was flattered by the public attention he received.

The years between his first visit to Los Angeles and his eventual emigration, in 1952, from the city back to Switzerland were marked by a multitude of public events and an enormous media presence. Mann's appearances were mostly politically motivated, even though his public speeches must always be thought of as connected to his literary works. We may assume that Mann's cultural curiosity about his new home also drove him to the stages of the auditoriums, theaters, cinemas, concert halls, churches, and universities of Los Angeles.

As Hans Rudolf Vaget has pointed out in his seminal work *Thomas Mann, der Amerikaner*, Mann had developed an increasing intellectual interest in America since at least the early 1920s. Walt Whitman's poetry and political writings left an enormous impression on him, but he was also familiar with the works of contemporaries such as Upton Sinclair, William Faulkner, and Sinclair Lewis. As we can see from his diaries, Mann took careful note of political debates in the *New York Times*, the *Atlantic Monthly*, *The Nation*, and the *New Leader*. Until the postwar period, he never tired of praising the excellence of contemporary American novels and literary criticism. He candidly confessed, "No, I don't love the European snark about transatlantic 'primitiveness.'"

A look at the novelist's various speaking engagements gives an idea of his public role in Los Angeles and how he interacted with different groups of people. He, of course, appeared on the city's major stages: he followed his lecture at the Shrine with three later appearances at the Wilshire Ebell Theatre (March 1941, September 1943, and May 1944), served as the keynote speaker for First Lady Eleanor Roosevelt at the Philharmonic Auditorium (April 1941), and addressed a memorial service for President Franklin Delano Roosevelt at the Santa Monica Municipal Auditorium (April 1945).

Mann also came into conversation with scholars and students, for example at Claremont Men's College (September 1940). His son Golo later was a professor of history at Claremont for eleven years. Mann was a frequent visitor to the UCLA campus in Westwood, where he gave his lecture "The War and the Future" (December 1941) to Phi Beta Kappa alumni at the University Club. Less than two years later (October 1943), the Hollywood Writers Mobilization, organized to motivate those working in the media to aid in the U.S. war effort, held a convention at UCLA's School of Education, attended by Mann, Lion Feuchtwanger, Hanns Eisler, and others. President Roosevelt sent a message of greeting, and the writers' associations of England, France, the Soviet Union, and China sent delegates. Mann spoke about his conflicted relationship with Germany and confessed that his homeland was becoming more and more alien to him.

Mann also addressed numerous gatherings of Jewish communities, such as the Zionist women's organization Hadassah, on "The Problem of Humanity in Our Time" (September 1943). At Rabbi Jacob Sonderling's progressive Hollywood Fairfax Temple, he read from his novella *The Tables of Law* (January 1945) and later from *The Holy Sinner* (January 1951), from which he also read at the Jewish Club of 1933 (February 1951).

During his years in exile, Mann developed a close, friendly relationship with the Unitarian Church. His connection to the Unitarians stemmed from his reception of the community's thought leaders, including

Ralph Waldo Emerson, as well as from the practical humanitarian work of the Unitarian Service Committee, which helped a number of European intellectuals escape to the United States, including Thomas's son Golo. Mann's grandchildren Frido and Angelica were baptized in the Unitarian Church in Santa Monica in 1942. Mann himself later climbed into the pulpit of the First Unitarian Church of Los Angeles to give a speech in March 1951.

While in Los Angeles, Mann participated in public meetings of various political and humanitarian initiatives and would take on a position of responsibility in some of the organizations. During the war years, the focus was initially on supporting Jews and other refugee groups upon their arrival in the United States. There are records of Mann's appearances at the American Committee for Christian German Refugees (April 1939), the European Film Fund (April 1939), and the Friends of the Hebrew University at Jerusalem (September 1941).

In March 1942, Mann and his colleague, the writer Bruno Frank, spoke at a public hearing of the so-called Tolan Committee. The occasion was an order issued by President Roosevelt authorizing the evacuation of all persons deemed a threat to national security from the West Coast to relocation centers farther inland. In a letter to Agnes Meyer, Mann praised what he saw as the exemplary work of the committee: "the studied courtesy with which we Germans were treated—it was quite charming and democratic." Mann and his fellow campaigners had succeeded in averting an internment of Germans, arguing that German refugees should not be victimized a second time. What Mann did not foresee, or deliberately ignored, was the subsequent internment of over a hundred thousand Japanese Americans, many of them U.S. citizens, in detainment camps in California and other western states.

After the end of the war, Mann remained politically active. His involvement soon came under the auspices of the East-West conflict and the increasing persecution of real or supposed Communists and their sympathizers. Mann spoke before the Independent Citizens Committee (December 1945); the Hollywood Peace Group (June 1948); the Hollywood Arts, Sciences and Professions Council (June 1949); and the National Council of the Arts, Sciences and Professions (January 1950), all left-wing pacifist organizations that advocated the observance of the First Amendment in the time of rising McCarthyism.

Given the enormous number of appearances in a wide variety of venues around the city, the question arises as to why Mann's active public role in Los Angeles receives so little recognition. To this day, the narrative of the lonely exile in "Weimar on the Pacific" dominates. Apart from the popular "Listen, Germany!" BBC radio addresses that Mann recorded monthly at NBC Studios in Hollywood between 1941 and 1945, the enormous presence of Thomas Mann and his family in American media is little known. In the archives of the *Los Angeles Times* alone, for example, there are several hundred reports on the Manns in the years 1938–1952. They speak of the enthusiasm of critics and readers not only for Mann but also for Erika and Klaus and Thomas's brother Heinrich. One *Los Angeles Times* critic wrote in his review of *Joseph and His*

Brothers, weeks before Mann first came to town: "Anything that I might say about Thomas Mann's epical narrative . . . must be prefaced with the statement, categorical if you will, that it is an achievement so great that superlatives are gratuitous." Of course, Mann's novels *The Beloved Returns* (1940) and *Doctor Faustus* (1948) were reviewed in the *Times*, but so were the novella *The Transposed Heads* (1941), his anthology *The Permanent Goethe* (1948), and reprints of his essays and lectures.

Erika's work *School for Barbarians: Education under the Nazis* was also received with interest. As a result, she led a lecture tour of dozens of American cities. In Los Angeles, she spoke at the Philharmonic Auditorium (November 1939) about family structures under Nazism and the indoctrination of German youth. A few months earlier, the famous gossip columnist Hedda Hopper even claimed to have observed Erika stealing the show from her father at a banquet in Hollywood. Erika had spoken with "ease and naturalness," and told of her youth in monarchist Germany. In December 1941, Erika even became the heroine of a comic strip in the *Los Angeles Times*: "TRUE THRILLER: THOMAS MANN'S DAUGHTER ERIKA COMBINED HER ACTRESS' SKILL WITH COOL NERVE WHEN SHE RE-ENTERED GERMANY DISGUISED AS A PEASANT AND RETRIEVED THE MANUSCRIPT OF ONE OF HER FATHER'S GREATEST BOOKS FROM UNDER THE NAZIS NOSES."

Erika and Klaus coauthored *Escape to Life,* on the history of German exile, which was also featured, along with a large profile picture, in the *Los Angeles Times* (April 1939). That September, Klaus addressed the Council of Jewish Women on "After Hitler, What?" In later years, he and Erika continued to maintain a media presence in the American public sphere. Klaus published reports from a devastated Europe on Nazism and anti-Semitism in Germany. However, in the last months of his life, stories of drug abuse and a suicide attempt took center stage.

In this city of stars and starlets, there was a pronounced interest in the Manns' private lives. The public grew informed about the most important events of the family's life in exile, including Thomas's appointment to Princeton (June 1938), the acquisition of the property in the Riviera district of Pacific Palisades (October 1940), and his milestone birthdays. Events such as his hearing to acquire American citizenship were accompanied by reports in the news (June 1945). For example, the clerk at the hearing questioned him intensively before asking for his autograph at the end: "She had exploited to the full the opportunity of holding a private conversation with the great writer. And who can blame her?"

Even visits to their grandson Frido in Northern California, a private invitation for the painter William Earl Singer, who had painted a portrait of Thomas, and a visit from Katia's twin brother Klaus from Tokyo were made public. In June 1948, the *Los Angeles Times* magazine even visited them at home on San Remo Drive. The reporter photographed Mann at his desk and commented on the classic furnishings of his bedroom: "Taste for Early American furnishings is evident in the bedroom. Rug is blue and quilted spread is rust colored."

The Manns' political role, however, was evident beyond their enormous public presence. As Alexander Stephan has pointed out, the American security services also took an interest in the Mann family early on in their American exile—as they did in most of the exiled German writers. Erika, in fact, worked for the Federal Bureau of Investigation (FBI) for several years beginning in 1940. She had offered the FBI her help in identifying saboteurs among the exiles. Golo worked for the Office of Strategic Services (OSS) in Washington, D.C., after training with the U.S. Army.

From the beginning, however, the Manns themselves were also under scrutiny by security authorities. When, in 1943, suspicions arose that Mann was using Moscow to position himself for political office in the postwar period, intelligence surveillance began that went beyond the ongoing documentation of correspondence with the State Department and President Roosevelt and his wife, Eleanor. As a result, the Manns received multiple visits from the OSS and FBI. One report suggested that the agents welcomed Mann's cooperation but were annoyed that their glasses of liqueur remained empty while the host refilled his own.

Especially in the postwar years, FBI reports become more critical. Mann's idealistic speech "The Coming Victory of Democracy" was now interpreted as "strongly radical, and particularly strongly pro-USSR." Authorities closely followed the writer's travels to Weimar in East Germany in 1949, his association with the leftist politician and former vice president Henry A. Wallace, and the article "The Moral Eclipse of Thomas Mann," published in *Plain Talk* magazine. Journalist Eugene Tillinger branded him a politically dangerous Communist, and the FBI subsequently labeled him "one of the world's most noted Communists." After the House Un-American Activities Committee (HUAC) publicly listed Mann as "affiliated with various peace organizations or Communist fronts," he noted in his diary, "Conversation with K. and Erika about the situation in America and our future there . . . with increasing chauvinism and persecution of every non-conformism. Revocation of passport quite certain." As such, the Mann family's public anti-Fascist activity became closely linked not only to their flight to the United States as an alleged safe haven but also to their second immigration, back to Switzerland, in 1952.

SHRINE AUDITORIUM
665 West Jefferson Boulevard
Benno Herz

On April 1, 1938, Thomas Mann made a stop at the impressive "colossal amphitheater" at 665 West Jefferson Boulevard to deliver his lecture "The Coming Victory of Democracy." Around six thousand people gathered inside the Shrine Auditorium to listen to him advocate against Fascism and for a stronger democracy. Interrupted at times by spontaneous applause, Mann reminded the audience, "Democracy wishes to elevate mankind, to teach it to think, to set it free. It seeks to remove from culture the stamp of privilege and disseminate it among the people." The political fundraising event was organized by the Hollywood Anti-Nazi League, formed in 1936 by professionals from the film industry to fight Fascism and the growing influence of anti-Semitic tendencies in the United States. Among other initiatives, the league tried to engage studios in producing anti-Nazi films and protested when Walt Disney invited the filmmaker and Nazi propagandist Leni Riefenstahl to Hollywood in November 1938.

That night, Mann shared the stage with fellow author and acquaintance Sinclair Lewis, who gave a "humorous" contribution, as Mann noted in his diary. Other speakers included his friend Bruno Frank and Thomas's daughter Erika, who, he wrote, "prepared all afternoon for an advertising speech for Austrian refugees. Touching." Following the show was a photo shoot with all participants, and Mann seemed more than happy with the turnout: "Money collected. Overall satisfaction." The *Los Angeles Times* reported on Mann's lecture in an article titled "Self-Exiled German Author Sounds Fascism Rebuke." In the audience were many famous émigrés and intellectuals, such as filmmaker William Dieterle and author Elizabeth Meyer, daughter of Mann's friend and supporter Agnes E. Meyer. Elizabeth wrote of the lecture: "Thomas Mann experienced the biggest success of his lecture tonight and was incredibly happy and even sprightly at the party afterwards, as Hans Vaget indicates in his book *Thomas Mann, der Amerikaner*.

Tired and hungry after the event, the Manns joined the Franks at their Hollywood home for beer, meatloaf, and eggs. Mann didn't go to bed until 2 a.m.

Opened in 1926, the Shrine is a fine example of Moorish Revival, a style that was inspired by North African and Spanish Islamic medieval architecture. Typical elements include horseshoe arches with numerous decorative elements, onion-shaped domes, and ornamental patterns. This type of revival architecture was very en vogue in the 1920s. The Tower Theatre on Broadway, which also opened in 1926, and the Lincoln Theatre at 2300 South Central

Avenue, which debuted a year later, are other L.A. examples.

The Shrine replaced the 1906 Al Malaikah Temple, destroyed by a fire in January 1920. The Al Malaikah was a division of the masonic society known as the Shriners, which itself originated from the Ancient Arabic Order of the Nobles of the Mystic Shrine in the 1870s. Still in existence today, the Shriners describe themselves as an American institution, adopting "oriental signs, tokens and costumes for the sake of pageantry." The group funds and supports over twenty-two hospitals, the

so-called Temples of Mercy, in L.A. and across the country, where upward of 800,000 children, regardless of race or religion, have been treated since 1922.

The auditorium has a long history and has been involved in many (pop) cultural events. Its stage was used as a set for the 1933 movie *King Kong* for the scene in which King Kong is first revealed to an astonished audience. In 1940, the nineteenth Academy Awards ceremony was held there; in 1952, scenes from the classic *A Star Is Born* with Judy Garland were shot in the auditorium; and in the 1960s and '70s, every major rock star, from Jimi Hendrix to Bruce Springsteen, performed there. In 1984, singer Michael Jackson's hair caught fire onstage while he was shooting a Pepsi commercial. The Shrine Auditorium remains an important live venue for Los Angeles today, hosting concerts and events year round.

Mann's April 1938 lecture wasn't his only appearance at the Shrine. On May 18, 1948, he saw the classical pianist Arthur Rubinstein play Prokofiev and Rachmaninoff in concert, and later writes in his diary "Tea at 6 p.m. and off to the Shrine Auditorium at 7.15 p.m. Arrived a little after 8. Difficulty with tickets, which were already 'picked up.' Finally seats, way in the back. Very crowded. Prokowjew's [sic] 'classical' played excellently. Rubinstein with the Concerto by Rachmaninoff, skillfully & indifferently. Met the artist during the intermission. "Luky [sic] people!" (. . .) Also heard Brahms' Fifth. Getting out of the parking lot. The drive home. Home around midnight. It was done. Chocolate. With Erika." Traffic, even back in 1948, indeed must have been bad that evening; it took him more than forty-five minutes to make his way from the Palisades to the Shrine.

King Kong is revealed to the public at the Shrine Auditorium

NBC STUDIOS
1500 Vine Street
Nikolai Blaumer

I n 1941, the BBC approached Thomas Mann while he was still at Princeton, asking if he would like to address his German compatriots in short radio speeches on a regular basis. He later reported that he could hardly believe this great opportunity at first: these broadcasts would enable the exiled writer to politically influence the German population in their native tongue. The offer was particularly appealing because broadcasting by longwave guaranteed that the speeches would be heard over the Volksempfänger, a radio receiver used by the Nazis for propaganda purposes.

Culture played a central role in war propaganda, for both the Nazis and the Allies. A paper by the BBC shows the goals that the British government associated with its German program: "to convince the audience that we are likely to win, to make them want us to win, to undermine the listener's morale by confusing him, and to invite listeners to passive and, later on, to active resistance." Even though Mann had the greatest possible freedom with his words, they undoubtedly fell in line with all these goals.

The first speeches were cabled from Princeton to London, where they were read out loud over the airwaves by a German native speaker. Soon after Mann relocated to Los Angeles, he was given the opportunity to deliver the words himself from NBC Studios in Hollywood. In his first personal address, he said: "What I had to tell you from afar, until now was brought to you by other voices. This time you hear my own voice. It is the voice of a friend, a German voice; the voice of a Germany which showed, and will again show, a different face to the world from the horrible Medusa mask which Hitlerism has

pressed upon it."

Mann's appeals for resistance, rejection of National Socialism, and liberation from totalitarianism remained the main concern of his programs. As early as 1942, he spoke from the Pacific about the extermination of Jews in German concentration camps. Years before the war ended, Mann reflected on the question of collective German responsibility and guilt. While Hitler was subjected to sharp polemics and ridicule, President Roosevelt remained the heroic figure in Mann's speeches.

The recordings were sent from L.A. to New York, and from there relayed by telephone to England and finally transmitted to Germany by longwave. Until his last speech, in November 1945, Mann drove every month from Pacific Palisades to the Recording Department at NBC Studios. The studios were located in a building designed by John C. Austin in the Streamline Modernist style, at the intersection of Sunset Boulevard and Vine Street, and were part of what was known as Radio City. ABC and CBS Studios were located in close proximity. In 1964, the iconic NBC building was demolished, and the station began concentrating its operations at its Burbank studios.

The Thomas Mann House in Los Angeles continues the tradition of the émigré writer's radio addresses. American and European intellectuals such as Francis Fukuyama, Deborah Feldman, Timothy Snyder, Chantal Mouffe, Colm Tóibín, and Daniel Kehlman have been among those invited to reflect on the renewal of democracy as part of the "55 Voices for Democracy" podcast and video series. Following in Mann's footsteps, for example, the German legal scholar Christoph Möllers said, "Democracy lives today, too, from those who doubt it and need to be convinced."

Radio engineer's control room, NBC Studios

ELEANOR ROOSEVELT
The Philharmonic Auditorium · 427 West 5th Street
Morten Høi Jensen

On April 28, 1941, following an introduction by Thomas Mann, First Lady Eleanor Roosevelt delivered a lecture on the ongoing war in Europe at the Philharmonic Auditorium in Los Angeles, located at 427 West 5th Street. The occasion was a slightly strained one; the Secret Service had received credible information about a potential threat to the First Lady's life, necessitating an additional police presence in the auditorium, something Mrs. Roosevelt found both unnecessary and inconvenient. In general, she never felt that she needed a bodyguard and, on many occasions, even preferred driving herself. But this time, given the severity of the threat, she relented.

The setting for the event could hardly have been more fitting. Not far away, clustered in the Hollywood Hills and Pacific Palisades, were the shaken survivors of an entire generation of German and Jewish intellectual and artistic achievement. More than a few of them had made it to this palm-canopied shelter on the Pacific thanks to the behind-the-scenes efforts of Eleanor Roosevelt and Thomas Mann, who had first met in 1935, when Mann and his wife, Katia, were guests at the White House. Since then, a cordial, if not exactly intimate, friendship had formed between the two couples; Thomas and Katia stayed at the White House on several occasions, sometimes for a few days at a time.

Eleanor Roosevelt was effusive in her public admiration of Mann's work. In her syndicated newspaper column "My Day" of September 24, 1938, she mentioned having just read *The Coming Victory of Democracy*, a short volume published not long after Mann's nationwide tour. "I feel sure that he feels as I do," Mrs. Roosevelt wrote, "that the World War and the attempts which we made at permanent settlements really left us with the seeds of the present complicated international situation. Because it seems difficult to make humanity rise to certain heights except in crises, nothing very much has been done up to now to correct the injustices that are, I think, inevitable after any bitter conflict."

But the true foundation of their relationship was the urgent matter of assisting refugees in Europe. This was an issue close to the First Lady's heart, even though the story of American support for refugees in the years before and during the Second World War is a dismal one; the rate of immigration in America reached its lowest at the exact moment when requests for U.S. visas were at their highest. Between 1931 and 1944, quotas would have allowed for over two million immigrants, yet only 377,597 were admitted. At one point, the number of emigrants from America even exceeded that of immigrants. Yet, refugee support remained substantial. In 1938, Mann and Mrs. Roosevelt were instrumental

Eleanor Roosevelt inaugurates her NBC radio series in Washington, D.C., April 30, 1940

in the establishment of the Emergency Rescue Committee (ERC), led by the journalist Varian Fry, who was sent to France with a list of names of endangered writers and intellectuals provided by Mann. The ERC was passionately supported by Eleanor Roosevelt, who pressured the president and the State Department to increase the quota of emergency visas. Although it focused on artists and intellectuals, the committee is nevertheless credited with saving somewhere between 2,000 and 4,000 Jewish refugees.

Mann and the First Lady's concerns continued to overlap even after the war and FDR's death in 1945. In 1947, for instance, HUAC member Richard Nixon ensured that the composer Hanns Eisler was placed on the Hollywood blacklist for his alleged Communist sympathies, going so far as to dispatch a subcommittee to Los Angeles to interrogate Eisler. (Nixon called him "the Karl Marx of communism in the musical field.") Mann was alarmed; he held the composer in high esteem and had engaged Eisler in

many long conversations, especially on the subject of Richard Wagner. During Eisner's show trial, HUAC representatives read aloud an exchange of letters from 1939 between former Undersecretary of State Sumner Welles and Eleanor Roosevelt regarding the matter of granting visas to Eisner and his wife. For HUAC, the fact that the former First Lady had been instrumental in campaigning for Eisner was something of a scoop: it bolstered the delusion that the Roosevelt administration had been infiltrated by Communist sympathizers.

Perversely, Thomas Mann and Eleanor Roosevelt, too, were targets of the postwar red scare. The FBI, under the paranoid and watchful leadership of J. Edgar Hoover, kept files on both of them. Mann, for his part, had long suspected that he was under FBI surveillance. In the dossier the agency kept on him, he was occasionally referred to as "a warm defender of Moscow" and believed to be "strongly radical and particularly strongly pro-USSR." In 1950, in a letter to the New York journal *Aufbau*, Mann defended himself. "I am not a Communist and never have been one," he wrote. "I felt it an honor and a joy to become a citizen of this country. But hysterical, irrational, and blind hatred of Communism represents a danger to America far more terrible than native communism."

Still, for a brief, flowering moment, there was fruitful collaboration between the wife of the U.S. president and the world's most preeminent anti-Fascist—a collaboration for which Los Angeles's Philharmonic Auditorium could well stand as a symbol. Unfortunately, the building was demolished in 1985 against much public outcry.

UCLA ROYCE HALL
10745 Dickson Court
Kalani Michell

The origin story goes that Royce Hall suddenly grew out of the Californian countryside. By the mid-1920s, the "Southern Branch" of the University of California, which would shortly thereafter become the University of California at Los Angeles, was in need of much more space than its existing location in East Hollywood could provide. This is where Western fantasies come in. During the dedication of the new location of the campus in Westwood 1926, as described in UCLA: The First Century, "[e]ach person there tried to imagine what the open barley field would soon look like and no one succeeded." It was at once a moment of uncertainty and of silent imaginings in a place—the university—that is usually associated with knowing. "By early 1929, majestic Royce Hall had risen on the once-barren land, proudly defying all obstacles," an almost magical process whereby "huge piles of brick somehow became Royce Hall [...]." But of course, it came from somewhere. Elsewhere. Many elsewheres.

In a case study of UCLA, University Planning and Architecture illustrates that "[h]istorical revivalism was then rife in America [...]. [...] Strikingly modelled upon San Ambrogio [Basilica di Sant'Ambrogio] in Milan, it [Royce Hall] has a two-story arcaded and vaulted loggia between paired irregular towers. [...] The plaza between these four [original] structures and the steps and terraces leading westward down the sloping terrain reflect the architects' [David Allison and George Kelham's] original vision to create an Italian hilltop town upon Beaux-Arts axial foundations." (Italian replicas were not uncommon in Los Angeles around this time,

with Thomas Mann's San Remo Drive neighborhood in the "Riviera" being another example.) As the first building at UCLA, Royce Hall provided the campus's primary classrooms and an 1,800-seat auditorium. It was named after "Josiah Royce, the native Californian philosopher who taught at Berkeley and then was lured to Harvard by pioneering American philosopher William James." The name was almost given to the library across the quad, but it was feared that students would just end up calling it "the library," not "Royce." If "Royce knows everything," as James apparently once said about his colleague, then this symbol of omniscience must not be forgotten over time; it should be inscribed into the primary place associated with knowing in this newfound institution.

These days, when one thinks of going to Royce, it can mean a few different things: the auditorium for invited guests, the public arena of the quad (often pictured against the uneven towers), and the portico in between–the arcaded hallway one must pass through in order to enter the building. When Mann wrote in his diaries that he visited "Royce Hall" for concerts, lectures, and ballets between 1944 and 1949, it might seem that he was referring to the auditorium, but it's actually the portico that helps us understand the historical complexity of this site with relation to Mann. It returns Royce to one of its points of origin in Milan: the cloister. Although Royce Hall is modeled after monastic architecture, this doesn't mean it's intended to house a monolithic community completely disconnected from the outside world. In fact, the cloister's architecture, as Verena Mund writes, "emphasizes access as well as separateness, the simultaneity of the inside and the outside [...], forming an arcadiac view into open space. [...] And even though you have only a limited view onto the outside [...], you do, from within the cloister, feel and hear and smell the atmosphere of the outside, like the summer sun, loud music or the wind."

While these diary entries about visiting Royce Hall might seem to describe temporarily entering an enclosed, exclusive community, for Mann, as an exile, thoughts about belonging were not inconsequential. From the liminal space of the Royce cloister/portico, one can start to make out the real and imagined communities Mann finds here, people who belong inside this structure (read: the institution, the exile circle, the realm of "high" art, the nation) and outside of it, without there being a harsh, impenetrable demarcation between the two. When Mann visits Royce, it's not just about who was there with him, in the flesh, on what date, even though the entries seem, at first, to be written this way, e.g., "April 28, 1944: To Westwood, Royce Hall,

for a concert by [Polish pianist] A. [Arthur] Rubinstein." This is the auditorium entry. What follows is the portico entry: "In the background of the podium a young man, brunette, serious and friendly in a childlike way, in which I thought I recognized Adrian [the protagonist of *Doktor Faustus*]." As we know from the UCLA origin story about the open field, imagining is also part of the process of site-building.

Royce Hall was a meeting place for art, criticism and culture but, as with the cloister, the outside is never fully shut out. As detailed in *UCLA: The First Century*, "[b]y July 1943, one in three UCLA students was in uniform, shifting the dynamics of campus life." On August 1, 1944, a year after the Allied bombing devastated Royce's prototype basilica in Milan, and not long after D-Day, Mann writes that he attended a recital at Royce Hall by Ernst Krenek with Theodor W. Adorno, a violinist (likely Grischa Goluboff), and the "rigid" conductor Otto Klemperer (a sonata performance which, according to Krenek, did not take place). He has dinner at Ernst and Karin Leyden's with Luise Rainer and Walter Slezak, arrives back home on San Remo Drive and, after a day with American student-soldiers in Europe, and Austrian, Dutch, German, and Russian immigrants and exiles in the Italian replicas of Royce and the Riviera neighborhood, writes about "Warsaw and Florence about to fall. Concern about the worsening of the robot plague [V-1 flying bombs]." Emotions, and fears, run high. Before Mann gives a lecture in Royce about Fyodor Dostoyevsky in 1945, he makes a note about a particular object he received at Berkeley in 1941,

Royce Hall, 1929

a gift to members of a prestigious academic honor society: "Shaved, [put on] tuxedo [.] Bathroom with Golden Key from Phi Beta Kappa. 7 p.m. quick bite. 8 p.m. to Westwood for lecture." It's an object of reassurance: access to an exclusive community and a public acknowledgement of academic achievements. Mann writes that the talk is very well received, but nevertheless laments "what it costs me, what I invest in nervous energy."

A year later, in February 1946, Mann is warned about the dangers to his life if he returns to Europe given his outspokenness during the war, attends a concert by celebrated contralto and civil rights icon Marian Anderson at Royce, and leaves early. He and Anderson knew each other from another university context in which they were thinking about exclusionary institutional politics. Together with Ralph Bunche, Albert Einstein, and Eleanor Roosevelt, they were on the first advisory board of Roosevelt College, established after over sixty faculty resigned from Central YMCA College in protest against racial, ethnic, religious, and gender quotas aimed at keeping minorities out of the institution. The accounts of Mann and/at Royce can be situated within a longer history of thinking, at this very place, about who belongs in the institution and who is told to stay outside of it.

Artist and writer Renée Green describes that she "like[s] architecture because there is in it the knowledge of building something up, as well as tearing something down—quite literally. [...] Living architecture means an acceptance of ruin to come. This differs from the historic notion of art, as matter made timeless, meant to last, an illusory wish, yet this somehow persists. [...] But with architecture and art, as with music, there is a plan, drawings, a score, based on what was designed or composed, something that can be reanimated by someone else at another time in another space." Thinking about Mann in this space can help us understand these visits as more than trips made by a great man of literature to a great monument of architecture, but rather as a possibility to recognize that greatness is never a stable category and a "work" of art is never set in stone. Architecture can help us remember that these ideas are constructed, and can therefore also always be deconstructed, and reconfigured.

ERIKA MANN
1550 North San Remo Drive
Irmela von der Lühe

At night, Hollywood is as quiet as Munich [...] If you want to see the nightlife you have to go to Los Angeles, to the Mexican quarter or to Chinatown." These witty sentences mark the beginning and end of one the early feuilletons that Erika Mann started writing for the Berlin daily *Tempo* in September 1928. Under the heading "Hollywood by Night," she gave her impressions of Los Angeles, the heart of the film industry, which she had visited with her brother Klaus in the winter of 1927 during their road trip. Although their hopes of being "discovered" in Hollywood, or at least of selling their father's novel *Königliche Hoheit* (*Royal Highness*, 1909) as a film script to MGM, fell flat, their experiences inspired the first book they wrote together. It was published by S. Fischer in 1929 under the title *Rundherum: Abenteuer einer Weltreise* (Round About: The Adventure of a Journey around the World) and received some acclaim. While this first encounter with Hollywood remained characterized by youthful exuberance and cheeky boldness (the siblings presented themselves as "the literary Mann-twins"), the spoiled globetrotters Erika and Klaus would become political émigrés only a few years later.

"For the first time since my flight from Germany I am almost at home somewhere. I have worked a lot, giving lectures and writing a book." These are the words of Erika in a fictionalized interview that opens the book *Escape to Life* (1939), also written with Klaus. At this time, Erika had been living in the United States for three years. She arrived in 1936, hoping to continue the success of her anti-Fascist political cabaret "Die Pfeffermühle" (the Peppermill). When that did not come to pass, she was able to start a new career as a political speaker, journalist, and eventually war correspondent with the U.S. Army. Her book *School for Barbarians,* which she mentions in the fictitious interview, was the first documentary report on education in the Third Reich and became a bestseller in the United States.

Erika expressed her admiration and respect for the "Land of Opportunity" in many forms: letters, essays, lectures, and the travelogue "Don't Make the Same Mistakes" (1940), which built on Sinclair Lewis's much discussed novel *It Can't Happen Here*. She had been trying to shake the American belief that Nazism was a purely German or European phenomenon that could never threaten the United States; the Atlantic Ocean seemed protection enough. In her travelogue, she writes of a train journey from Chicago to Los Angeles lasting several days, during which she encounters a well-educated and pleasant American who expresses these certainties. The young man sums up the results of World War I, the Treaty of Versailles, and German music and European culture in order to stress the historical and political singularity of the German road to Nazism. This, he claims, would be impossible in America. Proceeding from her personal history and the history of the final years of the Weimar Republic, Erika paints a different picture to her travel companion, countering that a "disease" may indeed spread into a life-threatening plague, even if it only affects one neighborhood. The fictitious

Erika Mann at tea with her parents, Katia and Thomas

conversation between the American and the German journalist émigré becomes a lesson in historical argument and contemporary history.

It is not by chance that this tale was based on a journey to Los Angeles. Erika accompanied her father and mother on his great lecture tour across North America and stayed with them at the Beverly Wilshire and later at the Beverly Hills Hotel. From her own activities, she was familiar with the social, cultural, and academic centers of Los Angeles. She often acted as interpreter and moderator of the question-and-answer sessions following her father's lectures. When Thomas addressed that audience of six thousand at the Shrine, Erika Mann gave a concise update of her father's speech at the "colossal amphitheater." She described the conditions in Austria after the German invasion, the sadistic barbarity of the persecution of the Jews, the random arrests, the hardships of the refugees, and the necessity of political solidarity and financial help. Vividly and emotionally, precisely and programmatically, she explained the situation to the audience and called on the United States to be the "conscience of democracy." President Roosevelt had been "concerned about the lot of hundreds of thousands of refugees," she pointed out, adding it was "the good fortune of democracy that the government is backed by a population of the greatest democratic independence." The Mann family's admiration for Roosevelt's America was unanimous, as Erika demonstrated when she expressed her support for countries invaded by Hitler's Germany. She appeared regularly in the lecture halls of Los Angeles, criticizing the isolationist policies of the United States and arguing emphatically for America's entry into the war. Inevitably this led to accusations of interfering in the internal affairs of her host country. Strong hostility and dangerous conflicts became part of Erika's everyday life.

After the end of World War II, however, she became disillusioned and her veneration for the U.S. Constitution and the American way of life was irreparably damaged. The Cold War and McCarthyism, her denouncement as a fellow traveler of Stalin, and frequent interrogation by the FBI led her to withdraw her application for citizenship. From Pacific Palisades, she wrote to the director of the Bureau of Immigration on December 11, 1950: "Nazism drove me away from Germany, the country of my birth where I had been fairly successful. Hitler's growing influence in Europe caused me to leave the continent where I had given over 1,000 performances with my own show; and now I see myself—without my own fault—ruined in a country that I love and whose citizen I had hoped to become."

GOLO MANN
Claremont Men's College · 888 North Columbia Avenue · Claremont
Friederike von Schwerin-High

Born in Munich in 1909, Golo Mann was the third of Thomas and Katia's six children. Possessed of a remarkable memory, he nevertheless experienced a somewhat withdrawn childhood within his highly gifted family circle and at the grammar schools he attended in Munich. Later, as a teenager, he transferred to Schule Schloss Salem, a boarding school, where he flourished. He took his academic high school exit exams in 1927, excelling in German and history. After several semesters of studying philosophy at the universities of Munich, Berlin, and Paris, he completed his doctoral thesis in 1930 at Heidelberg University under Karl Jaspers's supervision on the subject of Hegel's philosophy of history. Golo left Germany as early as 1933 and did not fully return to German-speaking Europe until 1958. He died in Leverkusen, Germany, in 1994.

Perhaps the formative years at the Salem school predisposed Golo, a lifelong avid hiker, toward the countryside in contrast to most of his family, especially his older siblings, Klaus and Erika, who were famous as children of the big city. Although reluctantly, Golo eventually found a home in the rural atmosphere of Claremont, the small Southern Californian college town, where he moved in 1947. He was further persuaded to pursue a career as a professor at Claremont Men's College (now Claremont McKenna College) by the prospect of being able to stand on his own two feet while engaging in pedagogical work. Golo, who believed that a thinking person wants their thoughts to be useful, taught classes that were very popular among students.

To be sure, Golo had not worked exclusively as a university lecturer. The length, uncertainty, and vagrancy of exile had not allowed him to build a normal academic career. Instead, he had proved himself a valuable collaborator, coeditor, and adviser on countless literary and publishing projects of his father, his uncle Heinrich, and his older brother, Klaus. Immediately prior to his employment at Claremont, he worked for the U.S. Army in military intelligence and helped establish new democratic public media in Hesse, West Germany. But even in the role and uniform of a U.S. Army officer, Golo could not envision himself living in Germany in the long run.

Golo Mann received his appointment at Claremont Men's College when the school was in its infancy. Its founding president, George C.S. Benson, assembled a faculty of distinguished, diverse scholars, with Golo an eminent representative of the German-speaking émigré community then making its mark in Southern California. Having published a well-received book, *Secretary of Europe: The Life of Friedrich Gentz, Enemy of Napoleon* (1947), Golo soon accumulated the credentials necessary to move quickly through the ranks from assistant to associate to full professor.

At Claremont, he taught modern European intellectual history, philosophy of history, problems of imperialism, political theory, and the Napoleonic era. Although he did not publish widely during this period, his class preparations would serve as the foundations of his later books on Wallenstein and on German history in the nineteenth and twentieth centuries, as well as countless political and historical articles and essays. Though he remained somewhat entrenched in provincial college life and did not necessarily network with the larger guild of prominent professional academic historians in the United States, he was highly regarded as an educator. His students voted him Professor of the Year in 1957. In the evenings, he sometimes invited colleagues and students for cheese and wine, delighting them with his accordion playing and old-fashioned European demeanor. Nevertheless, Golo never felt completely at home in Claremont. He always lived a little bit on the go, half-wishing to be appointed to a German university. There were, in fact, repeated negotiations with German universities. Yet, Germany had become a hopeless, disreputable place to which an exile and persecuted person did not necessarily want to return.

When his parents still resided in Pacific Palisades, Golo often visited them on weekends. Over the course of eleven years, he lived at seven different addresses in Claremont and neighboring Upland, all within a two-mile radius of the campus. Many of the places he rented still stand, but the College building where he had his office, Pitzer Hall, has been taken down, and Kravis Center and Gann Quadrangle now sit in its place.

Again and again, Golo received generous leaves of absence from Claremont Men's College. Combined with a prestigious Guggenheim Fellowship, these allowed him to spend increasingly more time on research assignments in Europe. Eventually, he received an appointment at Münster University and later at Stuttgart University, which led him to part ways with Claremont. Thanks to his long sojourn in California, however, he had become an expert on the United States and proceeded to write a best-selling book, *The Spirit of America* (1954). Written for a German audience, the book was dedicated to the faculty of Claremont Men's College. A thinker in decidedly transcontinental dimensions, Golo had written his earlier monograph on Gentz and the Congress of Vienna for an American audience; this new book on America was intended for a German readership.

As an educator, author of history books, and essayist, Golo has been consistently praised for his tremendous talent for storytelling, his elegant and engaging style of delivery, and his anti fatalistic approach to history. According to Golo, one can glean lessons from history by not regarding it not as a fait accompli but as a chain of events that could have turned out quite differently. Through a comparative-contrastive methodology, he argued, readers could appreciate history as a fundamentally open and contingent process, thereby preventing it from repeating itself. In some quarters, Golo was criticized for not providing extensive enough apparatuses of footnotes befitting scholarly writing. All the same, he became a sought-after and highly respected historiographer and political commentator who amassed numerous awards and international honors over the course of his long, distinguished career.

In 1981, Claremont alumnus Eugene L. Wolver Jr. ('51) established a lecture series named for Golo Mann at his alma mater. That, in turn, helped to launch the Athenaeum, the college's renowned venue for public speaking and debate. Golo himself gave a public lecture there on European politics on March 23, 1984, on the occasion of his seventy-fifth birthday celebration.

UNITARIAN CHURCH
2936 West 8th Street
Heinrich Detering

Thomas Mann's late, lasting embrace of the Unitarian Church—a church that ambitiously attempted to unite religious traditions from different parts of the world in a Christian perspective—has been long ignored. In 1951, the German novelist wrote that, for many years, Unitarianism had been "close to my heart," and "rarely, if ever," had he "taken so lively and militant an interest in the activities of any religious group." In many ways, he said, he felt connected to the Unitarians "personally and intellectually." Only a few months before his death in Switzerland, he wrote to the Unitarian minister Stephen H. Fritchman in Los Angeles, whom he considered a friend: "The spirit of your church [...]—it is this spirit that I find attractive since I got to know it." Mann did not speak of any other religious community in the same way. This partiality became apparent in his personal life. His youngest daughter, Elisabeth, and her husband were married in Princeton by a Unitarian minister, and the Unitarian Service Committee helped his brother Heinrich and son Golo escape from Europe during the war. All four grandchildren were baptized in the Unitarian Church. Mann wrote for the parish newsletter and spoke from the pulpit during a service. Fritchman remembered him as "one of our most cherished friends." There is little reason to doubt that Mann felt the same in return.

Mann's turn to the First Unitarian Church of Los Angeles epitomizes his effort to combine the political, philosophical, and religious traditions of his German background with an enlightened, universalist, and politically left-leaning tradition rooted in American culture since Ralph Waldo

Emerson and Walt Whitman. In preparation for his famous speech "On the German Republic" (1922), which marked his turn toward democracy, he studied Whitman's *Democratic Vistas*, which first led him to Emerson's transcendentalism and Unitarian traditions and provided him with an entirely new perspective on America.

Thus, at the beginning of his American exile, it was only a question of time before his personal convictions would take an institutional form. That came in 1940, when Golo and Heinrich fled Nazi Europe. Later, in 1942, Mann remembered the baptism of his four grandchildren as "the most gratifying experience in church I've ever had." Although his insistence on their Unitarian "baptism" was actually an act of heresy—the Protestant churches of the United States recognized neither the Unitarian Church nor its nonsacramental ceremonies as Christian—he continually insisted on the Christian origin and character of Unitarianism. At the crossroads of the Christian and nontheistic alignment, Mann plainly advocated a liberal Christian orientation. He published a "Christmas Message" in the congregation's newsletter as a summary of "what I personally mean by religion": a humanist, undogmatic yet pious, democratic endeavor.

While Mann and his family lived in Pacific Palisades, he became friends with Rev. Stephen Hole Fritchman, one of the most popular, most left-wing, and therefore most controversial figures in twentieth-century Unitarianism in the United States. Intellectually acute, relentlessly engaging in his political questioning, Fritchman had become chief editor of the most important Unitarian periodical in 1942, the *Christian Register*. Five years later, he lost this influential post after a sensational controversy, drawn out over a year and a half, in which he was denounced as a "Communist" because of his openly socialist leanings. The "Fritchman crisis" garnered nationwide public attention. In the wake of the scandal, Fritchman became a popular minister with the Los Angeles congregation. In his sermons, books, and radio shows, he advocated for African American equality, promoted social and political freedom, and spoke out against civil rights abuses during the anti-Communist hysteria.

As early as 1938, Fritchman's name had been at the top of the list of speakers at a rally in Boston, held under the motto "A Call to the People of Boston: Protest Nazi Terror against Jews and Catholics." The aims of his work as a minister in L.A. included reconciliation between Protestants, Catholics, Jews, theists, and atheists, because "communication with any person" is part of the "practice of our religion." Fritchman never relented in defending diversity and individual freedom, insisting that the true nature of religion lies in these maxims.

In Mann, the beleaguered Fritchman immediately found a supporter and, in the course of their six-year acquaintance, a friend. Mann, in turn, came to appreciate Fritchman as a fellow opponent of what he feared was the looming return of Fascism in American disguise. In October 1948, Mann and Frichtman published a protest note against the arrest of the "Hollywood Ten," who were suspected of being Communists. The paper had decisive consequences for both. On April 4, 1949, *Life* magazine, carried a sensational article, initiated by the FBI, depicting fifty mugshots with captions that gave only names and occupations in a format resembling a huge "Wanted" poster. The headline read: "Dupes and Fellow Travelers Dress Up Communist Fronts." The list was a who's who of liberal America. Apart from Norman Mailer, Albert Einstein, Leonard Bernstein, Charlie Chaplin, and Arthur Miller, it included "Thomas Mann, novelist" and "Stephen H. Fritchman, Unitarian clergyman." "To be a 'dupe' with them," Fritchman commented, "is the greatest honor I have yet had in my forty-six years."

The extent to which these events intensified the personal relationship between the two men can be seen eleven months later in a separate personal, even intimate, moment. On March 11, 1950, Heinrich Mann died. As if self-evidently, Thomas wanted to put the funeral in the hands of his Unitarian friend. In January 1951, when Fritchman was again a guest in Pacific Palisades, Mann commented on the visit the following day: "Fritschman [sic] yesterday: being American at its best." That year marked the high point in the alliance. In September, Fritchman was summoned before HUAC. Though

Mann himself was, in the end, spared interrogation, Congressman Donald Jackson denounced him, the liberal anti-Fascist, publicly as "one of the world's foremost apologists for Stalin and company." In this time of persecution, the two friends encouraged each other. "Men like you," Mann wrote to Fritchman, "are needed in this country today in greater numbers and they apparently are to be found."

In his autobiography, published in 1977, Fritchman described their friendship in detail. Letters from 1950 highlighted how much Mann, even at that time, actually identified with Unitarianism in general and with the L.A. congregation in particular. Under these circumstances, it came as no surprise that Thomas Mann himself should finally climb Fritchman's pulpit at the First Unitarian Church in March 1951. His reminiscences of both his intellectual and personal connection with the church soon gave way to passages characterized by a surprisingly confessional vehemence:

> By no means is it a matter of mere politeness or conventional courtesy, when I state that I am happy to be with you today. For many years past, Unitarianism has been close to my heart, and I have, more particularly, been rather intimately connected with the First Unitarian Church of Los Angeles. Last March, its Minister, the Reverend Stephen H. Fritchman, most movingly conducted the funeral rites for my dear brother Heinrich. My four grandchildren, native Americans all, were received into the Unitarian Church by baptism. And rarely, if ever, have I taken so lively and militant an interest in the activities of any religious group as I keep taking in the Unitarians' manifold efforts and doings. Why should this be so? I am a Lutheran, and owe a great deal to the German Protestant tradition into which I was born, as it were, and which contributed substantially to my spiritual and cultural make-up. Even so, and for my own person, I always inclined to see in religion something rather broader, more generally moral and ethical than that which could, as a rule, be expected to manifest itself within the confines of any one dogma.

Unitarianism here emerges not as another denomination but as the recognition of the human spirit—an interdenominational "unity of the human spirit"—which, as such, became the precondition for exemplary moral actions. Mann continued:

> Today, more urgently, perhaps, than ever before, what is needed is applied religion, applied Christianity—or, if you prefer, a new, religiously-tainted humanism, aggressively bent on bettering man's status and condition on earth, while at the same time honoring, and bowing in reverence to, the secret which lies at the bottom of all human existence and which must and will never be lifted for it is holy.

According to Fritchman's autobiography, this was "the most impressive pulpit editorial of my Los Angeles ministry, . . . [it] helped to define the concept of religion we were attempting to circulate in those days." Even after Mann's return to Europe,

Fritchman Auditorium, First Unitarian Church of Los Angeles

the friends stayed in touch. As late as December 1954, Mann recorded in his diary, among notes on world affairs: "Wrote message to Fritchman, Unitarian Church. Give money." In a letter written eight months before his death, he again remembered the familial relationship to the Unitarian Church and, quite solemnly, the private letter transformed into the "message":

> Leaving this aside, the spirit of your church, Christian humanism, which she advocates and which you humbly and bravely proclaim,—it is this spirit that attracts me since I learned about it and which I admire in true sympathy. Today, everyone speaks about the necessity to defend speech, freedom, and human dignity against totalitarian tyranny and coercion to conform, alien to western civilisation. . . . Without fail and at a sacrifice, the Unitarian church represents these western and Christian ideals in all their purity. These sacrifices have to and will be repaid. All those for whom your church is a source of spiritual inspiration will rally to provide

compensation. From abroad, I will contribute to this effort with the means of an author who does not write for a mass audience. And I ask you, dear minister Fritchman, to give my kindest wishes for Christmas and the new year to your congregation. They are wishes of peace and they are for a humankind united in their progress towards what is good.

Your friend
Thomas Mann.

No other document illustrated the spiritual affinity between the two men more clearly than a portrait photograph Mann sent to Fritchman in March 1951, with the handwritten dedication "To Stephen H. Fritchman. Defender of American evangelic freedom. Thomas Mann." Note he did not say "Protestant" but "evangelic"—meaning that he appreciated Fritchman's actions as according to a Gospel. The freedom he speaks of is democratic and, in this sense, an American freedom.

Fritchman himself would regard Mann as a good friend and as a teacher. When Mann died in 1955, Fritchman gave a moving memorial speech to his L.A. congregation, praising his selfless courage in the face of derisive attacks and even putting him in line with saints and prophets. He also spoke of the discreet financial contributions Mann continued to make from Europe "to resist the encroachment of the state upon the freedom of the church. He gave us all strength and courage, joy and pride in our limited personal human resources." Fritchman concluded, "His work will survive for years to come."

HOLLYWOOD MASONIC TEMPLE
6840 Hollywood Boulevard

Nikolai Blaumer

The history of Los Angeles is closely linked to Freemasonry. Although its heyday dates back decades, there are still many practicing lodges. Anyone driving through the streets of Los Angeles may discover numerous references to Freemasonry. One of the most outstanding architectural testimonies is the Hollywood Masonic Temple. A Masonic meeting place until the late 1970s, it has also been used for public events since its inception.

The temple was designed in 1921 by John C. Austin, one of the city's most eminent architects. Austin was responsible for Los Angeles City Hall, the Griffith Observatory, and the Shrine Auditorium, among other notable structures. The Hollywood Masonic Temple, formerly known as the Masonic Convention Hall, was home to Hollywood Lodge No. 355. In Thomas Mann's time, the 34,000-square-foot building was used for political meetings, such as those of the Independent Citizens Committee of the Arts, Sciences and Professions (ICCASP), which formed in the closing months of World War II to publicly oppose nuclear weapons and advocate for academic freedom.

Mann was a staunch supporter of the association's causes. Beginning in July 1945, he donated "20 dollars a month to the Indep. Citizens Comm. against the fascist agitation of Rankin, Smith, Reynolds in California." In another diary entry, the initiative was directed against the activities of representatives such as John E. Rankin, a cofounder of HUAC, and against the so-called Smith Act, which required all noncitizens to register their fingerprints and established criminal penalties for advocating for the overthrow of the U.S. government, primarily targeting Communists.

Mann was on the board of the ICCASP along with Duke Ellington, Eleanor Roosevelt, and other prominent supporters. In December 1945, he told

his patron Agnes E. Meyer that the organization was "a very well-behaved and all too necessary anti-Fascist corporation, of which I have become a member in horror at the state of democracy in this country. But it is on such occasions, in personal contact with the liberal forces of the country [. . .] that one regains courage and confidence. There was nothing like that in Germany after all, and one consoles oneself that the Smiths and Rankins and Reynolds will not have an easy time defeating this clear, firm, and manly, yet always humorously serene resistance."

Just one month later, on January 21, 1946, Mann appeared at another public meeting of the committee at the Hollywood Masonic Temple, the theme of which was "The Threat to Academic Freedom in California." He spoke after the Nobel Prize–winning chemist Linus Pauling, the committee's chairman. Mann's speech was a blunt attack on the so-called Tenney Committee in the California State Senate, which in those years forced the University of California to implement anti-Communist oaths for faculty: "Academic freedom does not only [. . .] mean the freedom to learn, but also the freedom to reach, the freedom of research and the independence of science. Where this freedom is chained by people who apply to it the improper and offensive standard of 'patriotic' or 'unpatriotic,' 'American' or 'un-American,' their culture, the soul of the country itself is in danger."

The following year Mann returned once again to the temple, this time for an address to the Hollywood Peace Group. He complained that he felt he was on increasingly unsafe ground in the United States. He had never been a Communist and would never be one. He sought, he said, "to restore the honor of America as a nation of well meaning intelligence and as a champion of progressive democracy."

In those years, the Hollywood Masonic Temple was an important meeting place for intellectuals who opposed the authoritarian tendencies of the emerging McCarthy era. Shortly after the Hollywood Peace Group meeting, a conference was organized by the screenwriter Dalton Trumbo to publicly protest the "treatment of minorities in film." After the Masonic Lodge's membership declined, the building was sold and later became a theater stage.

HOLLYWOOD FAIRFAX TEMPLE
525 South Fairfax Avenue
Nikolai Blaumer

When the United States entered the war in 1941, more than six thousand German Jews lived in Los Angeles, making the city the second largest center of German-speaking Jews in America. The Hollywood Fairfax Temple and its rabbi, Jacob Sonderling, created an important hub and community organization for Jewish art and culture. Thomas Mann met Sonderling multiple times during his American exile.

Sonderling was descended from a family of Galician Jews. He became involved in the Zionist cause at a young age and was one of writer and activist Theodor Herzl's earliest comrades-in-arms. After earning a doctorate in philosophy, he began serving as rabbi at the liberal Solomon Temple in Hamburg in 1908. There he worked to incorporate modern artistic, performative, and musical elements into religious services. Contemporaries called the temple "the cradle of Reform Judaism." Sonderling continued to pursue this approach, described as "both humanistic and innovative," when he immigrated to the United States in the early 1920s.

Rabbi Sonderling first settled with his family in New York before relocating west to found the Society for Jewish Culture–Fairfax Temple in Los Angeles in 1935. The community's members included numerous German and Austrian immigrants, and Sonderling took advantage of the arrival of outstanding composers of the musical avant-garde who found refuge in the California metropolis. He told the *Los Angeles Times* in 1938: "I saw tremendous possibilities with regard to the reinvigoration of our liturgical music." Sonderling commissioned a composition from Arnold Schoenberg and asked him to compose an arrangement for the Kol Nidre, the declaration recited before the evening prayer on Yom Kippur.

Connected through various mutual friends, Sonderling and Mann developed a good relationship over the years, born of an appreciation for each other's work. Sonderling invited Mann for multiple public talks at the Hollywood Fairfax Temple. During one such event in January 1945, Mann read from his story "The Law," which explores the exodus of the Israelites from Egypt. The five hundred people present had bought so-called war bonds as admission fees, which helped to finance the war against Nazi Germany. Mann's diary entry read: "introduced by Guggenheim, greeted standing by the audience. . . . Reading dramatic and exhausting, 1 hour and 10 minutes. Neumanns, Marcuse, von Hofe, Rabbi Sonderling, Singers and many others. Great impression."

However, Mann's appearances were sometimes controversial. For example, two gentlemen complained in the Jewish magazine *Aufbau* that children could be harmed by Mann's portrayal of Moses, and criticized Mann's allegedly historical-critical interpretation of the Bible. Rabbi Sonderling felt compelled to defend the writer in the March 1945 issue of *Aufbau*: "As a matter of fact, things are completely different. Thomas Mann, a novelist, chose a biblical figure for the subject of a book which he, as well as his readers, considers a work of fiction. His conception of Moses is the conception of a writer, and his book, in my opinion, can be appreciated or criticized only as a work of art [...] Accepting the fact that Mr. Mann did not claim he offered historical truth, but a novel on Moses—what is wrong with that?"

In 1951, Mann spoke again at Fairfax Temple, this time reading from his latest work, "The Holy Sinner." The philosopher Herbert Marcuse attended the lecture and wrote an article about it for *Aufbau*: "The Fairfax temple was overcrowded. In a speech, the host, Rabbi Dr. Sonderling, gave the highest and wisest praise to the novel 'Joseph and his Brothers': he did not say that Thomas Mann had brought the Bible closer to him again but that he had made it mysterious to him again [...]. Thomas Mann is a brilliant reader because he talks so well. His pleasure is contagious. He plays a whole theater: acoustically; he is a funny human voice imitator. What he put into the blue air that evening—blue, although smoking was not allowed in the temple—was a Mann medieval story: high-spirited and laid-back."

FLORENCE HOMOLKA
10788 Bellagio Road
Kaltërina Latifi

Florence Meyer Homolka (1911–1962), eldest daughter of Agnes E. Meyer and Eugene Meyer (a former publisher of the *Washington Post*), took some of the most impressive photographic portraits of artists, writers, and intellectuals of the 1940s and 1950s in U.S.-American exile. Charlie Chaplin, Judy Garland, Vladimir Horowitz, Lion Feuchtwanger, Arnold Schoenberg, Christopher Isherwood, and Thomas Mann were among her subjects. She was successful in capturing in an image what her mother had tried to do in her unfinished biography of Thomas Mann. In that work, Agnes was determined to represent the man and, to a lesser extent, the artist, for the character of a person, she believed, "is the greatest work of art altogether."

Both Mann and Homolka moved to the West Coast in the same year, 1941—Mann from Princeton to Pacific Palisades, Homolka to Los Angeles with her husband, the Austrian actor Oscar Homolka. Oscar had made a name as a first-rate actor in character parts in Berlin theater and in film. In 1935, he voluntarily immigrated to England and then, two years later, to the United States, where he managed to find work in Hollywood. Agnes Meyer had introduced her daughter to Mann, who grew fond of her. She was "as beautiful as a picture," he confessed in a letter to Agnes. He also admired her talent: "She has masterfully developed her photographic technique and has taken exquisite photographs of me." Thereafter, Homolka often visited the Mann family; she must have had her camera at hand all the time.

We take from Mann's diaries that he, too, often visited the Homolkas, who lived at 10788 Bellagio Road in Bel Air. In the summer of 1941, there is a record of several such encounters, be it at a "soirée at the Homolka's in Bel Air," or "for tea to Bel Air at the Homolka's." Agnes, who was visiting her daughter, also joined them: "Grand evening reception at the Homolka's in honor of Meyer. Cocktails, hors d'œuvres, buffet dinner, wild talking." Likewise, in 1943 Mann recorded such encounters in his diary, including a "reception at the Homolka's to meet the Ambassador and Mrs Davis," where he had a lively "conversation with [the ambassador] about Russia" and "the strategic options, [and] Hitler's difficulties with crude oil supplies."

Even in November 1948, the German intellectual continued to enjoy Homolka's company and her exceptional talent: "Florence has taken enchanting pictures of us and the little grandsons, a whole series." What was it that Mann so appreciated in Homolka's photographic style? Could Mann, the great storyteller, see in her almost intimate approach to family scenes a kind of narrative in sequence—in this particular case, a photo of the author telling a story to his favorite grandson, Frido? Another grandson lurks in the background, looking somewhat disgruntled, if not envious, of what is going on between his brother and his cheeky-looking grandfather.

It is part and parcel of Homolka's craft that

she depicts, for instance, Thomas and Katia with a gracious, almost regal air, as in her rendering of the couple in white on their terrace in Pacific Palisades in 1946. Homolka excels at blending the formal with the casual, exemplified by numerous photographs showing Thomas at work. Time and again, it was always Homolka's intention to portray Mann in the context of his family and work as a fully rounded personality; it might have been precisely that feature that attracted him most to her art.

Katia and Thomas Mann, by Florence Homolka, 1946

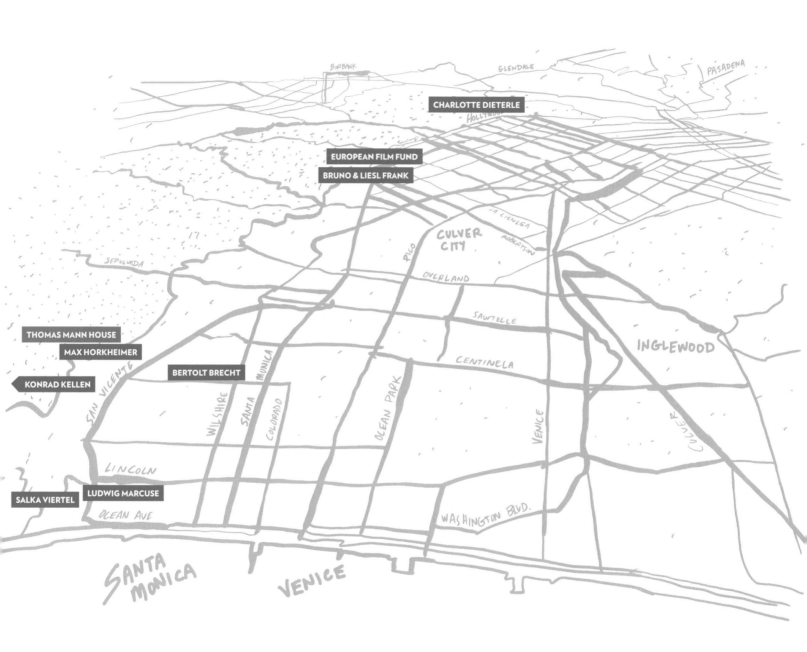

PART 2

CHARLOTTE DIETERLE

EUROPEAN FILM FUND

BRUNO & LIESL FRANK

THOMAS MANN HOUSE

MAX HORKHEIMER

KONRAD KELLEN

BERTOLT BRECHT

SALKA VIERTEL

LUDWIG MARCUSE

BURBANK

GLENDALE

PASADENA

HOLLYWOOD

CULVER CITY

LA CIENEGA

ROBERTSON

SEPULVEDA

OVERLAND

SAWTELLE

INGLEWOOD

SAN VICENTE

WILSHIRE

SANTA MONICA

COLORADO

OCEAN PARK

CENTINELA

VENICE

CULVER

LINCOLN

OCEAN AVE

WASHINGTON BLVD.

PICO

SANTA MONICA

VENICE

THOUGHT AND ACTION: REFUGEES, SUPPORTERS, AND THE NEW LEFT
Nikolai Blaumer

Everyone was fleeing and everything was temporary. We had no idea whether this situation would last until tomorrow, another couple of weeks, or our entire lives." Anna Seghers, in her novel *Transit* (1944), describes the utter chaos and fear faced by German refugees during the Nazi takeover.

Seghers, a self-confessed Communist, had already fled Berlin in 1933. The immediate threat to all Jewish and oppositional artists was tangible from the very first days of German Fascism. Weeks after the seizure of power, a public campaign against the "Un-German Spirit" began, which included the burning of books by dissenters and the denigration of modern art. A law was established requiring artists, musicians, writers, and other creatives to become members of the so-called *Reichskulturkammer* (Reich Chamber of Culture). Non-Aryans, Communists, and other opposition members were denied membership. Thus began an unprecedented exodus that encompassed most of the German cultural world.

Over the next few months, new centers of German exile culture emerged with their own publishing houses, theaters, and newspapers. Among them were the publications *Arbeiter-Illustrierte-Zeitung* (Prague), *Das Neue Tage-Buch* (Amsterdam), *Das Wort* (Moscow), *Mass und Wert* (Zurich), and *Orient* (Haifa). The center of German exile life was undoubtedly France. Alongside Paris, the southern French Mediterranean town of Sanary-sur-Mer became an intellectual German capital, frequented by Joseph Roth, Bruno Frank, Stefan Zweig, Alfred Kantorowicz, Lion and Marta Feuchtwanger, Ludwig Marcuse, Alma Mahler-Werfel and Franz Werfel, Bertolt Brecht, and, not least, the Manns.

Of course, the stream of exiles that spread around the world at that time not only included the German-speaking intelligentsia but also was a mass emigration of hundreds of thousands. The refugees' plight gained more international attention as the persecution intensified in Germany and the number of homeless and stateless people climbed rapidly, since many of the refugees were unable to find host countries. In the summer of 1938, President Roosevelt invited delegates from thirty-two countries to an international conference in Evian-les-Bains, France. Despite eager expressions of sympathy, not a single country except the Dominican Republic was willing to accept more refugees.

Across the United States, political forces sought to prevent the admission of Jewish refugees. According to the National Origins Law of 1924, the number of annual immigrants was strictly regulated by country. However, political resistance and sabotage in the administrative bodies ensured that those quotas were not reached. This affected the quota of German emigrants, under which Jewish refugees were counted according to their nationality.

With the annexation of Austria and the invasion of the Wehrmacht into what is now the Czech Republic, the situation of the persecuted further deteriorated. According to research by the United States Holocaust Memorial Museum, by September 1939 about 282,000 Jews had fled Germany and 117,000 from Austria. Of these, about 95,000 had immigrated to the United States, 60,000 to Palestine, 40,000 to Great Britain, and 75,000 to South America. There were about 350,000 Jews living in France at that time, of whom a whopping two-thirds

Varian Fry, seated right, in Marseille with André Breton, André Masson, and Breton's wife Jacqueline

were expelled from other countries. France's military defeat in June 1940 left them in a sort of deadlock.

France was divided into a German-occupied area and a self-governing zone with Vichy as its capital. According to the armistice agreement, the French administration was obliged to extradite foreigners at the behest of Germany. Thus, the Vichy government began interning first foreign-born and then French Jews. Since escape across the Mediterranean was not possible, the only way out was through Spain and Portugal and across the Atlantic. Three initiatives proved to be important rescuers in that situation, and Thomas Mann actively supported their cause.

The Emergency Rescue Committee (ERC) was founded in New York under the patronage of Eleanor Roosevelt in the same month that the Wehrmacht marched into France. Operating covertly from Marseille, the initiative's declared goal was to enable persecuted intellectuals, artists, and scientists to escape from occupied France to the United States. Its central figure was Varian Fry, who was only in his early thirties. He and his team arranged financial aid for refugees, helped obtain forged papers, and facilitated illegal border crossings into Spain. Mann provided a list of threatened poets and writers who were in France. It is estimated that the ERC was able to help as many as four thousand escape, including Marc Chagall, Max Ernst, Marta and Lion Feuchtwanger, and Alma Mahler-Werfel and Franz Werfel, as well as Mann's son Golo and brother Heinrich and his wife, Nelly.

On their journey from the French-Spanish border through Lisbon to the United States, many of the refugees were also assisted by the Unitarian Service Committee. The leaders of the initiative were Unitarian minister Waitstill Sharp and his wife, Martha. They, too, helped procure needed documents and were endowed with a generous fund from the American Unitarian Church. Mann was in direct communication with the Sharps and at times even signed on as spokesman for the committee. On September 20, 1940, he noted with relief in his diary, "At breakfast telegram from Golo and Heinrich from Lisbon, where they are waiting for a ship. Joy and satisfaction. Dispatches from the Committee, from the Unitarians who were helpful."

Entry into the United States was at the time fraught with numerous bureaucratic and financial hurdles for the fugitives. For example, they had to prove affidavits, job commitments, and financial reserves in order to obtain valid entry visas. Usually this was not possible without assistance. Even after their arrival, the newcomers were dependent on personal and financial help. The European Film Fund (EFF) was founded in response in 1938. Thomas Mann supported the organization financially, through general donations and donations that, mediated by the EFF, were directed to specific individuals—among them Heinrich Mann, Alfred Döblin, Leonhard Frank, and Walter Mehring—providing a precious lifeline.

Many of the refugees experienced their time in exile as a profound existential crisis. In Los Angeles, the philosopher Günther Anders had to eke out a living as a factory worker. He later recalled his dramatic situation as a "flourish of the infernal." Like many other refugees, Anders was constantly on the hunt for a residence permit, which he called a "life permit." For all those who were not particularly privileged, this certificate could paradoxically only be obtained if they simultaneously kept their heads above water with illegal moonlighting and meal cards. Life in exile was life on the edge.

In his essay "The Emigrant," published in the postwar period, Anders bemoaned that he had been denied a "lifewhole": "I could remember Paris only inadequately after I had reached the next station, New York; and since I have been living in Vienna, the factory to which I had to pilgrimage in Los Angeles lies in deep darkness—none of those who worked beside me is still known to me by name, none of the faces can I conjure up any longer. . . . What is true of every individual stretch within our lives is, of course, even more true of the whole of life. Its meandering pattern works as an effective hindrance to knowledge, the multiplicity of its bends makes its course completely inscrutable."

Anders's first wife, the political thinker Hannah Arendt, also reflected on her own experience of exile in New York. In the essay "We Refugees," written in 1943, she pondered the question of what constitutes a refugee and what this status means for one's own identity. Arendt observed that none of the exiles around her wanted to be called "refugee": "All our activities are directed to attain this aim: we don't want to be refugees, since we don't want to be Jews (. . .)." She called on her fellow exiles to acknowledge their Jewishness and their status as refugees: "Refugees driven from country to country represent the vanguard of their people—if they keep their identity. For the first time Jewish history is not separate but tied up with that of all other nations."

Likewise, Bertolt Brecht acknowledged his status as a refugee in his poem "On the Term Emigrants," expressing that the term did not fit his life in exile:

Always have I thought the name given to us was wrong:
Emigrants.
That means those who leave their country. But we
Didn't emigrate, on free will
Choosing a different country. Nor did we emigrate
Into a country in order to stay, possibly forever
But we fled. We are expellees, banished.
And no home, but an exile shall the country be
That accepted us.

Although Brecht did not see himself as part of American society, his political thinking was sharpened by his confrontation with social reality in Los Angeles. Brecht was shocked by the social contrasts in the city and by how writers here, as he perceived it, prostituted themselves for the film industry. Soon after his arrival, he captured in a poem how the glittering city on the Pacific could be both heaven and hell.

In Hell too
There are, I've no doubt, these luxuriant gardens
With flowers as big as trees, which of course wither
Unhesitantly if not nourished with very expensive water. And fruit markets
With great heaps of fruit, albeit having
Neither smell nor taste. And endless processions of cars
Lighter than their own shadows, faster than
Mad thoughts, gleaming vehicles in which
Jolly-looking people come from nowhere and are nowhere bound.
And houses, built for happy people, therefore standing empty
Even when lived in.

The houses in Hell, too, are not all ugly.
But the fear of being thrown on the street
Wears down the inhabitants of the villas no less than
The inhabitants of the shanty towns.

Arguably the most important work of social criticism produced in German exile on the Pacific is the seminal work *Dialectic of Enlightenment* by Max Horkheimer and Theodor W. Adorno, still one of the central texts of critical theory. Even though the book's main concern is a fundamental critique of the

Enlightenment's concept of reason, its assessment of the social reality of the time remains unmistakable.

The background foil for Horkheimer and Adorno's philosophical remarks was their shared experience as exiles in Los Angeles. The two sociologists, who had fled Frankfurt, found little to like about the popular culture of their host country. They criticized the industrially produced culture that robbed people of their imagination and deprived them of the ability to think. In their eyes, the people are reduced to consumers who are fobbed off with superficial trivia. Under these circumstances, questioning social order was becoming increasingly impossible: "Culture today is infecting everything with sameness," they declared. Hollywood was their main target. Laconically, Adorno stated that "every visit to the cinema leaves me, against all my vigilance, stupider and worse."

Yet their relationship to the film world is more ambivalent than one might think. As David Jenemann writes, Adorno and Horkheimer were by no means only hostile to Hollywood. Beginning in 1941, they worked for several years on a film project for the American Jewish Committee (AJC), the goal of which was to create a "typology of anti-Semitic traits." Distraught over the persecutions in Europe, they planned to galvanize viewers with a motion picture, employing suggestive means similar to those they themselves accused the "culture industry" of using. In a memo, they wrote that the shocking images in their film should convince all skeptics: "'Those devils must pay.' They are shown, their numbers increasing, finally merging with a symbolic picture of the whole American nation, marching united against the Axis."

Highly motivated to bring their project to fruition, Adorno and Horkheimer exhausted all possible contacts. They got in touch with the playwright Dore Schary, who would later become president of MGM. Schary dodged them for several months, feigning illness. The pair then unsuccessfully approached the writer Dalton Trumbo before using AJC funds to hire two less prominent screenwriters to bring the script to life based on their notes. The project dragged on into the postwar months before it was finally scrapped in 1946.

The Adorno and Horkheimer episode illustrates the paradoxical, critical yet productive way in which many of the exiles dealt with their own situation amid the social reality in Los Angeles. Looking back on his life, Adorno later noted that it was precisely his inability to adapt and his alienation in America that had given him an unbiased view on many cultural issues. Or as Brecht, once again, put it in *Refugee Conversations*:

> Emigration is the best school of dialectics. Refugees are the keenest dialecticians. They are refugees as a result of changes and their sole object of study is change. They are able to deduce the greatest events from the smallest hints—that is, if they have intelligence. When their opponents are winning, they calculate how much their victory has cost them; and they have the sharpest eyes for contradictions. Long live dialectics!

EUROPEAN FILM FUND
9169 Sunset Boulevard
Martin Sauter

The European Film Fund (EFF) was a refugee organization that emerged in response to the Nazi takeover in Germany. Founded in October 1938 in Los Angeles, the EFF's chief goal was to provide financial support to Jews from Nazi Germany working in Hollywood. It also offered emotional support, procured affidavits, and helped newly arrived refugees find work. Through the agent Paul Kohner, who was a cofounder, the EFF secured temporary writer's contracts with major film studios such as Warner Bros., which allowed émigrés to enter the country on a visa. Thomas Mann's brother Heinrich was one of the beneficiaries. As the EFF was first and foremost directed at refugees working in the film industry, it was instrumental when it came to negotiating these one-year "emergency contracts."

Though initially the brainchild of Kohner and the director Ernst Lubitsch, it was Liesl Frank, wife of the German-Jewish writer Bruno Frank, and Charlotte Dieterle, actress wife of the director William Dieterle, who in fact kept the EFF afloat. Evidence shows that the link between the Mann family and the EFF came down to one person in particular: Liesl Frank, the organization's executive secretary. The reasons for the strong bond between the Manns and Mrs. Frank were manifold. First of all, she was the daughter of one of Weimar Germany's most prominent and revered stage actresses, Fritzi Massary, whom the Manns knew and admired.

To say that Fritzi's fame rubbed off on her daughter would be an exaggeration. It did succeed in turning Liesl Frank into a sort of celebrity by proxy. Furthermore, Liesl had her mother's wit and

savviness, all of which may have fueled the mutual attraction between her and Bruno. They married in 1924 and lived on Munich's Mauerkirchner Strasse, a stone's-throw away from the Manns, who resided on Poschinger Strasse. Given Fritzi's prominence and the fact that the Manns and the Franks were neighbors—not to mention that Thomas and Bruno shared the same profession—it is not surprising that both families became close.

Though founded to support exiled film workers who had fallen on hard times, the EFF ended up supporting primarily writers, as their income was solely based on language compared to that of actors and directors. In addition, few of the émigré writers ever mastered the English language to a degree that allowed them to write and publish in English. Similarly, few were known well enough abroad to enable them to live on the proceeds of their books sold outside German-speaking territory. With their works banned in Nazi Germany, they could only rely on translations and the sale of the rights to their books to film companies. This, in turn, meant that their books had to be popular enough to be read outside their homeland. German and Austrian writers lucky enough to fall into that category were few and far between.

One of them was Thomas Mann, by far the most widely read German author in the world. The same cannot be said of Heinrich, whose novels were little known beyond his native country, despite the success of Josef von Sternberg's landmark movie *The Blue Angel* (1930), which was based on Heinrich's novel *Professor Unrat*, a fact practically unknown outside Germany.

Moreover, because Heinrich was a staunchly outspoken anti-Nazi, his bank accounts and his Munich apartment were seized by the regime after the Nazi takeover. With low foreign sales of his books, he quickly became dependent on outside aid, particularly once the contract the EFF had negotiated on his behalf had expired. Thus, Heinrich had to rely on financial support from Thomas in order to sustain himself and his wife, Nelly; occasionally, Thomas's monthly checks to his brother were issued through the EFF.

Thomas and Katia were also donors to the EFF, as that was how the organization worked: the better-off members of L.A.'s émigré community supported those who were in financial straits. From 1938 until its dissolution in 1946, the Manns donated $710 to the EFF (about $9,000 in 2022). The funds were usually administered by Liesl and Charlotte, and allocated depending on the financial situation of the beneficiaries.

Despite his donations, nothing suggests that Mann attended any of the organization's gatherings or meetings, though he did lend his name to efforts to raise additional funds to support Hollywood luminaries after their emergency contracts expired.

Just how close the Manns and the Franks were is highlighted by a telegram Katia and Thomas wired to Liesl following her husband's sudden death in summer 1945. In it, they stressed that they had no better friends and that Bruno would live on in their hearts. Thomas chose to sign the letter "Tommy," a moniker he is known to have used only with his dearest friends.

European Film Fund donor list, 1 May 1941 through 30 April 1942

BRUNO & LIESL FRANK
513 North Camden Drive · Beverly Hills
Friedhelm Marx

On a March 23, 1938, diary entry on his arrival in Los Angeles with his wife and daughter, Thomas Mann wrote of going "for lunch at Frank's. Nice little house." This first social invitation, coming near the end of Thomas's long lecture tour, took Thomas and Katia to the home of Bruno and Liesl Frank, at 513 North Camden Drive, Beverly Hills. The warm welcome from his fellow author, friend, and neighbor, combined with the sunny, warm, ocean-kissed air, made the city shine like no other. As a Jewish writer, Frank had left Germany immediately after the Nazi takeover in 1933 with Liesl, and had arrived in Los Angeles in 1937 via Austria, France, London, and New York. By this time, some of his books had been translated into English and his plays successfully staged in London and New York. Frank signed a screenwriting contract with MGM, securing a steady income, at least temporarily.

The next day, the Manns decided to extend their stay in the city. Through the month of April, Thomas, Katia, and Erika took up residence at the Beverly Hills Hotel, just a mile from the Franks' house. A kind of welcome party was held on April 3: "1/2 4 to Franks, big garden party, . . . talked to 100 people," Mann noted in his diary. Old acquaintances from Europe were among the guests, including the theater impresario Max Reinhardt and Carl Laemmle,

founder of Universal Pictures, in addition to many celebrities: "a sort of Vienna coffee house affair, with dozens of tables in her garden . . . and gallons of wonderful coffee and heavenly Kuchen and Kirschwasser . . . everyone proclaiming it the most charming event ever to happen in Hollywood," reported his friend Agnes Meyer. Bruno and Liesl made sure that the Manns were immersed in the glittering art and film scene of Hollywood during those weeks. The Manns' eventual decision to leave Princeton and relocate in Los Angeles, near that same "little house" on Camden Drive, was no doubt influenced by the numerous joint undertakings, walks, and dates for tea, lunch, and dinner. As former neighbors in Munich's Herzog Park, the Franks represented a little Munich in a foreign land, and Mann's children Erika and Klaus also perceived it that way during their visits to Camden Drive. Once the decision had been made in 1940, the family leaned on Liesl and Bruno for advice and support.

The Manns and the Franks were also united in their political commitment to the writers in Europe who were hoping for U.S. entry visas in the face of increasing danger. By March 1938, Bruno and Thomas had already made short political statements asking for financial support for the refugees from Germany. In the years that followed, they worked together on numerous initiatives that sought to secure visas, employment contracts, and donations for those affected, especially in the film industry. These included the American Guild for German Cultural Freedom, the American Committee for Christian German Refugees, and the EFF. After the United States entered the war, Mann and Frank lobbied the so-called Tolan Committee to ensure that Germans in exile were not counted as "enemy aliens." In 1943, each contributed a novella to the anthology *The Ten Commandments: Ten Short Novels of Hitler's War against the Moral Code.* For European writers in distress, the Frank house on Camden Drive became an important contact point; Ludwig Marcuse recalled that German-speaking exiles met there to listen to radio news from Europe.

Even after his contract with MGM was terminated in May 1939, Frank occasionally worked for the studios, including on screenplays for William Dieterle's *The Hunchback of Notre Dame* (1939), Mervyn LeRoy's *Madame Curie* (1943), and Ernst Lubitsch's *A Royal Scandal* (1943), but he soon returned to primarily pursuing his literary projects. Mann was his most important interlocutor; Frank's novel *The Daughter* (1943) and Mann's

Doctor Faustus (1947) were read to each other in turn, sometimes on Camden Drive, sometimes in the Manns' newly built house in Pacific Palisades. Bruno's life-threatening heart attack in April 1944, the constant suspicion that befell exiled authors, and the lengthy process of pursuing U.S. citizenship in January 1945 increasingly clouded the Franks' mood. On June 20, 1945, while preparing to move back to New York, Bruno Frank died as a result of a protracted bout of pneumonia. In an obituary for *Aufbau*, Mann wrote: "I will miss living side by side, the exchange, until my own last hour. I will miss his intelligent listening and fruitful commentary, his rich conversation, his European education and historical erudition, his laughter at stupidity, which he found very funny, yet knew in its gigantic malignity and danger."

Liesl and Bruno Frank in the garden of their house in Munich

CHARLOTTE DIETERLE
3151 North Knoll Drive
Diane Sippl

While Arnold Schoenberg composed a piece for German actress Charlotte Dieterle, and Bertolt Brecht wrote a poem about his friendship with her and her husband. It's doubtful, though, that either German émigré spent as much time with Charlotte and William, as Thomas Mann did. From the late 1930s to the mid-1950s, Mann entered at least fifty encounters with the couple in his diary—dining with them at his Pacific Palisades home or at their house in the Hollywood Hills, at the table, in the garden, or journeying to their farm through the "Topanga Pass" to attend soirées before and after film screenings in their library.

Whenever the Dieterles extended an invitation to a date in Beverly Hills (at the Beverly Wilshire Hotel) or Hollywood (at the Hotel Roosevelt), Mann often would get a ride from Bruno Frank or Ernst Lubitsch. He rarely drove, but that was not the reason for these particular escorts. Both he and Frank were active in the EFF, whose operations were essentially maintained by Charlotte and by Frank's wife, Liesl. Dieterle had organized the EFF just before WWII to support exiles from Hitler's Germany by arranging and funding the departures of exiles from Germany and placing them at Hollywood studios (primarily Metro-Goldwyn-Mayer and Warner Bros.) with one-year screenwriting contracts that would allow their entry into the U.S. She negotiated endless affidavits and financial agreements with Europeans in the industry who could afford to contribute. The refugees would be paid a weekly salary of $100.

By all accounts, Charlotte Dieterle was a mover and shaker in the émigré community and beyond. Hedda Hopper, the "buzziest" lady in Hollywood, wrote in 1939 in the *Los Angeles Times*, "And did you know that Dieterle's wife has probably done more for the Polish, Chinese and Jewish refugees than any other person in town? And the Dieterles helped back 'William Tell', which was given for the German refugees, to the tune of some 40-odd thousand dollars. And almost everybody in the cast got a job in Hollywood."

Whether it meant physical labor with the Citizens Committee for the Army and Navy to refurbish donated sofas at camps for isolated servicemen, or showing Girl Scouts how to safety-pin tags on clothes being sent overseas to war victims, Dieterle pitched in and did what was needed. She also gave speeches, hosted dinner-dances, and organized concerts and teas. She set up fundraising events throughout the Southland at ballrooms and banquet halls in Beverly Hills, swanky supper clubs, and private gardens. Whether at the El Capitan in Hollywood, the Embassy Club, the Warner Bros. KFWB Theatre, Max Reinhardt's *kaffeeklatsch* Workshop on Sunset Boulevard, the Victor Hugo Restaurant, the Book and Play Salon in Hancock Park, or the screening room in her own home in the Hollywood Knolls, her goal was to raise money. Yet a lot of her work was done behind the scenes.

Her initiative and ceaseless dedication to the EFF remain a key example of her commitment and accomplishments, but she also spearheaded countless campaigns to raise money for critical causes before, during, and after World War II. Some of these feats required more than coordinating people and venues and schedules; they required nonstop communication, from loud-and-clear publicity to covert operations, in order to produce effective results.

"Mrs. Dieterle," as newspapers such as the *Los Angeles Times* referred to her again and again, was a prominent figure, having worked as an actress in Berlin before she emigrated to Hollywood with her husband of fifteen years. Also an actor, William was known as the John Barrymore of Germany before he "defected" from the theater (Max Reinhardt's, no less) to the motion picture world in California, where he wrote, directed, and acted, getting to "[know] pictures from bow to stern." By 1932, the Dieterles had moved to 3151 North Knoll Drive, a spacious home in the Hollywood Hills with a splendid view of the canyons and easy access to William's work at Warner Bros. Studios.

In at least one case, William landed a job thanks to Charlotte's social imagination, shrewdness, and knack for bringing people together. She is said to have launched the ground-breaking 1935 million-dollar-plus production of *A Midsummer Night's Dream* for simultaneous release in twenty countries. Her husband would "assist" Max Reinhardt, who was credited as directing the film. The *Los Angeles Times* reported, "It was Mrs. Dieterle who tackled [producer] Hal Wallis, sold him wholesale, made and signed all the business contracts; bore with Max and William while they swatted over the adaptation and culled the Mendelssohn musical score; fed them pineapple pancakes" (the Dieterles had just returned from a trip to Hawaii). Charlotte's artistic enterprise and flair for persuasion fit hand-in-glove with her head for business. Surely Thomas Mann was inspired by her time and again.

SALKA VIERTEL

165 North Mabery Road · Santa Monica

Donna Rifkind

In her 1969 autobiography, *The Kindness of Strangers*, the screenwriter Salka Viertel confessed that she couldn't remember the first time she was introduced to her good friend Thomas Mann. She supposed that it must have been during the summer of 1940 in Los Angeles, most likely at a banquet for the Emergency Rescue Committee, whose work on behalf of European refugees both Viertel and Mann supported. Viertel called him "the representative, towering literary figure" of the exiled German-speaking artists and intellectuals who lived in Los Angeles during the 1930s and 1940s.

On Sundays they often met at Salka Viertel's house in Santa Monica, where they mixed with movie stars like Charlie Chaplin and Harpo Marx. When Viertel introduced newcomers to Mann, whom many Americans then considered the greatest writer in the world, she noted that Mann retained "the reserved politeness of a diplomat on official duty."

Mann referred to Viertel only fleetingly in his diaries. "Evening party at Salka Viertel's," reads a 1944 entry. "Excellent cooking. Wurst, soup, beer, hot coffee. Long conversation with [the philosopher Theodor] Adorno about the musical problematic of [*Doctor Faustus*]." And elsewhere: "Dinner at Salka Viertel's with [the director Ernst] Lubitsch and others. Excellent coffee. I spoke enthusiastically about Lohengrin, then a few Bismarck anecdotes."

A defining moment in the Viertel-Mann friendship occurred in May of 1941. Forty-five exiles gathered for dinner at Viertel's house to celebrate the seventieth birthday of Thomas Mann's elder brother, Heinrich, who had recently escaped from France with the help of the ERC. Before Viertel brought out her legendary chocolate cake, each brother gave a speech excoriating the National Socialists in Germany as the "defilers of humanity now ruling Europe." For Thomas and Heinrich, Viertel's house represented a last refuge from barbarism. "When the homeland becomes foreign," Thomas Mann declared that night, "the foreign becomes the homeland."

If Mann was the towering star of the Los Angeles exiles, Viertel was their ambassador, bringing them together and fostering alliances between them. For all his eminence, Mann never remained aloof from this intentional community. He understood its value and was grateful to participate in it. As he had written in *The Magic Mountain*: "A human being lives out not only his personal life as an individual, but also, consciously or subconsciously, the lives of his epoch and contemporaries."

Sergei Eisenstein and Salka Viertel on the beach in Santa Monica

MAX HORKHEIMER
13524 D'Este Drive
David Jenemann

Max Horkheimer, the exiled director of the Institute for Social Research (better known in the United States as the Frankfurt School), lived just down the hill and around the corner from the Manns in Pacific Palisades. That the Nobel Prize winner and the founder of critical theory were in such close proximity suggests nights of deep conversation, penetrating philosophical discussions, and probing efforts to come to grips with the European catastrophe and its potential aftermath. Though there were plenty of opportunities for such high-mindedness, what stood out about their relationship was their old-fashioned neighborliness.

Whom did Thomas and Katia call on to accompany them to their citizenship examination and serve as their character witnesses in 1944? It was Max and his wife, Maidon. Katia aced her exam—she had studied for it. Thomas had less than perfect results. Hence, a lot was riding on Horkheimer's response to the naturalization official's question as to whether "on his honor and his conscience" he believed Mann "would be a desirable citizen." Horkheimer's answer: "You bet." Short and sweet but not surprising for the sometimes laconic Horkheimer, who often signed off on correspondences with a simple "Alright."

In fact, compared to all his Frankfurt School colleagues, Horkheimer seemed to have adapted to America most easily, familiarizing himself with its lingo and adopting its directness. He and Maidon had made their way from New York to Los Angeles in a 1941 Buick at a time when many of his fellow exiles hadn't yet learned how to drive. He immersed himself in popular culture by clipping comic strips from the *Los Angeles Times*, and—unlike some of his fellow exiles—he sought to ingratiate himself with his American peers.

Horkheimer was perhaps, then, the perfect citizenship witness for the Manns. Their post-exam celebration was certainly in keeping with their new status. "Afterwards," Mann wrote in a letter to Agnes Meyer, "[we] had a vigorous American meal in a restaurant, pancakes with maple syrup, and coffee."

In the same letter to Meyer, Mann makes early mention of the development of the work that would become *Doctor Faustus*. "My concern now is with Adrian Leverkühn," Mann explained, referencing the tormented composer at the center of the novel, "and the problem of how to make the musical technicalities that come thrusting forward readable." Horkheimer would prove helpful in this matter as well, brokering a connection with his colleague and friend Theodor Adorno, whose draft of *Philosophy of Modern Music* and whose long talks with Mann would ultimately help solve the problem of making the compositional complexities of "the new music" narratively legible.

Four years later, the same week that Mann was receiving the first mimeographed copies of the English translation of *Faustus*, the Horkheimers once again featured prominently in his correspondence.

But this time, Mann did not commend any of Horkheimer's intellectual insights or express gratitude for introducing him to Adorno. Instead, in a letter to Bruno Walter, Mann lamented breaking his collarbone as a consequence of Max's long-standing neglect of home maintenance: "Many thanks for your sympathy. There is something quite embarrassing about receiving flowers, wine, and nice letters as the reward for such clumsiness. The step at Horkheimers is universally hated, and no doubt a good many others have stumbled over it, but still not quite in that way. I must have been exceedingly eager to be off."

Such is the way with neighbors. On the block, our public personas and our professional successes seem much less important than pancakes and maple syrup, busted front steps and broken collarbones, and cocktail parties that last into the night. This is the salvational charm of the exile experience, maybe even its minor miracle: In the midst of the monumental, down the hill and around the corner there was room for the mundane.

Cover of the first English edition of *Dialectic of Enlightenment*, one of the seminal texts of critical theory

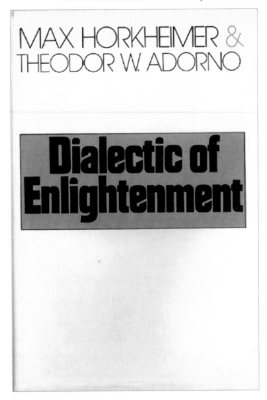

LUDWIG MARCUSE
451 San Vicente Boulevard · Santa Monica
Nikolai Blaumer

The philosopher and essayist Ludwig Marcuse recalled in his memoirs that moving to California was almost like being among friends in the Weimar Republic: "You don't feel such a foreigner when you're surrounded by friends who are also foreigners. And even if some of them weren't your friends, at least they weren't enemies. I hardly realized there were any Americans here. And I felt that a poor person isn't quite as poor in Los Angeles as in New York."

Marcuse hints here that he had landed in America as a stateless person without financial means. His formerly wealthy Berlin family had fallen on hard times in the 1920s, and the German Reich had expatriated him as a Jew in 1937. In the beginning, he was supported by the EFF with ten dollars a week. Max Horkheimer called him "the poor Marcuse," in distinction to his fellow philosopher Herbert Marcuse, who worked for the Office of Strategic Services in Washington, D.C., during the war.

Ludwig and his wife, Sascha, had friends in California, but they struggled with the English language and with Los Angeles as a city. Looking back, he wrote, "Until 1945 I still lived in Germany, though my address was Beverly Hills, California." He complained that Los Angeles bore little resemblance to his hometown, that it was an un-city in the drollest form, "inhabited by gangsters, movie stars and me." Ludwig and Sascha lived first at 340 North Oakhurst Drive in Beverly Hills, and later at 451 San Vicente Boulevard in Santa Monica.

The neighborly relationship between the Manns and Marcuses that had begun while both families were living in Sanary-sur-Mer grew closer and more intimate in L.A.. Mann enjoyed Marcuse's "good-natured chit-chat" but also appreciated their political discussions on topics such as the conditions of a German surrender or the European postwar order. Marcuse was an intellectual foil for Mann, especially regarding Mann's discussion of Nietzsche.

Marcuse began to teach German philosophy and literature at the University of Southern California shortly after his arrival in California. In 1945, he attained tenure at USC as a full professor and wrote regularly for the German-Jewish monthly *Aufbau* in addition to authoring books on the history of philosophy, including *Plato and Dionysius* (1947) and *Philosophy of Happiness* (1948). His reflections on the classical philosophers developed in light of his own experiences. At the same time, Marcuse took issue with the general expectation that philosophy and literature should be thrown into the service of the war against Nazi Germany: "And if the German thinkers of the exile have a political task, it is not this: to refute Alfred Rosenberg for the thousandth time. They should rather thoroughly clean the unclean area between novel and theology. For here is the Augean stable of our time. This, however, requires more courage than refuting Hitler—or Marx."

Marcuse's older sister Henni immigrated to Palestine, but his mother, Paula, and younger sister Edith lost their lives in Germany during the Nazi era. They had been hiding in a hostel in Berlin Charlottenburg in 1941–1942. After learning of the death of two friends who had chosen suicide the night before their deportation, his mother suffered a heart attack. His sister was deported and died on May 8, 1945, the day of the Russian liberation.

Despite this terrible history, Marcuse settled down near Munich after his retirement in 1961. The famous literary critic Marcel Reich-Ranicki remembered him with these words: "He never wanted to know anything about the non-conformism at all costs that was so fashionable in the Federal Republic of the sixties. But he was one of those permanent disturbers of the peace whom Germany has always needed, mostly feared, often chased away, and never loved."

BERTOLT BRECHT
1063 26th Street · Santa Monica
Steven D. Lavine

The German playwright and émigré Bertolt Brecht detested Thomas Mann, an attitude that Mann reciprocated but expressed less fiercely, frequently, and colorfully. Brecht and Mann's mutual dislike—to put it mildly—dates back to the early 1920s. Mann, already a celebrated figure, received further acclaim around the publication of *The Magic Mountain.* Brecht, with virtually no produced plays at the time, was nevertheless hailed by the Berlin critics as the savior of German theater. Mann, in fact, reviewed two of the playwright's early works without enthusiasm, summarizing Brecht as "a strong but careless talent who has been pampered by the German public."

This conjunction of their careers, with the accompanying press attention and literary community small talk, was enough for Brecht to settle on Mann as the very model of the bourgeois artist, absorbed in a late romantic attention to art and selfhood and, in the process, standing in the way of the serious attention to the social and political progress to which Brecht was devoted. On that basis (for Brecht never read *The Magic Mountain* or any of Mann's subsequent novels, and Mann did not attend Brecht's plays), plus perhaps Mann's coldly worded reviews and his patrician manner, Brecht took every occasion to attack and ridicule Mann. By 1930, Mann had even entered Brecht's poetry, in "Ballad on Approving of the World":

> "The writer lets us read his Magic Mountain,
> And what he writes (for money) is well described!
> What he conceals (for nothing) might have been the truth. I say that Mann is only blind, not bribed."

Brecht justified his assaults on literary and social grounds: "I single out Mann's books solely because he is the most successful type of the bourgeois producer of vain, artistic, useless books." Mann dismissed his fellow émigré with condescension and scorn, though he did on occasion use only slightly less patronizing terms such as "beast" and "partyliner."

When Brecht came to the United States, he first rented at 817 25th Street in Santa Monica. Later, with the $10,000 he earned working with the director Fritz Lang on the script for *Hangmen Also Die!* (his only successful entry into film), the playwright purchased, through a rent-to-own arrangement, a much more comfortable home at 1063 26th Street. Despite his disgust with the crass commercialism of the movie industry and his scorn for what he saw as the artificial landscapes of Southern California, Brecht genuinely liked his new home, in particular its ample work space and its garden, of which he wrote, "In this garden it becomes possible to read Lucretius again."

In Germany, Brecht and Mann had friends in common but traveled in different circles. In Southern California, and socializing in the same émigré community, they could not avoid bumping into each other. Not long after settling in Santa Monica,

Bertolt Brecht and Lion Feuchtwanger at Villa Aurora, 1947

Brecht wrote to his friend Karl Korsch, "I meet Thomas Mann at best by chance and then 3000 years gaze down on me." As much as they might have tried to avoid each other, there were events that simply could not be missed: Alfred Döblin's birthday party, a memorial for Max Reinhardt, and Salka Viertel's Sunday tea parties, in addition to the many social gatherings at the homes of mutual friends such as Lion Feuchtwanger and Hanns Eisler, who tried unsuccessfully to mediate between the two. It must have been galling for Brecht to encounter someone with whom he so completely disagreed. Mann was already being marketed by his U.S. publisher Alfred Knopf as the greatest living representative of the best of German culture. Worse yet, Mann was generally accepted as the leader of the émigré community and was perceived to have a direct line to the Roosevelt administration.

A far deeper ground for animosity was soon to emerge. Mann was publishing essays and making speeches that treated the rise of Hitler as "stemming from deep roots in Germanic culture." He began suggesting that all Germans shared in the guilt, if not the responsibility, for the evils of Hitler's regime.

Brecht found these views a crime against the German people. For him, capitalism and the conservative bourgeois elite—with whom he had associated Mann all along—were the responsible parties who had victimized the general populace, employing propaganda to pull the wool over their eyes and terror to stifle any sign of resistance.

Their passionate disagreement came to a head in August of 1945, when Mann first signed and then removed his signature from a declaration Brecht was circulating in support of the National Committee for a Free Germany, which had been formed the previous month by German émigrés and prisoners of war in the Soviet Union This declaration included the statement: "We too deem it necessary to distinguish clearly between the Hitler regime and the classes linked to it on the one hand and German people on the other." Mann offered several reasons for not signing on but in the end he simply did not believe there were viable democratic forces in Germany capable of establishing a democracy on their own.

For Brecht and many others in the émigré community, Mann's actions were, especially given his presumed influence in Washington, tantamount to asking that Germany be occupied and punished by the Allies before any attempt was made to establish a democracy. Brecht even reported that Mann had told Feuchtwanger that as many as a half million people might have to be killed.

Of course, no one in Washington was even listening. There was an occupation, but democracy was established in short order.

KONRAD KELLEN
540 Paseo Miramar
Helmut K. Anheier

Some lives are full of strange twists and unexpected turns. The political scientist and analyst Konrad Kellen lived such a life, one replete with an unlikely parade of people coming together, drifting apart, reuniting, and separating again while moving from country to country and occupation to occupation. In reviewing this parade, one is easily reminded of Shakespeare's *The Tempest*: "misery acquaints a man with strange bedfellows." Kellen, the penniless, drifting young exile, and Thomas Mann, the world-renowned author, were such strange bedfellows.

Kellen was born Konrad Moritz Adolf Katzenellenbogen. The Katzenellenbogens were a prominent and respected Berlin family who owned a villa in town and an estate outside the city. Kellen grew up in luxury. Albert Einstein and the economist Albert O. Hirschman were among his relatives, and the likes of actress Marlene Dietrich, painter Max Liebermann, boxer Max Schmeling, race car driver Rudolf Caracciola, and numerous business and political leaders were part of the family's social circle. While attending the prestigious Mommsengymnasium, he read several of Mann's works. In particular, *Der Zauberberg* left an impression on the young Kellen, who developed a lasting admiration for the *Zauberer*, or "magician,"

as he privately referred to Mann years later.

His father's bankruptcy in 1932 and his parents' divorce uprooted his young and privileged life. After spending a year studying law in Heidelberg and Munich, he abruptly left Germany for Paris in 1933 upon witnessing a Nazi rally. In Paris, he led an unsteady existence, drifting, living in semipoverty, with intermittent stays in the Netherlands and Yugoslavia. He met Mann's son Klaus, and they struck up a friendship that later brought him to the Mann family in New York. Kellen arrived in New York in 1935, working odd jobs before becoming a broker on Wall Street and frequently visiting Einstein at Princeton. At that time Kellen was introduced to Thomas Mann. He moved to Los Angeles in search of work, became a U.S. citizen, and changed his name to Konrad Kellen.

In Los Angeles and now married, Kellen ran into Mann's daughter Erika on the Santa Monica promenade in July 1940. She told him that her parents would be in town for a while, living in rented accommodations in Brentwood. Living off odd jobs and competing with other exiles for work, Kellen was eager to connect with the Manns, who were relatively well off and well connected. When the Manns moved to L.A. permanently in April 1941, Kellen was delighted when Thomas hired him as his private secretary, a position he held until the summer of 1943, when he was drafted into the U.S. Army.

Kellen lived in rented accommodations in Santa Monica, which at the time was a much less expensive area than Brentwood, Pacific Palisades, or Beverly Hills. The secretarial job seems to have paid about $1.50 an hour, enough to live on but not enough to be truly comfortable. But working for the "Magician" was a most welcome opportunity for the cash-starved Kellen and offered an opportunity to make connections.

Kellen focused first on typing the manuscript for *Joseph the Provider.* He then moved on to managing Mann's correspondence in both German and, increasingly, English. On a typical day, Kellen would arrive early in the afternoon and collect two or three pages of text—handwritten in *Süterlin*, a historic form of German script—that Mann had composed in the morning. Kellen would return them the next day, neatly typed on a typewriter at his Santa Monica home (Mann hated the distracting sound of typewriters), and pick up the next installment. They also reviewed the novelist's correspondence: letters in German to which Mann replied in longhand, which were typed by Kellen; and letters in English to which Mann dictated the gist of his response, which Kellen formulated and brought back the next day for signature.

In between were countless lunches and invitations for tea and dinner at the Mann home, with many exiles visiting along with members of the "Hollywood crowd." He began moving closer into Mann's inner circle and became a friend of the family. When Kellen left for the army, Mann wrote a heartfelt letter of appreciation, and they parted on positive terms. Thomas and his former secretary would meet again briefly, and for the last time, in Zurich in 1952, two years before Mann's death.

During the war, Kellen participated in the Normandy landings and later served as a U.S. intelligence officer in defeated Germany. Like his cousin Albert O. Hirschman, he interviewed former Nazi officials and participated in denazification activities. For several years, he worked abroad for Radio Free Europe as the Cold War took hold. Upon his return to the United States, he worked in military intelligence for the Hudson Institute before joining the RAND Corporation and becoming an expert on terrorism, collaborating with leading figures including the futurist Herman Kahn on forecasting and foresight models that are standard tools today.

Unlike his former employer, Kellen never became a public figure. While working for RAND he was regarded as a contrarian who challenged the rationales and assumptions of American foreign policy. He gained some political prominence when, in the 1960s, he criticized the American war effort in Vietnam, declaring it unwinnable. History proved him correct. Yet, how well did he understand American society, and Los Angeles in particular?

In his memoirs *Mein Boss, der Zauberer*, we find in the chapter "Living in Los Angeles" this curious passage: "Of course, there are areas with a higher concentration of black people. However, there are no formal and legal limitations. Whoever has the money, can live wherever he wants to buy a house. Alas, most blacks cannot afford to do so." It is a perplexingly naïve description of housing policies in wartime Los Angeles, and the difficult conditions for the Japanese, Chinese, and Latino populations are not even mentioned. One wonders how fully Kellen understood the tensions underlying American society at the time.

Perhaps both Kellen and Thomas Mann somehow remained strangers in their own adopted land.

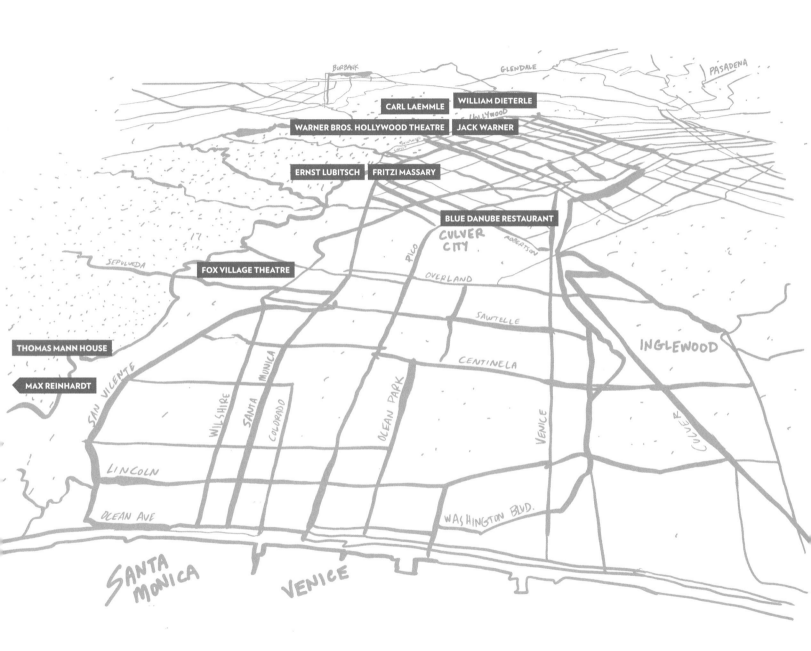

PART 3

THOMAS MANN HOUSE

MAX REINHARDT

FOX VILLAGE THEATRE

CARL LAEMMLE

WILLIAM DIETERLE

WARNER BROS. HOLLYWOOD THEATRE

JACK WARNER

ERNST LUBITSCH

FRITZI MASSARY

BLUE DANUBE RESTAURANT

BURBANK

GLENDALE

PASADENA

HOLLYWOOD

CULVER CITY

ROBERTSON

PICO

OVERLAND

SAWTELLE

CENTINELA

INGLEWOOD

SEPULVEDA

17

SAN VILENTE

WILSHIRE

SANTA MONICA

COLORADO

OCEAN PARK

VENICE

CULVER

LINCOLN

OCEAN AVE

WASHINGTON BLVD.

SANTA MONICA

VENICE

FILM IN EXILE IN HOLLYWOOD

Benno Herz

On August 21, 1941, Thomas Mann made the following entry in his diary: "To dinner in Beverly Hills at Sir Cedric Hardwicke's. Mr. and Mrs. Singer are among us, along with the fat producer Hitschcock [*sic*] with his blonde wife. He snored after coffee. Sleeps in his chair at night, too. — Talked about acting, Kean, Garrick."

Mann's misspelling of Hitchcock tells us a few things. First, in 1941, the esteemed novelist still felt estranged from what Hitchcock stood for: a new aesthetic language for moving images that fused high art and cinema, the rise and importance of a new medium, and a film culture that was becoming increasingly globalized, with its heart and center in Mann's adopted hometown of Los Angeles. Second, Mann distanced himself from Hollywood and this particular cultural scene. He deliberately moved to Pacific Palisades, away from the studios and glamorous film premieres.

It seems odd, though, that he would give the great British film director the cold shoulder in his diary, considering that, at this point, Mann had already seen (and commented positively on) two of Hitchcock's movies, *Saboteur* and *The Lady Vanishes*. Mann's spelling of Hitchcock's name (with the German *sch*) can be read, on the one hand, as his attempt to present himself as a foreigner with respect to the new discourse on film, symbolized by the name Hitchcock, and, on the other hand, as an attempt to embody it in a way that made sense for him. It represented something unnatural and revealed that the concept of the narrative "high arts"—which he previously thought pertained exclusively to literature and theater—was undergoing a cultural transformation. Mann was grappling with the rise of  a new medium and how it could change perspectives on literature and the conditions of artistic production and distribution, which were of central importance in Los Angeles. The dinner scene described above and the little spelling "mistake" illustrate the writer's at once ambivalent and intense relationship with "the industry."

Mann had long been a passionate filmgoer even before he was charmed by Hollywood during his first visit to L.A. in 1938. But he also was a harsh critic of the medium, which had influenced the chapter "The Dance of Death" in his 1924 novel *The Magic Mountain*. In it, the protagonist, Hans Castorp, visits a theater in Davos to see a film that sounds exactly like Ernst Lubitsch's 1920s silent classic *Sumurun*, which Mann himself saw in Munich in 1922. While the film was not depicted favorably in the novel, it was not a reflection of Mann's real-life relationship with the director. In 1939, Lubitsch, who was already one of the most accomplished directors and studio executives in Hollywood, gave Mann a ride to his lecture at a fundraising dinner at the Beverly Wilshire Hotel. Afterward, the two enjoyed a casual dinner with the director William

Dieterle and other notable industry figures. "Highly acclaimed by Hollywood's elite," Mann commented on April 5, 1939.

Mann met many European members of the Hollywood elite on his trip to Los Angeles. From left: Thomas Mann, Carl Laemmle, Max Reinhardt, and Ernst Lubitsch, April 3, 1938

There is no doubt that Mann felt drawn to the world of film. The host of that dinner party with Hitchcock, Cedric Hardwicke, was an accomplished British actor who was most likely shooting *The Ghost of Frankenstein* (1942) at the time with horror icons Lon Chaney Jr. and Bela Lugosi. The fact that Mann chatted about acting with him and Hitchcock indicates his interest. In a letter to his son Klaus shortly after his first visit to California, he wrote: "I'm a little afraid of the scholarly atmosphere back at Princeton, and the movie riffraff (*Movie Gesindel*) is basically preferable to me."

Though it is uncertain whether Mann truly believed in the binaries he suggested, it is clear that he was intrigued by the Hollywood scene, which he positions as a welcome respite from the world of academia. His first week in Los Angeles read like a starstruck tabloid magazine: Bruno and Liesl Frank took Thomas, Katia, and Erika on a tour of Paramount Studios, where they were introduced to Paramount president Adolph Zukor; briefly met Fritz Lang, who was working on the movie *You and Me*; previewed the latest Lubitsch film; and were fortunate enough to be allowed on set during a film shoot.

Shortly after their Paramount tour, Mann was invited to a fundraiser benefiting Jewish refugees at Warner Bros. executive Jack Warner's home. Mann noted on April 1, 1938: "Tuxedo toilet. Picked up for soiree at rich film producer Warner's. $100 dinner for the refugees. Stars. Pompous house and park. Beautiful library room, church candles on dining room tables. [. . .] Colossal sums of income." Later that week, Mann visited Walt Disney at his studio, where he watched a preview of "The Sorcerer's Apprentice," loosely based on Goethe's 1797 poem "Der Zauberlehrling." The animated segment would be incorporated into Disney's classic *Fantasia* (1940). Mann's observation of Disney the man is remarkable: "Strange, the personality of Disney. Fatigue. Almost silent." Only a week earlier, Mann had visited a cinema in San Francisco to see Disney's *Snow White and the Seven Dwarfs* (1937), describing it as "without style, but pretty and as a work amazing, attractive for me in view of Joseph." The latter was an allusion to the fact that Mann was already thinking about a screen adaptation of his novel *Joseph the Provider*, which was not realized during his time in Los Angeles.

Mann's relationship with film was complex and deep. Over the next decade, he was in touch with many people in the industry, perhaps also because of their shared European heritage. In the 1920s, the German film industry, starting with Universum Film AG (a major German film studio founded in 1917) and the

Babelsberg studios in Berlin, was a competitive force and an attractive market for the big Hollywood studios. Lubitsch's *Madame Du Barry* (1919) and *Anna Boleyn* (1920) found U.S.- distributors as early as 1921. The *New York Times* included both films on its list of the fifteen most important movies of 1921. Robert Wiene's T*he Cabinet of Dr. Caligari* (1920), Fritz Lang's *Metropolis* (1927), and Robert Siodmak and Edgar Ulmer's *People on Sunday* (1930) are other examples of internationally acclaimed successes of the time. By the end of the 1920s, most of the major Hollywood studios had offices in Berlin and kept an eye out for new talent in the city. As for Lubitsch, he would set sail for Hollywood on his own terms in 1922 to pursue a career.

When the Nazis seized power in 1933, more than two thousand Jewish professionals working in the booming German film industry of the Weimar Era feared for their lives. Many fled to other European film capitals such as Vienna, London, and Paris. After the outbreak of World War II in 1939 and the ongoing terror waged by the Nazis in Europe, more than eight hundred of them made their way to Hollywood. A strong connection between Hollywood and the German film scene had already been established once the first wave of these political refugees arrived after 1933. The beginning of professional disqualifications and the ostracizing of Jews in 1933, the Nuremberg Laws in 1935, and the start of the war brought various waves of refugees who relied on a network of supporters within the Los Angeles film industry. Directors, writers, cinematographers, composers, and actors not only found a safe haven in the city but also hoped to continue their careers and achieve artistic success.

By 1938, the Hollywood agent Paul Kohner, Lubitsch, and Laemmle had founded the European Film Fund to help émigrés with much-needed affidavits, financial assistance, and job opportunities. The studios were giving contracts to many of the exiles. Screenwriters, directors, actors, and even novelists such as Alfred Döblin and Heinrich Mann were dependent on their screenwriting contracts with MGM, Warner Bros., and Universal. These were the key to survival for many, since most of the exiles were financially suffering, having left behind all their belongings. The exiles faced many other challenges from different industry hierarchies and workflows in the Hollywood studio system. For example, directors were not given as much artistic freedom as they were accustomed to back in Germany at Universum Film. In addition, they met resistance from unions and guilds that wished to protect the job market for U.S. workers. And there was, of course, the major obstacle of learning a new and foreign language that writers, directors, and especially actors had to face. Moreover, actors were increasingly confronted with a moral dilemma: offered roles as Nazi officers and SS troopers, they had to decide if they were willing to take up the role of their own persecutors. Given their financial constraints, it was not much of a choice. The Jewish German Austrian actor Alexander Granach played not only Julius Streicher, founder and publisher of the anti-Semitic propaganda newspaper *Der Stürmer* in Paramount's 1944 *The Hitler Gang*, but also the Gestapo officer Alois Gruber in Fritz Lang's *Hangmen Also Die!* (1943).

The studies themselves took different stances on the exiles and the political tumult in Nazi Germany. As Jack Warner had been born to Polish Jewish parents, his company, Warner Bros., stopped distributing films to Germany as early as 1935. MGM and Paramount continued to cater their films to a German audience by simply removing Jewish names from the credits. This changed after the attack on Pearl Harbor and the U.S. entry into World War II. Hollywood then actively engaged in the production of anti-Nazi propaganda films, with over 160 produced between 1941 and 1945, most famously Michael Curtiz's

William Dieterle, Max Reinhardt, and art director Anton Grot review a model set for *A Midsummer Night's Dream*, 1935

Casablanca (1942) and Lang's *Hangmen Also Die!* (1943), the latter written by Lang and Bertolt Brecht. But the U.S. involvement brought new obstacles to the fore, such as curfews, a general suspicion of foreigners, and a hostile work environment for refugees from Germany. Despite successful careers in their native countries, many exiles and refugees from Europe were prevented from fully participating in the American film industry.

Some managed to leave their mark on Hollywood. The Austrian director, producer, and screenwriter Billy Wilder, who immigrated in 1934, is considered one of the most influential filmmakers of classic Hollywood cinema. The credits of his works contain a who's who of European film exiles, and his filmography includes some of the best movies of all time, *Double Indemnity* (1944), *Sunset Boulevard* (1950), and *Some Like It Hot* (1959) among them. One genre in particular became a playground for exiled filmmakers: "They made horror films, crime pictures or melodramas. But within the confines of their genres they helped create a new and disturbing vision of the U.S.: the 'film noir.' They brought the harsh black and white tonalities so characteristic to the nightmare visions in German expressionist films of the Weimar Republic, to the hardbitten urban melodramas as well as to the sexually-repressed fantasies of the horror cycle," writes Jan-Christopher Horak in his seminal article "The Palm Trees Were Gently Swaying: German Refugees from Hitler in Hollywood." But it wasn't only the directors who had a major impact on Hollywood. Composers such as Franz Waxman, Erich Korngold, Ernst Toch, and Max Steiner found much work writing film scores. Steiner, of Austria, wrote more than two hundred scores between 1920 and 1965 for such classics as *Casablanca* and William Dieterle's *The Life of Emile Zola* (1937). Back in Weimar Germany, the Hungarian actor Peter Lorre, born László Löwenstein, was the lead in Lang's 1931 international hit *M*. Like Wilder, he arrived in 1934 and, after improving his English, launched an incredible career, becoming a Hollywood icon with his eerie performances in *The Maltese Falcon* (1941) and as the Japanese secret agent Mr. Moto in eight movies. The list of films, professions, and names involved in exile Hollywood goes on and on, especially if one considers the many overlooked émigrés working as camera operators, set designers, and editors in the dream factory under the Southern California sun.

Mann had his share of personal interactions in Hollywood, but he also frequented theaters, film premieres, and private screenings at studios all over the city. It is fair to say that between 1941 and 1952, his love of American cinema. He reveled in, watching films like *A Streetcar Named Desire* (1951), *The Big Store* (1941) starring the Marx Brothers, the war movie *Air Force* (1943) and Disney's anti-Nazi film *Der Fuehrer's Face* (1943). He also found time for European productions like the French romantic drama *The Idiot* (1948). Mann even made his own attempts at Hollywood fame. In 1942, he worked on a screenplay based on the story of Odysseus for Twentieth Century-Fox. In 1944, he was asked to be on the writing team for a film with the working title "The Woman with the Hundred Faces." Neither project was ever realized.

As much as Mann enjoyed going to the movies, he could be a very harsh critic. He straightforwardly wrote about more than twenty of them in his diaries. He remarked positively on Marlon Brando's performance (and torso) in *A Streetcar Named Desire* while criticizing other aspects of the film: "Brutal, hysterical, symbolist, the sensuality quite vividly appealing, especially by the ever-exposed magnificent torso of a young husband, primitive and of compelling sex appeal. The whole thing quite hollow and overplayed, pretending meaning. The audience laughs jubilantly, although it sees a tragedy." Of the war movie *Hitler's Children* (1943), he opined, a "pathetically stupid Nazi movie," preferring the film *Air Force*, which was filled with "flying fortresses and good pilot types." He dismissed *The Idiot* as "quite thin, quite weak." Also on Mann's watchlist were Lubitsch's *Ninotchka* and *Heaven Can Wait*, Hitchcock's *Jamaica Inn*, and several Disney films. *Bambi* (1942) was his favorite Disney movie; he saw it twice, in cinemas in Los Angeles and San Francisco, describing it as a "beautiful play of animals" and "adorable."

In his diaries, one can find upward of fifty entries that mention "went to Westwood to the cinema," followed by a short, poignant remark about the film he saw that night. But he also went to theaters in Santa Monica and Hollywood, attended many private studio screenings, and was invited to myriad Hollywood premieres. Despite his many derogatory comments on certain films, the movie "riffraff"' and the medium's still inferior status compared to literature, it is hard to deny that he was passionate about and interested in the film world, leading one to wonder whether it makes sense to take his diary entries at face value. Whether there isn't greater meaning to be found in the way Mann summarizes a film in fragments, as with his frequent commentaries on actors' bodies. Many contradictions about the cinematic medium in these diaries are not resolved but are given voice: admiration and rejection, fascination and criticism, naturalization and estrangement. In the end, "Hitschcock" and Mann might not be as estranged from each other as one might think. Mann considered this possibility, too. After all, both sometimes snored in their chairs, didn't they?

CARL LAEMMLE

Universal Studios · 100 Universal City Plaza

Jaimey Fisher

As one of the film industry's founding fathers, Carl Laemmle was among Hollywood's great innovators, transforming the industry, its personnel, and even its ethos. Born Karl Lämmle in 1867, "Uncle Carl" may also have been the highest-profile German American in Hollywood, so his intermittent interactions with Thomas Mann are revealing both for the U.S. film industry and for the German author's 1940s exile. Culture was interwoven with a duty beyond mere distractive entertainment, something their encounters on both sides of the Atlantic underscore.

Like many film pioneers in the United States, Laemmle's origins lie far away, both geographically and professionally. Born in Laupheim, Germany, in 1867, he immigrated as a teenager, landing in Chicago. He eventually found his way to Oshkosh, Wisconsin, where he worked as a bookkeeper for a clothing company and soon rose to manager. He returned to Chicago and opened his first nickelodeon there in 1906. He developed a chain of them and started a business in film distribution, and by 1910 ran the largest distributor in the country. In 1912, just six years after entering the industry, he founded and became the first president of Universal Studios.

The story of Uncle Carl, however, transcends commercial success, for he helped create the culture of Hollywood itself. Both the star system and the development of the expansive, variegated movie backlot likely owe more to him than to any other individual. Among his 1910s watershed transformations of early cinema were the emphatic promotion of specific actors in Universal films, generally regarded as the first step in the star system still dominant today. Before this innovation, actors tended to be left unnamed in film credits. Laemmle began promoting them in new, individual ways: Florence Lawrence, formerly known as "The Biograph Girl," was touted as "the first star." Laemmle also helped lead the fateful migration of early film production from the East Coast to California, establishing a headquarters at what was then the world's largest studio complex, in the newly dubbed Universal City in the San Fernando Valley. Although he did not invent the film studio, he did invent the studio city, according to scholar Bernhard Dick. Over a span of 250 acres, Laemmle established an unprecedented number of sets, as well as workshops that constructed and supplied those sets, complete with a sawmill, blacksmiths, even a zoo. Finally, the list of collaborators and employees contains some of the biggest names of the 1910s and 1920s: Mary Pickford, Rudolph Valentino, Irving Thalberg, and John Ford, to name a few.

Besides these cultural and industrial achievements, he was unusual among top studio heads for the degree to which he kept up relations with his "foreign" origins in his hometown of Laupheim, to which he would make near-annual pilgrimages. As a result, one of his longest-lasting contributions was his influential balancing of the cultural-industrial and the philanthropic-activist modes.

It was apparently on one of his regular trips back to Europe that he met Thomas Mann in Zurich,

Universal City c. 1937

where he pitched the novelist on a movie project based on the Joseph tetralogy. This 1934 proposal underscored how Laemmle's civic-mindedness intersected with not only his philanthropy but also the content of his films. One of Universal's most famous undertakings was the award-winning yet controversial *All Quiet on the Western Front* (1930), for which Laemmle returned to Germany to negotiate with Erich Remarque, the author of the novel on which it was based. Despite, or maybe because of, the violent Nazi riots against the antiwar novel and its subsequent ban, Laemmle would later declare that the film was the work of which he was most proud. The film garnered various accolades, including Academy Awards for best director and best picture (then called Outstanding Production). At the Oscars ceremony, MGM studio executive Louis B. Mayer said the film might just go on to win the Nobel Peace Prize.

This formula for a politically minded literary adaptation of a novel by a major German author seemed to be what Laemmle had in mind when he pitched Mann in Zurich. The project never came to fruition, however, since Mann's later diary entries on seeing Laemmle in Los Angeles in the 1930s make no mention of it. For example, on April 21, 1938, during a month long stay in L.A., Mann recounted how he and Katia enjoyed a private screening with Laemmle of "Meyerling," actually *Mayerling* (1936), a French historical drama about nineteenth-century Vienna directed by Anatole Litvak and produced by Seymour Nebenzahl, of *Westfront 1918* (1930), *M* (1931), and *The Testament of Dr. Mabuse* (1933) fame. Mann only cites, in his assessment of the screening with Laemmle, the entertaining film and Charles Boyer's excellent performance as Prince Rudolf. A few days later, on April 23, Mann told of another screening courtesy of Universal, at Universal Studios at 100 Universal City Plaza, but there, too, no mention of the *Joseph* project.

Earlier that same month, Mann had seen the "*alte[n] Lemmle* [*sic*]" (old Laemmle) at a high-profile fundraising dinner hosted by Jack Warner after Mann's lecture "The Coming Victory of Democracy." Scholar Douglas Gomery has observed that "Warner's soiree for Mann marked something of a turning point for up-front, no-apologies incursions into politics around Hollywood," but Laemmle had foreshadowed this watershed with his own 1920 philanthropy on behalf of the vanquished Germany, his declaring himself a pacifist around *All Quiet on the Western Front*, and his activist work on behalf of refugees. At the event, Laemmle, ever the showman, smiled in a picture with Mann, Max Reinhardt, and Ernst Lubitsch. Laemmle and Mann would meet again in Switzerland that summer, on a trip that, rarely and notably, did not take Laemmle to Germany or Austria. "Uncle Carl" died a little over a year later, on September 24, 1939, at age seventy-two in Beverly Hills, far away from Laupheim and from the new war in Europe just starting.

ERNST LUBITSCH

268 Bel Air Road

Kai Sina

Thomas Mann's diaries were written as private documents, but for all they tell us about the political thoughts, personal feelings, and literary and essayistic works of the celebrity author living on San Remo Drive, they also read like a brilliant society novel set in the beautiful Pacific Palisades and its surrounding areas.

A recurring figure in such a novel would be Ernst Lubitsch, one of the first European directors in Hollywood. Already in 1923, Lubitsch had immigrated to the United States, where he came to enjoy great success, most notably with the 1939 comedy *Ninotchka* starring Greta Garbo. His name appeared quite frequently in Mann's diaries—and rarely without the added notation "dinner," "dinner party," or "lunch." These mostly informal get-togethers were frequently attended by an assortment of exiles and émigrés, among them the singer Fritzi Massary, Alma Mahler-Werfel and her husband the writer Franz Werfel, the actress Salka Viertel, the director William Dieterle, and the producer Eddie Knopf, in addition to regulars Lion and Marta Feuchtwanger, Max Reinhardt, and Bruno and Liesl Frank. The places where they met included the spectacular Lubitsch residence in Bel-Air, the elegant and high-end Beverly Wilshire Hotel, Salka

Viertel's salon in Santa Monica, and the Mann villa in Pacific Palisades. Sometimes their gatherings were combined with private film screenings, either in Lubitsch's own in-home "studio" or at the actual Twentieth Century-Fox studios, where the Mann family often would be chauffeured in true style, "in 3 cars," as occurred on Katia's sixtieth birthday.

The personal connection between Lubitsch and Mann began in 1938, when Mann visited L.A. to give the keynote speech at a fundraiser for the American Committee for Christian German Refugees. Lubitsch insisted on picking up the Nobel Prize winner at his hotel and taking him to the event. The friendly gesture was an expression of the high regard in which Mann was held by Lubitsch's world. "With and through Lubitsch," explains Hans Rudolf Vaget in his brilliant study of Mann's years in American exile, "it was essentially Hollywood that did the honors."

Unlike Theodor Adorno or Bertolt Brecht, Mann was open-minded about the American film and entertainment industry. His statement in a letter to his son Klaus in 1938 that he preferred the California "movie riffraff" to the "scholarly atmosphere" of Princeton is actually quite funny: it speaks of a bourgeois artist whose aesthetic inclinations and social preferences, disreputable and delightful, have fallen into disarray. (Conversely, Lubitsch, who had no academic background, admired Mann for his impressive erudition.) Mann was genuinely interested in the medium of film and in Lubitsch's works in particular, which had started long before his move to the United States and had already found literary expression. *The Magic Mountain*, for example, describes a screening of a "thrilling drama of love and death," where the scenes "galloped past, full of gorgeousness and naked bodies, thirst of power and raving religious self-abnegation; full of cruelty, appetite, and deathly lust," causing "smarting eyes" for the visually overwhelmed residents of the Davos sana-

Ernst Lubitsch in the 1920s

torium. This passage took its cue from Lubitsch's silent film *Sumurun* (1920), which Mann had viewed "with quite some repulsion" at the Lichtspieltheater am Sendlinger Tor in Munich.

Did the writer and the director ever talk about the fact that the former, in his novel, had used the latter's film as the basis for a satirical media critique? There is nothing to lead us to assume that this was the case, especially as there is no mention in Mann's diaries that the two ever discussed artistic interests or aesthetic issues. Mann hardly ever referred to a Lubitsch work by its title, nor did he go into any great detail about it. His comment after a screening "of Lubitsch's latest comedic film" on July 24, 1943 (probably *Heaven Can Wait*), was rather typical: While he considered the film to be "colorful," containing "lovely ideas" and "nice dialogue," there was no mention of a deeper aesthetic satisfaction; it was "only a movie, after all." Mann's diaries leave no doubt that literature always ranked more highly than film in his hierarchy of the arts.

And yet, his relationship with Lubitsch should not be underestimated, for it offered Mann a certain continuity during entirely unforeseeable, often fearful times. A diary entry on September 10, 1940,

begins with that morning's news of "horrible attacks on London." It goes on to note the pressing worries of a paterfamilias: "Deeply shaken and hardly able to work. Erika in the midst of the explosions and the destruction. She cannot cable us daily that she is alive." What can provide solace in such an unbearable situation when all one can do is wait and hope for the best?

Mann made the psychologically wise decision to spend his evenings with familiar people, to cling to comforting rituals, and to seek some form of distraction. Even if it could not lay to rest his worries about his daughter and the global situation, an evening out with good food, fine drinks, and camaraderie at least offered a certain degree of relief from his inner distress.

We would not be able to guess that, however, from his diary entry of December 1, 1947. Amid his usual notations about the weather, the progress of his work, and his daily rituals, Mann wrote, without any apparent dismay, "News of Ernst Lubitsch's death." The unemotional tone may come as a surprise; they had met only two months earlier, discussing "much about this country, against and for." But perhaps it is precisely the business-like tone that is revealing: it gives a safe external form to an event whose emotional impact cannot be foreseen at the moment of writing. In this respect at least, keeping a diary and attending dinner parties with Lubitsch were not so different after all.

WILLIAM DIETERLE
3151 North Knoll Drive
Noah Isenberg

Though he was not quite as well known as some of his more illustrious German- and Austrian-born counterparts working in Hollywood during the studio era—one thinks, for instance, of Ernst Lubitsch, Fritz Lang, and Billy Wilder—William Dieterle was an enormously prolific, highly acclaimed director whose German and American careers spanned close to half a century. Like Lubitsch, Dieterle and his wife, Charlotte, arrived in Hollywood before the massive exodus from Nazi-engulfed Europe. Dieterle had made his first films in Weimar Berlin, where he had begun his career as an actor, having trained with the great theater impresario Max Reinhardt, before earning a string of screen credits as a director. Reinhardt and Dieterle would codirect *A Midsummer Night's Dream* in 1935 for Warner Bros., where Dieterle received his first major studio contract in 1930 and where he continued to direct for more than a decade. It was during the 1930s, when the studio fortresses became increasingly flooded with film professionals in flight from Hitler, that Dieterle gained his reputation as an early pioneer of the socially conscious biopic. These films include *The Story of Louis Pasteur* (1936), *The Life of Emile Zola* (1937), and *Juarez* (1939), all starring Paul Muni and all made in Burbank at Warner Bros.

Among his dearest friendships within the burgeoning émigré and refugee community of Los Angeles was the one he formed with Thomas Mann, a frequent dinner guest and impassioned interlocutor on all things political, cultural, literary, and cinematic. The two maintained close ties starting in the late 1930s and continuing throughout the 1940s, when Thomas and Katia took up residence on San Remo Drive and William and Charlotte were living on North Knoll Drive, just above the Hollywood Hills. Mann's diary entries from the period recounted numerous social gatherings, screenings, soirees, and *kaffeeklatsches* with the Dieterles. Writing from Beverly Hills on April 4, 1938, Mann commented on a private screening—a double feature of Mickey Mouse and Dieterle's *Zola*—held at the Dieterle home and attended by Walt Disney himself and actor Paul Muni. Mann remarked that he didn't make it to bed until 2 a.m. Over the next two years, he would make entries again and again of these encounters, from watching Dieterle's *Pasteur* to driving to Burbank with the Dieterles and Bruno and Liesl Frank for a preview of *Juarez* ("a first-rate achievement").

During this same period, the Dieterles and the Franks, along with Lubitsch, the renowned screenwriter, actress, and salon hostess Salka Viertel, and the agent Paul Kohner, helped to establish the European Film Fund. Because of his anti-Nazi activities and the perceived propagandistic nature of his films, Dieterle became the target of a campaign by Martin Dies, the rabid anti-Communist congressman from Texas. Of particular concern to Dies and his fellow congressional committee members were two films, *Juarez* and *Blockade* (1938), Dieterle's Spanish Civil War picture starring Henry Fonda as a freedom fighter on the side of the loyalists (his most poignant line, "Where is the conscience of the world?," struck a resonant chord in the Hollywood colony). Harry Warner, president of Warner Bros., would eventually be brought before Congress to testify, accused of beating the drums of war and, if one can believe the term today, of being "prematurely anti-fascist."

Over the next several years, Mann's relationship to the Hollywood film industry continued to be one of mild fascination, considerably less fraught than it was for other members of the émigré community, and one in which he held a personal stake. In September 1941, around the time that Harry Warner was testifying before Congress, Mann wrote about an "optimistic" conversation with Dieterle about adapting his Joseph trilogy to the screen. Owing to the commercial success of his novels published in English by Knopf—notably the 30,000 copies of *Joseph the Provider* (*Joseph, der Ernährer*), the third book in his trilogy—he continued to harbor the same positive outlook he had after discussing the idea with Dieterle. A letter from Mann to Charlotte, written on Halloween 1944, noted that things had gone silent regarding the film adaptation but that now, after the war, the $4 million to $5 million investment needed should be more feasible. Alas, like many ideas that involved the émigré community in Hollywood—including an alleged plan for Bertolt Brecht and Dieterle to team up on a series of propaganda shorts aimed at German prisoners held in U.S. detention centers—the adaptation of Joseph never panned out.

Mann's diary entries from this period veer from seemingly banal observations gleaned from the dinner table shared with the Dieterles ("Very good chocolate pudding with whipped cream") to the more poignant commentary on momentous historical events, including a palpable fear of Russophilia taking hold among members of the émigré community (a fiery debate ensued after watching Michael Curtiz's *Mission to Moscow* in June 1943), the Nuremberg trials in 1945, the Communist takeover in Prague, and the independence of the Jewish State in 1948. By the winter of 1952, just months after what appeared to have been a "lifeless" Thanksgiving dinner with the Dieterles at the famous movie industry haunt Chasen's on Beverly Boulevard, Mann had begun to shift his focus from remaining in his adopted homeland to escaping an increasingly inhospitable McCarthy era and the merciless wrath of the House Un-American Activities Committee (HUAC).

Two years later, writing from the Hotel Hassler in Rome, Mann expresses his final hope—in vain, it turns out—that Dieterle will still somehow manage to adapt his Joseph novels and that he in turn will be paid the princely sum of $20,000 for their rights. By that time, Mann had permanently relocated to Switzerland, where he would bid his final farewell in a Zürich hospital in August 1955, while Dieterle returned to Europe that same decade, churning out mostly unremarkable, by now altogether forgotten, movies and television programs for the West German entertainment industry. Like Mann, he passed away in Europe, at his Bavarian home south of Munich, in December 1972.

JACK WARNER
Warner Bros. Studios · 5800 Sunset Boulevard
David Wallace

Anti-Jewish sentiment was fairly common in America in the 1930s, stoked by such popular figures as Charles Lindbergh and Henry Ford. As a result, hundreds of thousands of Jewish refugees were refused entry into the country. Joe Breen, the virulently anti-Semitic head of the (motion picture) Production Code Administration (PCA), was actually charged by his boss, Will Hayes, with enforcing a ban on anti-Nazi films, one that

lasted until the outbreak of World War II. Hayes's action was taken at the request of Josef Goebbels, Hitler's minister of propaganda, and carried out by Georg Gyssling, the Nazi consul in Los Angeles, who was allowed to remove any anti-German material from a film. Ironically, the largely Jewish-controlled movie studios complied. Money was the issue, and though Goebbels and Hitler were fans of Hollywood films, Goebbels had threatened to ban them in Germany, the American film industry's second-largest international market.

But one studio refused to go along. In the early 1920s, a small film company was founded by four pioneering brothers named Warner. Other than a series of popular films starring a trained German Shepherd named Rin Tin Tin, the studio grew slowly. Then, in 1927, it hit celluloid gold with the production of *The Jazz Singer*, generally credited with being the first film to incorporate sound. Filmed at their studio, located at 5800 Sunset Boulevard in Hollywood, the movie made Warner Bros. into a major operation.

As descendants of Polish Jews who had fled anti-Semitism, Jack, who was president, and his brothers Harry, Albert, and Samuel were worried about the rise of Nazism in the 1930s and decided to use their studio to fight it. The result was a decision to buck the PCA's rule with a series of anti-Nazi films, starting with *Confessions of a Nazi Spy* (1939) starring Edward G. Robinson.

It created an uproar. Pare Lorentz, the writer and director whose socially conscious documentary films included *The Plow That Broke the Plains*, said: "The Warner brothers have declared war on Germany with this one." Hitler, who screened it, was outraged.

Under pressure from the Roosevelt administration and isolationists, Warner agreed to shelve several planned anti-Nazi films, including *Underground*, a noir film about anti-Nazi resistance, but soon changed his mind. As the conflict heated up, Warner Bros. went to war with Germany. Literally.

In 1940, in addition to greenlighting new anti-Nazi productions, Warner Bros. paid for two Spitfire fighter aircrafts (named the *Franklin D. Roosevelt* and the *Cordell Hull*, after FDR's secretary of state) that almost certainly fought in the Battle of Britain, the valiant air conflict that stopped Hitler's planned invasion of England.

By then, Thomas and Katia Mann and their six children had moved to the United States. Mann had first met Jack Warner in the spring of 1938 during Thomas's lecture tour. Wrote Rennie Davis in the *Los Angeles Examiner*: "To honor the Nobel Prize winner and Mrs. Mann, (the Jack Warners) bid a brilliant dinner party of Hollywoodites to gather 'round last night at their Bel Air home, including Gladys and Edward G. Robinson, Alan Campbell and Dorothy Parker, the Jimmy Cagneys (Cagney made 38 films for Warner Bros. which made him a major star) . . . the Irving Berlins . . . Ernst Lubitsch . . . etc."

Considering the national and local publicity surrounding Mann's lecture tour, it was clear that in America he would enjoy a broad-based social and literary eminence. Los Angeles, with its large German-speaking population of emigrants from the Third Reich, was a particularly comfortable choice. Mann also loved movies, and his new acquaintance, Jack Warner, was a major moviemaker with a take-charge personality. As described by the actress and Warner star Bette Davis, "[Jack] was the father. The power. The glory. And he was in business to make money." Their friendship was inevitable.

After Warner Bros. relinquished the Sunset Boulevard site in 1950 and moved its operations to Burbank, the studio has had several owners, including the musician and actor Gene Autry. The studio's film (and later television) success has continued to the present day.

Filming at Warner Bros. Studios, 1935

MAX REINHARDT
15000 Corona Del Mar
Nikolai Blaumer

ike my ancestors, I walked dry-footed through the sea into the desert and spent seven lean years in Hollywood. There, Warners and other non-believers recognized me as too ponderous for the dance around the golden calf," Max Reinhardt wrote to his friend and former assistant Francesco von Mendelssohn in August 1943.

The forced new beginning for the world-famous director had begun promisingly in America. After the Nazis forced him out of his theater empire and expelled him for his Jewish origins, Reinhardt found tremendous success in 1934 with his live production of *A Midsummer Night's Dream* at the Hollywood Bowl. The director rebuilt the entire area around the auditorium, removed the shell for the orchestra, created an artificial hill, and lit the stage with thirty thousand incandescent lights. The ensemble was top-notch and the Los Angeles Philharmonic played to a sold-out audience of twelve thousand.

Warner Bros. agreed to a film adaptation, to be helmed by Reinhardt and William Dieterle. The budget was generous, and the fee for Reinhardt was princely by the standards of the time. Reinhardt invited the Austrian composer Erich Korngold to Los Angeles to adapt Felix Mendelssohn's music to the length of the film. The production, released in 1935, was artistically ambitious but a commercial fiasco, and permanently damaged Reinhardt's reputation in America. Such was his status when Thomas and Katia reunited with the theater impresario and his second wife, Helene Thimig, as exiles in America.

Mann and Reinhardt had known each other for more than thirty years and were connected through numerous contacts. In 1938, at a soiree at his home at 2201 Maravilla Drive in the Hollywood Hills, Reinhardt advised Mann to settle in the vicinity of the Hollywood dream factory. Mann recorded in his diaries, "Beautiful house in splendid location. Sea of lights of the city." A few years later, the Manns relocated to California from Princeton.

Disappointed by the reception of the film version of *A Midsummer Night's Dream*, Reinhardt had rented a Columbia Broadcasting System (CBS) building at 6121 Sunset Boulevard, where he established the Max Reinhardt Workshop for Stage, Screen and Radio to train actors and directors. The Mann family was invited several times to public performances at the workshop. Reinhardt had to shut down the operation in 1941, noting sorrowfully, "in a city where the surface dominates [. . .] one cannot justly expect the development of the three-dimensional arts of the theater."

With the lack of professional success, financial resources became scarce. Reinhardt also had to support his first wife, Else Heims, who was living separately in Santa Monica, and with whom he was engaged in a grueling divorce. Reinhardt therefore decided, out of necessity, to move from the Hollywood Hills to what was then the more affordable

Pacific Palisades—to a stately house with a view of the sea. Mann remarked, not without envy, that it was a "house furnished with true stagecraft, against which ours is of sober practicality."

A few weeks after his seventieth birthday, in October 1943, Reinhardt died after suffering a stroke. Mann spoke at his funeral service and later made the following diary entry: "How our life gradually becomes impoverished in its personnel and depopulates itself before we ourselves go, the death of Max Reinhardt has made me feel quite strongly. [...] Our starting points and spheres lay far apart, but again and again, from a young age, our paths led together momentarily, and to see him at work, at his clever and colorful, sublime and sensational work, was one of the most interesting pleasures of my life."

Panoramic photo of *A Midsummer Night's Dream* cast at Hollywood Bowl, 1934

FRITZI MASSARY
520 North Canon Drive · Beverly Hills
Verena Mund

Thomas Mann and the retired operetta star Fritzi Massary knew each other long before Massary immigrated to Los Angeles in 1939. He was a good friend of Bruno Frank, who had married Massary's daughter Liesl in 1925. No wonder, one might think, that Mann spent so much time at each of the four houses where Massary resided in Beverly Hills. Yet, Massary was more than just one of Frank's relatives. The former "Princess of Olala" had been famous for the nuances of her "Tralala la la-la-la" (from the song "In the Case of Love," or "Tralala Song," from the 1904 revue *Die Herren des Maxim*) and her skill at walking the line of suggestiveness. Alfred Polgar, who was part of Mann and Massary's circle, said she, like no other, created a "delicatessen of shamelessness" in her performances.

According to Albrecht Joseph, who accompanied Massary in her early days in Beverly Hills (and who also worked as a secretary for both Massary and Mann), she maintained a powerful erotic aura well into her later years. In Berlin and in Frankfurt, girls and women alike, according to Joseph, endeavored to wield a handkerchief the same way she did, not to mention dress, walk, take a seat, and even smoke like her. In his memoirs *Ein Tisch bei Romanoffs,* Joseph delineated the diva's cultural impact: "there was no higher praise for a lady than to call her, 'like la Massary.'"

Beyond the circle of émigrés, however, Massary's fame did not extend to Hollywood, and the soprano was not well known outside German-speaking Europe. After leaving Berlin, her career was over. Yet, she obviously had not lost her regal comportment and her ability to entertain. Mann loved the "air of operetta" she generated. Her presentation of "Lubitsch stories" and other amusing accounts made it into his diaries several times. Even when visiting her daughter, he brought "flowers for la Massary." Following Bruno Frank's death, Massary moved in with Liesl. Mann's reports of his visits there place Liesl in the background or rarely include her at all. Together with Massary, the Franks, and others, Mann would attend the cinema or private screenings with "the Dieterles" at Warner Bros. Studios of films such as *Juarez* (1939), which he summarized as an "excellent achievement in every regard, a glory to the industry. La Massary in tears."

German journalist and author Kurt Tucholsky had seen Massary perform on stage: "Not one has ever burned their gob [Schnauze] with champagne"—and focused on Massary's accentuation of the word *Schnauze*: "with a kind of satisfaction, a joy of the subsurface, that forced one to an instant curiosity." Mann seemed to agree. He enjoyed her soirees or even just "lunch at the lovely house" of hers at 606 North Bedford Drive, often with the Franks, and "champagne." Not long after she had moved into "her new very elegant house" at 520 North Canon Drive, he relished a "good feast" at "Mme Massary." Nothing changed even after she relocated to 615 North Rodeo Drive, where he, as always, appreciated her "champagne and excellent food," not to mention the "champagne cocktail." Sure enough, the zenith of it all was the "elegant champagne-goose-liver-chocolate combination" he once received from Massary at Christmas.

Fritzi Massary, postcard, Berlin, c. 1918–1927

phot. Nicola Perscheid, Berlin.

FOX VILLAGE THEATRE
948 Broxton Avenue

Benno Herz

Reading Thomas Mann's diaries, one finds two common reasons why he drove the fifteen minutes west from his home on San Remo Drive to Westwood, home to UCLA and the closest neighborhood that provided him with the infrastructure of a city. The most common reason was to get a haircut. "To Westwood for haircut" is almost a catchphrase, repeated over a hundred times in the author's diaries. It was often combined with other errands, such as banking, buying clothing, or doctor's visits. The second most common reason was: "To Westwood to the movies."

Tucked between the hills of Bel Air to the north, Santa Monica to the west, and Beverly Hills to the east, Westwood became the home of the vast UCLA campus in the late 1920s. With many students living in the neighborhood, by 1940 the town was one of the three major movie markets in L.A., along with Downtown and Hollywood. By the 1970s, Westwood had the largest number of first-run theaters compared to any neighborhood in the city.

The Fox Village Theatre is a remarkable structure built in 1930 in the Spanish modernist style. Located at 948 Broxton Avenue, it was designed by the architect Percy Parke Lewis, who was responsible for other buildings in the Spanish Mission style in the surrounding area. Fox was constructing many locations at the time, and the Westwood venue became a symbol for the neighborhood and the Mediterranean-style atmosphere of "the Village," as Westwood's city center is often called. The 170-foot tower, with its glowing art deco "FOX" neon sign, can be seen from afar. In 1988, the theater was named a Historic-Cultural Monument by the Los Angeles Cultural Heritage Commission.

Mann often would venture with Katia and daughter Monika "to Westwood to the cinema: pilot film" (June 20, 1941), "after dinner with K.[atia], Golo and Moni to Westwood to the cinéma: excellent film" (January 27, 1942), "with Erika, Golo und Moni to the cinéma in Westwood" (June 29, 1942), "with Heinrich to Westwood to the cinéma: Parisian occupation and Gestapo film, not bad!" (May 7, 1942), or with his friends the Borgeses to watch the "impressive navy war movie" *In Which We Serve* (March 8, 1943). Trips to the movies were a family event for the Manns, and an important part of their experience in Los Angeles. Between 1941 and 1952, Mann mentioned over fifty such trips "to Westwood to the cinéma."

In his diaries, Mann also would refer to a "Fox Cinéma." Though he never mentioned any characteristic features, this would likely have been one of only

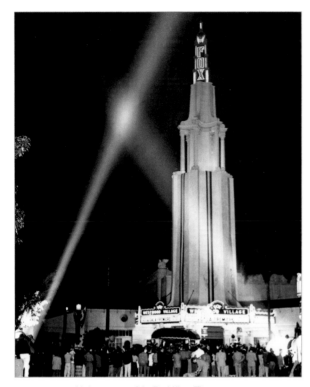

Nighttime view of the Fox Village Theatre, 1951

two options in Westwood at the time: the Bruin Theatre, across the street from the Fox, opened its doors in 1937 and is still operating today, or the beautiful UCLAN Theater, which opened on Christmas Eve 1940 on Westwood Boulevard just south of Wilshire.

Mann's proximity to the cinema center of Westwood is described in detail in his diaries, following the same stylistic formula: First he mentions the person with whom he saw the film ("To Westwood to the cinema with X"). Then he records which film he saw, sometimes mentioning the name but most often describing the plot in a few words or making allusions to certain actors or themes. This is usually followed by a short, poignant, sometimes funny critique.

The "Fox Westcoast Theatres" listing in the *Los Angeles Times* on March 2, 1942, advertised the 1942 film *Shanghai Gesture* by Austro-Hungarian director Josef von Sternberg. On March 4, Mann wrote: "6 p.m. tea and snacks (...) and off to Westwood to the cinéma: Shanghai-Society film and *Suspicion*. The best thing was the correctness and naturalness of the guys."

Mann's diaries reveal his opinions on a wide range of films. It is hard to pin down his favorite genre, but some of the more notable films included were *Dr. Jekyll and Mr. Hyde*, which he described as "not flawless, of course, but poignant as a moral tragedy" (October 10, 1941). He later remarked, "Saw excellent English film: Mister D. with Leslie Howard, Adventures in Nazi Germany" (April 6, 1942). Mann was most likely referring to *49th Parallel*, which had its U.S. release in the first week of April 1942.

The novelist left another comment about a potential movie adaptation of his Joseph trilogy, indicating he was envisioning what that would look like. His April 11, 1944, entry read: "Afterwards for a cinéma visit to Westwood: *Lady in the Dark*, psychoanalytical dream show, not very enjoyable. Interesting though the color technique in regard to Joseph. At home chocolate and tree cake." This 1944 musical film made use of the color production process known as Technicolor.

But Mann by far did not like all the movies he went to see in Westwood. For example, the 1943 anti-Nazi propaganda flick *Hitler's Children* was deemed "pathetically stupid" ("*erbärmlich dummen Nazi-Film*") (April 7, 1943). Even Thomas Mann, a staunch anti-Nazi himself, would not be completely beguiled by the Hollywood dream factory.

WARNER BROS. HOLLYWOOD THEATRE
6433 Hollywood Boulevard
Benno Herz

On September 15, 1943, celebrities of the émigré community were spotted at a premiere at the Warner Bros. Hollywood Theatre. As scholar David Jenemann recounts in his book *Adorno in America*, the *Hollywood Reporter* covered the evening: "Exiled Notables at Showing of the Rhine. World-famous authors, consuls-general, and educators forced to flee from Germany (…) joined motion pictures stars last night at a unique 'Premiere in Exile' at the Warner Bros. Hollywood Theatre. They saw the Motion Picture version of *Watch on the Rhine* starring Bette Davis and Paul Lukas. Present as the guests of Harry M. Warner were Thomas Mann, Heinrich Mann, Bruno Frank, Emil Ludwig, Lion Feuchtwanger, Bert Brecht, Dr. T. Adorno and Prof. Max Horkheimer."

We know that Mann thoroughly enjoyed movies and that he went to screenings as often as twice a week. What is surprising is that Max Horkheimer and Theodor Adorno, the grouchy members of the Frankfurt School, and Thomas's rather socialist-leaning brother Heinrich joined in. To better understand why so many politically engaged exiles went to this premiere, one must consider the film on the ticket: the 1943 Warner Bros. production *Watch on the Rhine*, directed by Herman Shumlin, a Broadway director and producer. Based on Lillian Hellman's 1940 play of the same name, Dashiell Hammett's screenplay transported Max Schneckenburger's 1840 poem "Die Wacht am Rhein" to the politically troubled times of the 1940s. The patriotic work, written during the Rhine Crisis between France and Germany, made a "thunderous call" in five verses to defend the German

Rhine so "no enemy sets his foot on the shore of the Rhine."

In the film, the anti-Fascist German engineer Kurt Muller and his American wife, Sara, portrayed by Paul Lukas and Bette Davis, have returned to the United States in 1940 after Kurt served in the German underground resistance fighting the rising Nazi regime. At home in Washington, D.C., a guest of Sara's family discovers Kurt's secret and threatens to expose him.

This very German source material and its political actualization in the 1940s might be one of the reasons why many of the exiles attended the premiere. Stories like this could have happened to some of their own friends and families. In addition, many of their acquaintances were named in the credits, including the Austrian composer Max Steiner, who wrote the score, and the German-Jewish editor Rudi Fehr, who worked for Warner Bros. for more than forty years. The movie was produced by Hal B. Wallis, who a year earlier landed a massive box office hit with *Casablanca*, which also featured many of the exiles. *Watch on the Rhine* was nominated for an Academy Award for best picture and won the New York Film Critics Circle Award. In 1946, Mann saw another film directed by Shumlin: *Confidential Agent* (1945) with Peter Lorre.

Mann described the remarkable evening in his diary: "(. . .) 7 o'clock chicken soup. Then as invited guest to Warner Theatre, Hollywood Boulevard, Première of *Watch on the Rhine*. Franks, Bassermanns etc. Countless photographic shots. After the performance in the foyer with Warner, the actors. Interviews. At home chocolate. — Listened to swing. Situation at Salerno slightly improved. One seems

Film poster, *Watch on the Rhine*, 1943

to hold out until the English arrive. Colossal air bombardments."

It is interesting how he jumps from the social aspects of the glamorous event to the serious topic of the political situation in Italy—another hint that the film's story resonated with him. We don't know for sure if Mann visited the Warner Bros. Hollywood Theatre again. In his diaries, he mentioned going to "Warner Bros. to see a movie" several times, but this could also refer to the private previews at the studio.

Nevertheless, the Hollywood Theatre, at 6433 Hollywood Boulevard, has long been a major showcase. Also known as the Hollywood Pacific Theatre or Warner Hollywood Theatre, it was built in the French-inspired Beaux-Arts style in 1928 by the architect G. Albert Landsburgh, who was famous for many luxury theaters and cinemas of the time. It opened on April 26 with *Glorious Betsy*, one of the first Warner Bros. films that included sequences with audible dialogue, making use of the Vitaphone sound film system. The two radio towers on the roof of the building made it instantly recognizable: they were placed by Warner Bros., which at the time still owned the radio station KFWB. Unfortunately, the theater closed in 1994 after suffering damage from both the Northridge earthquake and the construction of the Red Line subway. The building has since been declared a Los Angeles Historic-Cultural Monument and can still be seen when walking the Walk of Fame on Hollywood Boulevard. Just look for the iconic transmitter towers on the roof.

BLUE DANUBE RESTAURANT
1904 South Robertson Boulevard
Jan-Christopher Horak

The headline read "From Diamond Else to the Blue Danube," and referred to the failed Hollywood career of the Viennese émigré film director Joe May, who produced an almost unending series of hit films in Berlin before 1933 but crashed and burned in America. His doomed restaurant, the Blue Danube, was the final chapter before he died a pauper in 1954. The story of Joe and Mia May's Blue Danube was endlessly repeated within the émigré community and in almost every biographical sketch of the once world-famous director who was forced to flee Germany with his wife—herself one of Germany's most popular silent film stars—after the rise of Hitler and the expulsion of all Jewish filmmakers from the film industries in Berlin and Vienna.

The story of the Blue Danube's lack of success became a symbol of Joe May's specific fate in Hollywood, and of a Central European émigré community hopelessly mired in nostalgia for their prewar past. But like all anecdotes that mix rumor, myth, truth, and fiction, this story lacks specificity, one writer even stylizing the restaurant as a place where émigré intellectuals like Thomas Mann gathered to indulge their obsession with good food and political satire while discussing the fates of those stranded in Europe.

Of course, the truth is much more complicated and layered. Despite one author characterizing May's film work as comprising a handful of abysmal B-films, May participated in no less than fifteen films as a writer and director at Universal, including some commercial and critical hits such as *The Invisible Man Returns* (1940) and *The House of the Seven Gables* (1940). If the job offers dried up at the end of the 1940s, this probably had more to do with the fact that May (born 1880) was of retirement age, a problem that would also eventually befall almost all of his American colleagues in an industry that favored a continual infusion of young blood.

Though the restaurant failed, it was not for lack of trying. Opened on April 2, 1949, at 1904 South Robertson Boulevard in West Los Angeles, in a primarily residential neighborhood, it was probably intended as a garden restaurant, similar to the "Heurigen" restaurants in Vienna's Grinzing district. The menu featured a mixture of American fare—steaks, lamb chops, veal scallopini, and typical Viennese dishes like Wiener schnitzel, beef goulash, veal Paprikash with spaetzle, boiled beef with horseradish, and Sauerbraten, topped off with desserts that included Apfelstruden, Palaschinken, and Nussnudeln. Prices were moderate, ranging from $2 to $4 (about $23 to $46 in 2021) for entrees. Mia May was a wonderful cook, but the area, which lay south of Wilshire and Pico Boulevards, didn't lend itself to success. Given that more than half of all restaurants fail, even in high-traffic commercial areas, the German-speaking community alone could probably never have sustained a restaurant.

The Mays had financed the operation through a subscription program, raising approximately $12,000 (about $137,000 in 2021) from friends and colleagues at $500 a share, guaranteeing 2.5 percent of the eventual profits. The effort was spearheaded by the agent Paul Kohner and the director Billy Wilder and coordinated through the European Film Fund. While Wilder gave $3,000 and Kohner and Robert Siodmak each contributed $2,000, single "half shareholders" included John Auer, Henry Blanke, the Friedrich Hollanders, Hedy Lamarr, Anatole Litvak, Joe Pasternak, Otto Preminger, Arnold Pressburger, Gottfried Reinhardt, Walter Reisch, Sam Spiegel, Robert Thoeren, and Henry Guttman from the émigré community. Lending support from outside the community were John Huston, Hugh F. Herbert, Lewis Milestone, Ayn Rand, and Lou Wasserman, among others. Based on pledges, May had taken out a private loan from Fred Brosio, which needed to be paid off even before the restaurant opened. The shares, essentially loans, were to be repaid in monthly installments within two years, including 6 percent interest.

However, the Blue Danube remained undercapitalized. In a letter of February 18, 1949, to Kohner, May indicated that the purchase of the property and renovations had cost more than anticipated, seriously diminishing his initial operating capital. As a result, the Blue Danube closed after only a few months. Until May's death in April 1954, the couple was dependent on subsidies from the European Film Fund. Mia outlived her husband by twenty-six years, passing away in November 1980 at the age of ninety-six, still dependent on the kindness of strangers.

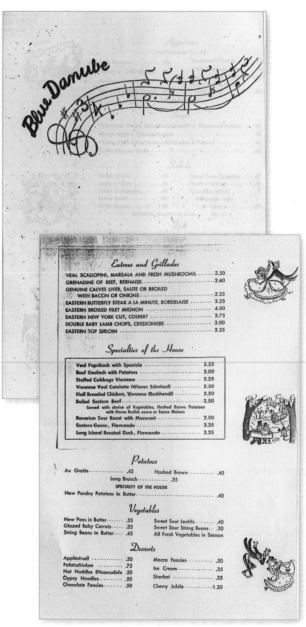

Menu, Blue Danube Restaurant

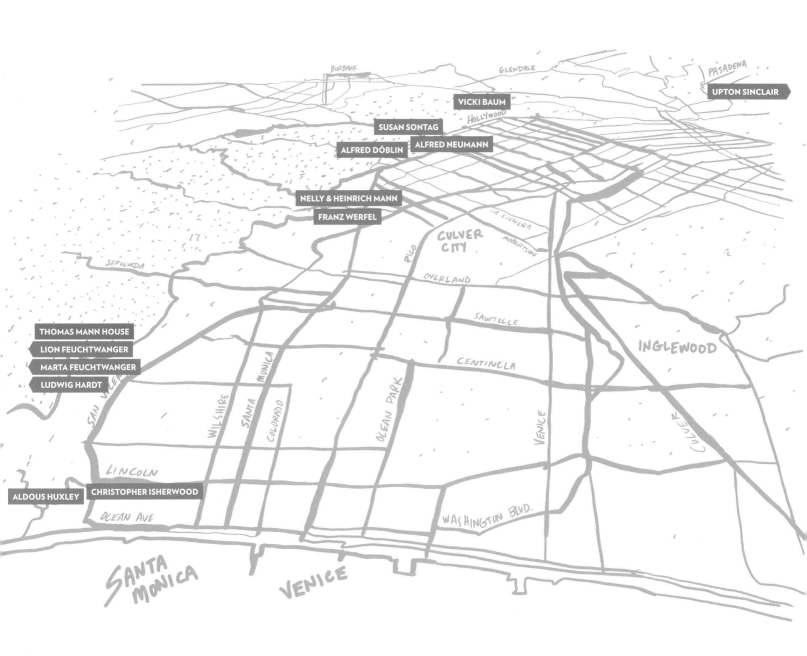

PART 4

UPTON SINCLAIR

VICKI BAUM

SUSAN SONTAG

ALFRED DÖBLIN   ALFRED NEUMANN

NELLY & HEINRICH MANN

FRANZ WERFEL

CULVER CITY

THOMAS MANN HOUSE

LION FEUCHTWANGER

MARTA FEUCHTWANGER

LUDWIG HARDT

INGLEWOOD

ALDOUS HUXLEY   CHRISTOPHER ISHERWOOD

BURBANK   GLENDALE   PASADENA

HOLLYWOOD

LA CIENEGA

ROBERTSON

PICO

OVERLAND

SAWTELLE

CENTINELA

VENICE

CULVER

SEPULVEDA

17

SAN VICENTE

WILSHIRE   SANTA MONICA   COLORADO

OCEAN PARK

LINCOLN

OCEAN AVE

WASHINGTON BLVD.

SANTA MONICA

VENICE

LOS ANGELES'S LITERARY RADIANCE

Benno Herz

West Los Angeles in the 1940s "effectively became the capital of German literature in exile. It was as if the cafés of Berlin, Munich, and Vienna had disgorged their clientele onto Sunset Boulevard," according to music critic and author Alex Ross. The road to exile began just a decade prior, in April 1933, when the Office for Press and Propaganda of the German Student Union instigated the "Action against the Un-German Spirit," a campaign that led to the public burning of thousands of books. Whatever the Nazis regarded as left-leaning, democratic, communist, or Jewish was burnt in Berlin, Frankfurt, Munich, Hannover, and other cities. Works by Heinrich Mann, Lion Feuchtwanger, Alfred Döblin, and Bertolt Brecht were among those classified by the Nazis as literature "worthy of burning" (*verbrennungswürdig*). Among the rallying cries, the German students shouted, "Against decadence and moral decay! For discipline and decency in family and state! I surrender to the flames the writings of Heinrich Mann, Ernst Glaeser, and Erich Kaestner!" while the SA and SS played marching music on Berlin's Bebelplatz.

In the aftermath of the burnings, blacklists were continuously supplemented and expanded; a year later they would carry more than three thousand titles of banned books and writings. A "list of harmful and undesirable literature" finally contained 12,400 titles and the complete works of over 150 authors. The highly symbolic acts of public burnings and the subsequent cleansing of German libraries, publishing houses, and universities made it clear to every writer in and outside the Reich that post–Weimar Germany had no room for writers who were not aligned with the Nazi Party's ideology. This marked the beginning of a literary exodus out of Germany. By the end of May 1933, almost fifteen thousand respected and acclaimed authors had left the country or were forced into exile. In November, the Nazis implemented a so-called Reich Chamber of Culture (*Reichsschrifttumskammer*) that served as a direct instrument through which they could influence and control the authors remaining in Germany. Those who did not apply for membership were automatically excluded from publishing in Germany. Even exile did not spare many authors from the Nazis' grasp: names of authors in exile were published and used to strip them of their German citizenship, among them Thomas and Heinrich Mann. But this fierce suppression aroused an even fiercer response from the émigrés: the processing of this trauma, the experience of exile, and the strong positioning against the ideology of the Nazis are themes that can be found in what is often referred to as "exile literature," or *Exilliteratur*. The German-language publishing house Querido Verlag was established in Amsterdam in reaction to the developments in Germany. It was founded by Fritz Landshoff, former publishing director of the respected *Kiepenheuer Verlag* in Berlin, and the politically committed Dutch social-democratic publisher Emanuel Querido. Its purpose was to provide persecuted and banned German authors with publication opportunities. The company was an important mouthpiece for many refugee authors until its destruction during the Nazi occupation of Holland in 1940. Between 1933 and 1940, it published works by many of the authors who would eventually settle in L.A., among them Feuchtwanger, Döblin, Theodor Adorno, Max Horkheimer, Ludwig Marcuse, and Erika Mann.

Before many of these exiled authors reunited under the Southern California sun, they would gather in the fishing village of Sanary-sur-Mer. The list of those seeking refuge in this southern French village by the Mediterranean Sea is long, and includes Marcuse, Lion and Marta Feuchtwanger, Bruno Frank, and Franz

Beach of Port-Issol and the Lido, Sanary-sur-Mer, c. 1933

Werfel and Alma Mahler-Werfel, as well as Thomas, Katia, Heinrich, Golo, and Klaus Mann. The town soon also attracted other international writers, such as the British author Aldous Huxley and his wife, Maria. Huxley wrote his dystopian futuristic novel *Brave New World* in Sanary-sur-Mer. It was also where he first encountered Thomas Mann in the summer of 1933. Upon the declaration of war in 1939, the idyllic writing retreat was no longer a safe haven. The exiles were suddenly treated as enemy aliens. In September, the concentration camp known as Camp des Milles opened near Aix-en-Provence, some forty miles inland from Sanary; Lion Feuchtwanger would be interned there. Later, many of the prisoners were transferred to a temporary tent camp near Nîmes, where Feuchtwanger was smuggled out—disguised as a woman—by employees of the U.S. consulate in Marseille aided by his wife, Marta. Another exodus began, sometimes by foot over the Pyrenees, to Spain and Portugal, with the hope of embarking from Lisbon on one of the ocean liners to New York or Latin America. Some were not as fortunate: when denied passage by the Franco government's border patrol in Portbou, Spain, on September 25, 1940, Walter Benjamin, the philosopher and author of *The Work of Art in the Age of Mechanical Reproduction,* committed suicide. To avoid capture by the Nazis, he took an overdose of morphine, his travel visa to the United States—obtained with the help of Horkheimer—still in his pocket.

Those authors who made it to the United States arrived at ports on the East Coast. What sparked this literary trek to Los Angeles? For one, the city was the center of the booming film industry, offering many screenwriting job opportunities for novelists. Hollywood was always in need of a good story: *The Blue Angel*, starring Marlene Dietrich, had already been an international success in 1930 and was based on Heinrich Mann's 1905 novel *Professor Filth*. From Döblin and Brecht to Franz Werfel and Vicki Baum, many novelists signed short-term contracts with movie studios. Whether they liked this new opportunity or not, employment was essential to get the necessary visas and provided financial stability. In addition, Los Angeles had a different intellectual and cultural infrastructure than that in New York or other cities on the East Coast. In "The Haunted California Idyll of German Writers in Exile," Alex Ross suggests that L.A. "allowed refugees to reconstitute the ideals of the Weimar Republic instead of competing with an existent literary scene." Also, real estate wasn't as expensive. Many of the refugees were stripped of all their accounts and belongings by the Nazis or had to leave everything behind in order to escape. Since the first ambassadors of a German-Jewish literary community had come to L.A. in the 1920s and early 1930s, there was already an established network of émigrés that the newly arrived authors could tap into, from Salka Viertel's salons and parties on Mabery Road to organizations like the European Film Fund. Considering all the available support and the year-round pleasant weather, it was no surprise that 1940s Los Angeles was teeming with talented writers, poets, and novelists. Both local writers and those from all over the United States came to mingle with the fugitives from Europe.

The literary microclimate in L.A. was heating up; many German writers were working on monumental novels, using the backdrop of medieval or ancient settings as a projection screen for timely political interpretations. Feuchtwanger was a master of this, with works such as *The False Nero* (1947), *Goya* (1951), and *Jewess of Toledo* (1955). Mann wrote his Joseph saga, a four-part novel written over the course of sixteen years that tells the biblical story of Joseph and his brothers. His American colleague Upton Sinclair, born just three years before Mann in 1878, was looking at more contemporary topics. *Dragon's Teeth* (1942), for which Sinclair won the Pulitzer Prize in 1943, was set in Nazi Germany. With the beatnik generation on the horizon, which would profoundly change U.S. literature and culture, there was already a younger generation of rebellious newcomers pushing toward a more colloquial, subcultural style of urban novel. Christopher Isherwood's 1939 *Goodbye to Berlin*, a veritable success praised by many of his fellow writers, was exemplary of a more gritty, cosmopolitan realism. As Isherwood wrote in one passage: "I am a camera with its shutter open, quite passive, recording, not thinking." The author as a passive camera, recording his surroundings and emotions, can be seen in contrast to the extensive historical research that Feuchtwanger or Mann would conduct in order to vividly depict the fabric of medieval Spain or ancient Egypt. Looking at this motley group of writers with their various origins, ages, and cultural backgrounds, it becomes quite impossible, and rather unproductive, to try to pin down a monolithic literary genre or style in 1940s L.A. This scene was as multilayered and complex as the biographies and background stories of its protagonists.

How was Mann able to stand out in this mass of talented writers? As German studies and Mann scholar

Hans Rudolf Vaget illustrates in his seminal work, *Thomas Mann, der Amerikaner*, Mann's novels were often assumed to be philosophically overloaded and therefore exhausting to read for U.S. audiences. Still, Mann's dense "novels of ideas" were extremely popular among that readership. Their essentially human motifs resonated with an audience reeling from war and the Great Depression. By 1941, *The Magic Mountain* had sold over 125,000 copies and *Joseph in Egypt,* 47,000 copies. The latter was even included in the biggest book club of the country, the Book-of-the-Month Club, after which it sold another 210,000 copies. His later works *Doctor Faustus* and *The Holy Sinner* were also featured in the club. Promoted by his publisher, Knopf, Mann experienced much success in his adopted country. He came to represent the "other" Germany. In opposition to Hitler and the Nazis, from exile he publicly championed democracy. Tobias Boes points out in his critically acclaimed book *Thomas Mann's War: Literature, Politics, and the World Republic of Letters*: "This idea corresponded not so much to a flesh-and-blood individual as it did to a network entity, created through the labors of literary agents, translators, editors, publishers, journalists, literary critics, and of course, ordinary readers. Thomas Mann became a cipher in which America could see itself." As early as 1934, before his move across the Atlantic, Mann was featured on the cover of *Time* magazine—a sensation for a German author.

This fate was not shared by most of Mann's fellow exiles. His brother Heinrich, for example, had difficulty making ends meet even while receiving financial support funneled to him by Thomas through the European Film Fund. Brecht, Döblin, and Feuchtwanger couldn't repeat the success they once enjoyed in their home country. Economic inequality, foreign-language complications, and the competitive and unfamiliar American book market created tensions in the exile community. These conflicts of class and recognition certainly played a role in the dynamics among the exiled writers. Döblin, for example, accused Mann—who was well-off compared to many of his peers—of dealing only with the "problems of villa owners." There were many infamous (and entertaining) fights between Brecht and Mann. Their feud produced some of the punchiest taunts. In a letter to Karl Korsch in 1941, Brecht wrote: "Whenever I meet Thomas Mann, 3,000 years of tradition look down upon me." Brecht's criticism of Mann's reverence for canon and high-art snobbery and Döblin's remarks about the Manns as elite villa owners make visible these conflicts of class and social background within the émigré community.

Of course, there were also strong ties and lasting friendships within the community. There was a caring bond between Thomas and Katia Mann and Lion and Marta Feuchtwanger, who visited each other quite frequently, often reading from their most recent works. The Austrian-Jewish writer Vicki Baum was also among Mann's friends in L.A. Her international best-selling novel *Grand Hotel* was adapted into a film starring Greta Garbo and Joan Crawford, which won the Academy Award for outstanding production in 1933. The Austrian Bohemian novelist, playwright, and poet Franz Werfel quickly made a name for himself in Hollywood after his book *The Song of Bernadette* was made into a film. The list of novelists-turned-Hollywood-screenwriters goes on to include Alfred Neumann, one of the most widely read authors of the Weimar Republic; Tobias Boes discusses his close friendship with Mann.

Not all of the exiles were as fortunate. Many struggled and weren't able to make it. Brecht collaborated with Fritz Lang on *Hangmen Also Die!* (1943) but did not give Hollywood another shot. Döblin, contracted as a screenwriter at MGM, provided ideas and suggestions for the screenplay of the (later Oscar-winning) film *Mrs. Miniver* (1942) and *Random Harvest* (1942). In both cases, his German scripts were translated into English and incorporated into the screenplays. Nevertheless, his yearlong contract expired in 1941 and wasn't renewed. Other exiled authors who were still writing, speaking, and thinking in German were facing similar problems: Ludwig Hardt, one of the most famous German-language reciters of his time, wasn't able to translate his language-based art for an English-speaking audience. Unable to write in English, many relied on translators. In an open letter to his colleague Walter von Molo, Mann described his feelings as an author detached from his native language as the "heart asthma of exile." In his own book, Vaget points out that Mann lamented the fact that his "books eke their lives in English now."

Despite his own struggles with English, Mann was interested in contemporary U.S. literature and knew some of L.A.'s finest novelists. He was honorary president of the German-American Writers Association, and in a speech delivered at the congress of the American Writers League at Carnegie Hall in June 1939, he praised American literature as the "deepest and most inspiring kind," naming the works of Walt Whitman, Edgar Allan Poe, Ernest Hemingway, and Upton Sinclair as examples. Sinclair and Mann had met as early as April 1938 on the latter's first visit to L.A. He noted in his diary on April 18: "Drove to Pasadena to see Upton Sinclair. In the garden with the family, in the living room with Sinclair and Mr. Brown [author Lewis Brown] (. . .) Dinner at the great hotel of P. Sherbet." Like Mann, Sinclair was an important figure in both politics and literature. A socialist writer, his novels were often based on or inspired by real events and were critical of modern-day capitalism. His influential 1906 exposé *The Jungle* pulled back the curtain on the harsh conditions in Chicago's slaughterhouses and revealed how the meat industry exploited immigrant labor. Mann was well aware of his colleague's work, writing in December 1942, "Appreciation for Upton Sinclair's new novel," probably a reference to *Between Two Worlds* (1941).

The British writer Christopher Isherwood lived at 145 Adelaide Drive in Santa Monica Canyon, not far from the Mann home in Pacific Palisades. Isherwood had arrived in 1940, around the same time as Mann, the culmination of a six-year odyssey that had begun with his German boyfriend, Heinz Neddermeyer. After fleeing Berlin in 1933, they were seeking not only a safe haven from the Nazis but also a place where they could live peacefully as a homosexual couple. Their journey had taken them to the Canary Islands, Copenhagen, Brussels, Amsterdam, and Sintra in Portugal, until Neddermeyer was arrested and detained by the Gestapo in 1937. Before Isherwood settled in L.A., alone, he worked as a screenwriter with the Austrian director Berthold Viertel, husband of Salka Viertel, in London. Isherwood's work inspired him to write his novel *Prater Violet* (1945). Set in Vienna, it provides an ironic commentary on the Nazi annexation of Austria. Isherwood was well aware of Mann's work and familiar with *Death in Venice* and *The Magic Mountain*.

But there was another angle to their relationship. When he was a journalist in Berlin, Isherwood was friends with Erika and Klaus Mann. After the Nazis revoked Erika's citizenship in 1935, Klaus had asked Isherwood to marry his sister so she could obtain British citizenship and a valid passport. He demurred, and approached his friend the British poet, W.H. Auden, instead. Auden did not know Erika but agreed to the marriage in a telegram, saying he would be "delighted." (Isherwood later confirmed this in his memoirs.) Even though the marriage was regarded as a formality, a cordial relationship developed between Auden and the Mann family, and Erika held on to her British citizenship until the end of her life.

Isherwood, who was working as a screenwriter at MGM, would frequently meet Mann for lunch, tea, and dinner at Salka Viertel's home. At the time, Isherwood was dating the photographer William "Bill" Caskey.

From left, W.H. Auden, Christopher Isherwood, and Stephen Spender, 1937

After a dinner in March 1949, Mann noted harshly in his diary: "Isherwood very much in need of drinks with his formless and charmless Bill. Hard to understand." Nevertheless, Mann was interested in the young British writer's work. Mann read *Prater Violet* and later praised Isherwood's contribution to a volume dedicated to Klaus, who tragically overdosed on sleeping pills in Cannes in 1949: "Very good, portrait-like contribution to the memorial book for Klaus by Christopher Isherwood. Moving."

Another British writer and friend in California was Aldous Huxley. For a short time in the early 1940s, the Huxleys lived across the street from the Manns on Amalfi Drive, and Huxley occasionally worked for MGM as a screenwriter. Probably Mann's youngest admirer was fifteen-year-old Susan Sontag, who would later become a world-renowned writer, filmmaker, philosopher, and cultural critic. Sontag, who considered *The Magic Mountain* among her favorite books and had an early encounter with Mann that proved to be a defining moment in her life.

But the interactions between Mann and other

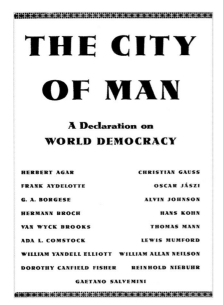

THE CITY OF MAN

A Declaration on WORLD DEMOCRACY

HERBERT AGAR	CHRISTIAN GAUSS
FRANK AYDELOTTE	OSCAR JÁSZI
G. A. BORGESE	ALVIN JOHNSON
HERMANN BROCH	HANS KOHN
VAN WYCK BROOKS	THOMAS MANN
ADA L. COMSTOCK	LEWIS MUMFORD
WILLIAM YANDELL ELLIOTT	WILLIAM ALLAN NEILSON
DOROTHY CANFIELD FISHER	REINHOLD NIEBUHR
GAETANO SALVEMINI	

Thomas Mann et al., *The City of Man: A Declaration on World Democracy*

writers, and between the European émigrés and their American counterparts, are more than anecdotal and extend beyond Los Angeles. Political alliances were forged to create a literary and philosophical counterbalance to Nazi Germany and the rise of Fascism. As early as 1941, a group of U.S. and European writers, journalists, historians, and public intellectuals worked together to publish the manifesto *The City of Man: A Declaration on World Democracy*. It was intended as a response to Nazi Germany, affirming there was now a global responsibility to heed the dangers of Fascism and stand in solidarity against it. The writers thought about how a new world could be structured peacefully and how totalitarianism could be avoided for future generations. Among the seventeen signatures on *The City of Man* were those of the educational reformer, social activist, women's-rights supporter, and best-selling U.S. author Dorothy Canfield Fisher, women's education pioneer Ada Comstock, U.S. literary critic Van Wyck Brooks, Austrian writer Hermann Broch, and Thomas Mann.

Weaving together all these anecdotes, connections, and political collaborations between these many authors and novelists of different backgrounds and histories, one can discern the large, complex network of writers who inspired and challenged one another during this time and contributed to the literary radiance of this city.

NELLY & HEINRICH MANN
301 South Swall Drive
Michaela Ullmann

Nelly Mann, the second wife of Thomas Mann's older brother Heinrich, wasn't exactly what Thomas and Katia expected in a sister-in-law. Nelly, who grew up in humble social circumstances, had moved to Berlin and landed a job as a barmaid. Her appearance—blond, tall, curvy—attracted the much older Heinrich in 1929. Heinrich was inspired by Nelly and her life full of deprivation and hardship, and he memorialized her in his novel *Ein ernstes Leben* (A Serious Life).

As the Nazis assumed power in February 1933, Heinrich was one of the first intellectuals to flee Germany. Like Thomas and Katia, he initially found refuge in southern France. Nelly stayed behind in Berlin and, despite being arrested and interrogated, attempted to secure Heinrich's manuscripts, money, and valuables. She eventually followed him to France, where they married in 1939. Once the country fell to German occupation, they fled Europe for the United States.

Like most German exiles during World War II, Heinrich and Nelly faced great financial difficulties here. While it is widely known that Heinrich received support from Thomas and other émigrés, including his close friend Lion Feuchtwanger, it is rarely acknowledged that Nelly took loving care of her elderly husband, that she learned to speak English and to drive a car, and that she worked long hours as a milk-delivery driver in Los Angeles, as a nurse, and as a seamstress of soldiers' uniforms.

The embarrassing "awful trollop" and Heinrich lived at 301 South Swall Drive, a few miles from the Mann family. It was probably there that Marta and Lion Feuchtwanger arrived for a party one night and were greeted at the door by a naked and drunk Nelly. This episode made it into Christopher Hampton's play *Tales from Hollywood* and, throughout the literature, Nelly is portrayed as an alcoholic who was no match for the Mann family. Diary entries and letters from Thomas and Katia reveal their embarrassment that Nelly was part of the family, and their plans to rid themselves of her by sending her to New York or by splitting the couple up. One can imagine the pain this situation must have caused Heinrich. But Heinrich loved Nelly, and she was not as simple-minded as she is often portrayed. She was interested in learning new things, and worked hard to support herself and Heinrich, who was in his seventies with very few opportunities to get his work published in the American market.

Sadly, Nelly's mental health problems and alcohol consumption only worsened. On December 17, 1944, at age forty-six, she succeeded in her fifth suicide attempt. Afterward, Heinrich moved into an apartment at 2145 Montana Avenue in Santa Monica and lived in seclusion, suffering indescribably from the loss and spending countless hours by her grave at Woodlawn Cemetery nearby. Salka Viertel wrote to her husband that Nelly had been Heinrich's "sunshine."

On March 12, 1950, in the midst of preparations to return to Europe to accept a position as president of the Academy of Arts in East Berlin, Heinrich passed away. His funeral took place two days later at Woodlawn.

Tragically, even in death Nelly would not be fully accepted as Heinrich's wife. In 1961, Heinrich's remains were exhumed from Woodlawn and reinterred at the Dorotheenstädtische cemetery in Berlin. All that is left of Heinrich in Santa Monica is his gravestone. However, Nelly's remains were left behind. A plaque on Heinrich's new grave in Berlin is the only hollow reminder of his devotion to Nelly.

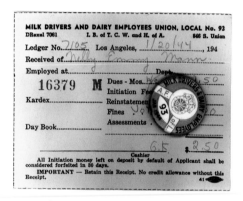

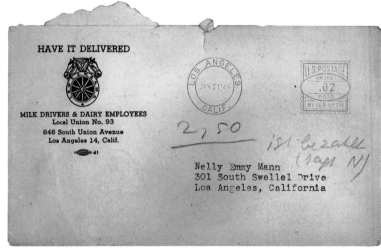

Nelly Mann's Milk Drivers' Union Card, 1944

LION FEUCHTWANGER
520 Paseo Miramar
Claudia Gordon

As you've probably noticed, I am fond of you.
—THOMAS MANN, ON LION FEUCHTWANGER

When Thomas Mann and Lion Feuchtwanger first met in Munich around 1907, they were merely passing acquaintances moving in the same circles. In the 1920s, they both signed a petition "For the Freedom of the Arts" and fought for the release of a young Communist who had been unjustly incarcerated. Still, both artistically and politically, they had little in common. In contrast to Mann, who in 1918 had published his treatise *Reflections of a Nonpolitical Man*, Feuchtwanger was known as a "committed and courageous [...] campaigner for freedom of speech, independence of the arts, social justice and political decency," according to Andreas Heusler in his book *Lion Feuchtwanger: Münchner-Emigrant-Weltbürger*. An early outspoken critic of National Socialism, whose rise to power in his native Munich he caricatured in the 1930 novel *Success*, Feuchtwanger was labeled "Enemy Number One of the German People" and was first on the list of Germans who lost their citizenship in 1933. Mann shared this fate in 1936. German students burned the works of both authors during the nationwide "Action against the Un-German Spirit" on May 10, 1933.

That same day, Thomas and Katia arrived in Bandol in the South of France, where Lion and Marta Feuchtwanger were already residing. As part of the involuntary community of exile in Sanary-sur-mer, they started meeting regularly. In Los Angeles, the relationship between the two authors grew even closer. Mann mentions Feuchtwanger as an authority on business dealings and contract law, betraying a tinge of jealousy at his friend's financial success. Still, their relationship was very much based on their shared profession and centered around sharing excerpts from their works at each other's houses. In 1943, the Feuchtwangers had purchased a neglected property, designed in 1928 by Mark Daniels as the Los Angeles Times Demonstration Home.

Marta Feuchtwanger was able to see its potential, in contrast to Peggy Guggenheim and Katia and Thomas, who passed on the listing. Today, the house is known as the artists' residency Villa Aurora. On account of its stunning ocean views and striking architecture, Mann called it "a veritable castle by the sea." Like its occupants, some of the building materials and architectural features had been imported from Europe. Interior design was clearly not a priority; royalties and advances paid to the then best-selling and widely translated author immediately went to purchases for Feuchtwanger's third and final library. Whereas Mann's own desk was quite ornate and imposing, Feuchtwanger simply put together four small secondhand desks for himself and his secretary, creating what Thomas called the "most useful and best organized literary workshop I have ever encountered." Both authors worked on a strict schedule, which in Mann's case extended to his social life. Whenever Mann attended readings at the Feuchtwanger residence, evenings started promptly at eight, since Mann wanted to be home by 11 p.m. sharp.

Although Mann could never understand Feuchtwanger's fondness for dictation, taken by his long-time secretary Hilde Waldo, both kept to a rigid writing schedule. Before the war, Mann had dismissed Lion's writings as mediocre and, according to Marta, was rumored to have spoken out against Feuchtwanger being considered for the Nobel Prize. Even so, George Tabori's report of a 1948 encounter with Mann at Villa Aurora, during which Mann allegedly used an uncharacteristic expletive to describe Feuchtwanger's novels, must be taken with a grain of salt. In contrast, on the occasion of Lion's sixtieth birthday, Mann states that it was high praise to proclaim a work "almost as good as Feuchtwanger" and offered enthusiastic praise for the Goya novel *This Is the Hour*: "The whole of Spain is in it [...], thoroughly studied, a monumental painting." Katia also attested to her husband's appreciation of Feuchtwanger's works.

In Los Angeles, Mann and Feuchtwanger once again joined forces when it came to civic engagement. According to Feuchtwanger, "the younger Thomas Mann had declared himself not very interested in political and societal relations/connections [...]. The older Thomas Mann left the ivory tower for the market square and spoke." Both men supported fellow émigrés through the European Film Fund, recorded radio addresses as part of the allied propaganda effort, and joined in a futile attempt at sparing Hanns Eisler from deportation. They felt bitterly misunderstood when they were branded "premature anti-Fascists" and placed under FBI surveillance, thus going "from Undeutsch to Un-American," according to Anthony Heilbut in *Exiled in Paradise*. Like Feuchtwanger, who had published the account *Moscow 1937* after meeting Stalin at the height of the Show Trials, earning him the reputation of a "compliant apologist of the Stalinist dictatorship," Mann was suspected of being a Communist. When the Mann family returned to Switzerland as a result, the Feuchtwangers, unable to obtain American citizenship during Lion's lifetime, remained in the United States. Undoubtedly, the experience of Feuchtwanger's close friend Charlie Chaplin, whose reentry permit was pulled after he had left the country, served as a cautionary tale. While Mann yearned for the villa on San Remo Drive and the California climate, Feuchtwanger longed to be surrounded by the sounds of spoken German once again. And, clearly, they missed each other. Feuchtwanger wrote, "My life here has gotten rather lonely, since Thomas Mann and Charlie Chaplin have left the country." For his part, Mann thought it "very, very sad that it is over now with the reading to each other from our works. I am always afraid that you will not find your way to Europe anymore and neither will I find the reverse one." Sadly, this prediction would come true. Lion Feuchtwanger died in 1958 and is buried at Woodlawn Cemetery in Santa Monica, where his headstone can be found next to the marker for the original burial place of Heinrich Mann.

MARTA FEUCHTWANGER
520 Paseo Miramar
Friedel Schmoranzer

n her notes on the year 1961, Marta Feuchtwanger reminisces about the true nature of the relationship between Lion Feuchtwanger and Thomas Mann, only to conclude that she might never have a clear answer for it. In a series of recorded interviews conducted by Lawrence Weschler in 1975, she recalled how that friendship evolved through the years, from its difficult beginnings when the Feuchtwangers were friends with Thomas's brother Heinrich, to the couples becoming closer. During their time in exile in France, they established a bond that led to discussions about politics, literature, and their own work, as well as the pleasures of new technology. Marta distinctly mentions Thomas's keen interest in the advantages of the electric BBQ. In his personal letters, he did not forget to praise Marta's cooking skills.

In Los Angeles, the Manns were frequent guests at the Feuchtwangers' home, a Spanish Revival villa at 520 Paseo Miramar. The Manns and the Feuchtwangers celebrated every birthday together. After Bertolt Brecht and Helene Weigel returned to Europe—Mann and Brecht famously didn't get along—the Feuchtwangers even spent every Christmas evening at the Mann residence.

Asked to write about Mann on what would have been his one hundredth birthday for a panel at the University of Southern California, Marta opened her essay as follows: "Thomas Mann has been celebrated for his work and for his attitude in politics, and most of all for his utterances as a refugee from Hitler terror. I would like to speak about him as a woman about a man." For her, he was a model of correctness: "his appearance reminded you rather of a diplomat." He, on the other hand, felt comfortable speaking with her about daily troubles such as his aversion to making his own bed and how best to shoo away coyotes who were disturbing his sleep with their howling and hunting at night.

Marta found Mann to be more pessimistic and bitter in contrast to her husband, especially in regards to the future of Europe. However, " (. . .) he who was known as aloof and reserved, could be warm and interested when he was in a small gathering of good friends. He seemed to prefer listening to others than to speaking himself. This was changed entirely when he read from his work. His performance was masterly, he indulged in his fine irony, and you could see how much he enjoyed his own work."

The after-dinner readings at the Feuchtwangers were held in Mann's favorite room, "the German Library," a small space with a wooden ceiling and a fireplace that, as the name suggests, holds the library of the classics of German literature as well as those of their contemporary fellow writers. When the two authors presented their new works to a larger group of friends, Thomas was the guest of honor and moderator of the German portions of the evening,

Lion Feuchtwanger at Villa Aurora, 1947

his writings were not representative of German literature. Even if these rumors were true, their bond seemed far more than a partnership of convenience between two exiled writers and their wives who had to start over in a new country. What seems certain, looking back, is that the Feuchtwangers and the Manns were longtime companions who respected one another. They discussed issues both work-related and personal, their work, questions of day-to-day life, and together they navigated life in exile during some of the most difficult times of the last century.

Marta Feuchtwanger at Villa Aurora

whereas Charlie Chaplin had the first word at the English readings.

After Mann grew increasingly disappointed by the political developments in America and his interviews in front of the House Un-American Activities Committee, the Manns decided to move back to Europe. Even separated by the Atlantic, the two couples continued a lively exchange of letters. Marta recalls that both Thomas and Katia wrote more than once about how much they missed their evenings of dinners and collective readings in America.

As in most social circles, there were rumors and criticism. One was that Mann once suggested that Feuchtwanger did not deserve a Nobel Prize because

VICKI BAUM
2477 Canyon Oak Drive
Alexis Landau

The most remarkable thing about Hollywood is that it does not exist," the Austrian Jewish novelist Vicki Baum wrote in her memoir *It Was All Quite Different* (1960), explaining the clash between her imagined Hollywood and what she actually found there. Upon her arrival in Los Angeles in 1931, Baum experienced, as did many refugees, the contradictory sense of Los Angeles as an idyllic seductive dream, a humming locus of talent, creativity, glamour, money, and natural beauty as opposed to the reality of haggard, overworked screenwriters and the smattering of small towns—loosely connected but lacking any true center. Baum noted that the odd touristic fascination with prints in concrete of movie stars' hands and feet gave off an aura of "atavistic magic" reminiscent of the handprints found within the Lascaux caves, and she felt sorry for anyone who came here for the magic, as she had.

At the same time, Baum found beauty, magic, and, most important, work. In Berlin, she had left behind a career as an editor at *Ullstein Verlag* and as a commercially successful novelist. Her first novel, *Stud.chem. Helen Willfuer* (1928), was about a young, ambitious woman who breaks into the male-dominated world of academia, epitomizing the "New Woman" who revels in the newfound sexual, economic, and political freedom of the Weimar Republic. Baum reflected on this time period, before the rise of Fascism, with fond nostalgia: "It was a great time to grow up, in that last era of European peace, there was so much beginning in its daybreak air, such a good, fertile dawn. It was for us, my generation, to bring about the liberation of women, of love, of sex. . . . We were not satisfied to tear down the obsolete, we did our best to create something better."

After the publication of *Stud.chem.Helen Willfuer* came the massive success of *Grand Hotel*, Baum's best-known novel, the one that brought her international fame. It was subsequently staged as a play in Berlin (Baum wrote the script herself) and then adapted for Broadway in 1931, becoming its biggest hit in thirty years. Later in life, with her characteristic biting wit, she reflected on living in the shadow of such a commercial success: "You can live down any number of failures, but you can't live down a great success. For thirty years I've been a walking example of this truism . . . a success, moth-eaten as it may be, will pop up among old movies, or as a hideous musical or in a new film version, or in a Japanese, a Hebrew, a Hindu translation—and there you are."

Despite her misgivings about her success, the start of production on the film version of *Grand Hotel* (1932) brought Baum to Hollywood, and the novel's popularity is ultimately what saved her life. After filming wrapped, Baum returned to Berlin where her family and her editorial job awaited her, but she quickly saw that something had changed. Berlin was no longer the city of her youthful dreams and aspirations, of artistic and sexual freedom that so many had enjoyed; it had become a place she sensed was unsafe for Jews and artists. Being both, as well as armed with a keen intuition, she wrote: "I looked at the faces of the demonstrating mobs on the streets; the haggard sharp-jawed faces and sagging old trench coats of the disenchanted veterans and the unemployed; I saw hatred and fanaticism every-where in this world, so well painted by George Grosz and expressed by Bert Brecht, and I thought: I have two nice boys; what will Germany make of them?" Despite not even having a contract set up in Holly-wood, Baum made the fateful decision to leave her homeland well ahead of many others who struggled to leave, or who couldn't leave, years later.

Spending the next decade writing for the movies before returning to novel writing, Baum lived in various places in Los Angeles. From 1933 to 1942, she resided at 1461 Amalfi Drive in Pacific Palisades, after which she tried Pasadena, which she found claustrophobic, before finally settling in the north Hollywood Hills at 2477 Canyon Oak Drive. A nature lover dedicated to her garden, she described her beloved home as rife with exotic plant life, a refuge from what she felt was the noise and ugliness of the city: "A bit of the tropics grows in front of my house; a few royal palms, fern trees, a thick stand of proud shell ginger fourteen feet high, a jacaranda tree, a blue cloud when in bloom, and through it all twists the gray and silver snake of a sycamore trunk".

Not much has been written about Vicki Baum and Thomas Mann's interactions from Baum's point of view, but Mann mentioned Baum at least six times in his diaries when each lived in Pacific Pali-sades, often frequenting the same dinner parties and literary salons. One warm day in 1938, Mann wrote: "At noon. Very warm. To the tea the new summer suit. Soiree with writer Vicki Baum. Almost only German-speaking guests. The architect Neutra, the comedian, musician, actor, Dr. Klemperer, Schon-berg, etc. Long conversation before dinner."

On another afternoon, after he had finished writing for the day, Mann described visiting Baum and her husband at their home. After discussing "the bleakness of this particular part of the country," they concluded it was "tiring and energy reducing" and yet "so much preferable to the eastern climate."

Even though Baum and Mann moved in the same circles, Mann was often referred to as "emper-or of exiles." It appears Baum thought of herself as not even close to his sphere of lofty literary bril-liance and international fame. In her memoir, she cast Mann in the same category as Dostoevsky and Tolstoy, writers whom she read with "undiminished joy." When speaking of her own work, however, she would lower herself a notch, a tendency not shared by her male counterparts, Lion Feuchtwanger, Franz Werfel, and Mann among them. Baum always appeared to be winking sardonically at her own suc-cess, which seems the healthiest way to be a writer. She concludes, "A sense of modesty has prevent-ed me—thank Heavens!—from thinking that I am writing the great pre-war novel, or the great postwar novel, or any other damn representative novel of any kind."

ALFRED DÖBLIN
1347 North Citrus Avenue
Stefan Keppler-Tasaki

The very first word concerning the Berlin novelist Alfred Döblin in Thomas Mann's diaries is "hostile," and was symptomatic of a history of tensions that eased up only during their time of shared exile in Zurich in 1933 and L.A. from 1941 to 1945. The trained psychiatrist, never short on diagnoses of his contemporaries' state of mind, accused Mann in various hurtful comments of dealing merely with "problems of villa owners" at

provincial places, of holding on to idyllic forms of the epic, and of neglecting the brute forces of modernity. Döblin even broke with Lion Feuchtwanger in 1935 because of the latter's appraisal of Mann's *Joseph and His Brothers*. Mann, for his part, was repeatedly irritated by Döblin's writings, such as the "harrowing novella" "Sermon and Burning of the Jews" (a section from Döblin's novel *Wallenstein*) and the exuberant review of Heinrich Mann's essay collection *Power and Humanity*, which played a part in the brothers' political quarrel. However, the German-Jewish avant-garde writer earned Thomas's gratitude when he protested courageously against Heinrich's removal as president of the literary division of the Prussian Academy of Arts in February 1933.

Döblin immigrated to Los Angeles after an excruciating escape from Paris. The exile community welcomed him at a ceremony held at the First Unitarian Church on October 26, 1940. In *Destiny's Journey*, his unsettling testimony of the exodus, Döblin attributed himself to the "nation of the poor." In accordance with his proletarian self-understanding—Mann once called him a *Bildungsproletarier* ("proletarian of education")—he prided himself to be living "in the middle of the real Hollywood." The location of his two-bedroom bungalow, at 1347 North Citrus Avenue, built in 1923, supported at least some of the aspects of urban life that he was seeking. Döblin, who never owned a car, was not fond of the garden city character of Los Angeles, as he expressed in his infamous saying "One is amidst greenery frequently and extensively. But am I a cow?"

The first encounter between the fellow émigrés took place on May 2, 1941, at the home of Salka Viertel at 165 Mabery Road in Santa Monica. About forty people convened that night to celebrate Heinrich Mann's seventieth birthday. Döblin's name was high on the guest list, suggested by Lion Feuchtwanger, who once described Thomas Mann's and Döblin's work as two sides of the same coin of modern novel writing. As usual, the "bitter and denying" man, as Mann considered him, did not use the occasion to make friends. Rather, he mocked his nemesis, the "man of paper," for formally congratulating his own brother by reading from a lengthy manuscript. Döblin and Mann at least had in common a tendency to follow a policy of distance and solitude, albeit in very different ways.

Perhaps their most significant meeting unfolded at the El Pablo Rey Playhouse, at 1211 Montana

Avenue in Santa Monica, on August 14, 1943. The rental place for art events, opened in 1937, was a venue of the Music-Arts Society of Santa Monica and other institutions. Elisabeth Reichenbach, wife of the UCLA scholar Hans Reichenbach, and Helene Weigel chose it as the location to celebrate Döblin's sixty-fifth birthday. The event featured a "long artists' program" (as stated in Mann's diary) for about 180 guests, strange in light of the fact that the guest of honor had very few social ties. Heinrich and Bertolt Brecht delivered speeches about the "profound connoisseur and lover of Berlin," the explorer of the "essence of the epic." Pieces by Schoenberg and other exile composers were performed with the suggestion that atonal music corresponded with Döblin's modernist work. The actor Fritz Kortner read from *Wallenstein* and the actor Peter Lorre from *November 1918*. Thomas contributed a message to the birthday book expressing "all heartfelt admiration for so much bold, new, energizing" that Döblin had brought to narrative fiction in German. He even credited him on the "recent destiny of the occidental novel," referring to the "return of the modern novel to myth" that he pursued in his Joseph trilogy and that he also found in Döblin's *Babylonian Wandering*, a "very remarkable" work, as he told Karl Kerényi.

Döblin's employee ID as screenwriter for MGM Studios, 1941

Mann drew inspiration from the event for *Doctor Faustus*. In the book's final chapter, on a Saturday evening, protagonist Adrian Leverkühn summons "a large number of people, most of whom were strangers, both inwardly and outwardly, to join him [...] for the purpose of introducing them" to his secret: the deal with the Devil. He starts his confession "very softly, in a murmur, so that only a few could understand what he said or make much sense of it," and he accuses himself of pride and presumption and places himself under higher powers. "An embarrassed, tense silence now reigned in the room." Some leave the place with signs of protest. Similarly, Döblin crashed his own party that night when he expressed regret for his former intellectual pride and committed himself to the firm moral standards of Catholicism. Hanns Eisler left the gathering under protest. Mann was one of the few who could handle this confession, and later that night he assured Döblin that Jews and Catholics alike can speak more easily of God than Protestants can. In *The Genesis of Doctor Faustus*, Mann recalled Döblin's speech as "sympathetic." The same source reveals that Mann visited Döblin's home at least once: in April 1944, to visit his fellow writer on his sickbed.

FRANZ WERFEL

610 North Bedford Drive · Beverly Hills
Adrian Daub

Thomas Mann and Franz Werfel arrived in Los Angeles in 1940 as part of the great literary migration from Germany. Originally, after the Nazis annexed Austria in 1938, Werfel and his wife, Alma Mahler-Werfel, moved to France. When the Germans invaded in 1940, the Werfels fled across the Pyrenees by foot, accompanied by Heinrich and Nelly Mann Thomas's son Golo. From Portugal they were able to obtain passage to the United States. When their ship, the *Nea Hellas*, pulled into the dock at Hoboken, New Jersey, on October 13, 1940, Thomas was there to meet them.

Not long after, Mann and his family moved to Pacific Palisades. Werfel first settled in the Hollywood Hills, on Los Tilos Road, in a grand Spanish-style house with a two-car garage and a gardener. He and Alma later relocated to 610 North Bedford Drive in Beverly Hills. The distance from the Mann home on San Remo Drive notwithstanding, Mann would visit the Werfels with some regularity. Alma soon restarted the salons she had hosted in Vienna, and soon figures like Arnold Schoenberg, Igor Stravinsky, Bruno Walter, Soma Morgenstern, Lion Feuchtwanger, and Lotte Lehmann were frequent guests.

The milieu they were part of has been mythologized as "Weimar on the Pacific." But Weimar's paths to the shores of the Pacific were various. Many of the émigrés found themselves safe but adrift. Mostly avant-garde modernists with deep roots in German language and culture, they had a difficult time fitting into a cultural scene dominated by the film industry. Mann and Werfel were two exceptions. Mann arrived as a kind of cultural elder statesman, a Nobel Prize winner, an important, internationally recognized voice against Fascism. In his diaries, the author could jot down a quote about himself he had seen in a book: "Idealists dream of Th. M. as the president of the second German Republic." It speaks to the man's ego that he does not comment further. Werfel, meanwhile, arrived to immense and immediate success.

During their flight from Europe, Franz and Alma had briefly sought refuge in Lourdes, in southern France, where Franz pledged to write a novel about Saint Bernadette should he make it safely to America. *The Song of Bernadette*, written in just five months after his safe arrival, was published in 1941 and would become his most commercially successful novel, spending more than a year on the *New York Times* bestseller list. A 1943 film version from Twentieth Century-Fox was the studio's most expensive production that year, recouped three times its budget, and won four Academy Awards. Franz Werfel's success was a true Hollywood story.

Neither the novel nor the film's success seemed to have sat easily with Mann. Perhaps he was put off by the book's unironic religiosity. Perhaps he (the gentile) found it strange that Werfel (who was

Jewish) should turn to such a Catholic story when others (Schoenberg and Mann included) sought out Jewish topics. The European émigrés were a restless community; the gossip and backbiting could get rather intense. A general sense of competition and jealousy pervaded. After all, for every writer, composer, or director who had made it here, there was someone else who was stuck in Europe, or was living in poverty, or had died. In October 1940, Mann heard of the death of another friend in Europe. In his diary, he noted, "The friends are falling. The desert expands. And the garbage that lands here." In a letter around the same time, Werfel wrote to his friend Willy Haas, who had found refuge in Bombay: "We live, and I don't know how. Poor Walter [Hasenclever] is dead. And so many others with him."

While Mann's friendship with Werfel was genuine, Mann's own diaries speak to a profound ambivalence between them when it came to artistic matters. In an entry from his trip west, Mann mentioned that fellow émigrés were attempting to lobby for Werfel to receive the Nobel Prize; Mann declined to participate. As Erhard Bahr points out, many of Werfel's admirers were perplexed by *Song of Bernadette*—Werfel had been abandoning his earlier modernism in fits and starts, and *Song of Bernadette* seemed nothing less than anti-modernist.

That was before the movie premiered. In February 1944, Mann reported seeing *Song of Bernadette* in a theater. "The figure of the heroine is poignant. The whole thing rather awkward." There may have been some envy at work that his friend was fitting in so well. In his diary, Mann proudly mentioned the visit of a "Mr. L. from MGM" who wanted to talk with him about turning the Joseph novels into a movie, which never came to pass. More generally, he seems to have simply regarded Werfel's late novels as middlebrow, and Werfel himself a bit of a sellout. Werfel's next big novel was *The Star of the Unborn,* a science-fiction story modeled on Dante's *Divine Comedy*. It was about a writer whisked from his home, which happens to be at 610 North Bedford Drive, hundreds of thousands of years into the future, guided by the spirit of his friend B.H. (Willy Haas).

Mann's diary entries about Werfel capture the contradiction of émigré existence in L.A., swerving from news from the war, almost all of it bad, to seemingly incongruent stories about walks on Santa Monica beaches with Katia and dinners at the Werfels' house. By the end of their California association, the news of the war was entirely good. On July 11, 1945, two months after the end of the war in Europe, the Manns shared what would be their last dinner with Franz Werfel. The night of August 26, 1945, Mann learned that Werfel had been found dead in his study. "Dumbfoundedness" was the reaction Mann recorded in his diary. He added, with his characteristic exactitude and coldness, that at least "his novel is done."

ALFRED NEUMANN
1527 North Stanley Avenue
Tobias Boes

For much of his time in exile in the United States, Thomas Mann was hailed as both the "Greatest Living Man of Letters" and "Hitler's Most Intimate Enemy." He had another nickname, which remains in use even today when his other epithets have largely been forgotten: "the Magician." Mann acquired this moniker when he cured his young children Erika and Klaus of a recurring nightmare. From that point on, he would defend it by staging readings from his manuscripts almost every night in his own living room. Once the lights had been dimmed and the family poodle, Niko, had settled down at his feet, Mann would light a cigar and begin casting his "pedagogical enchantment," filling the minds of his assembled family—and on occasion, his friends—with "magical landscapes."

We owe these descriptive phrases to Alfred Neumann, a fellow writer who, with his wife, Kitty, was one of Mann's closest friends and a frequent guest in his home. Mann and Neumann started exchanging letters in 1917; their real friendship began in 1924, however, when the Neumanns moved into a house in the immediate vicinity of the Mann residence in Munich's Poschinger Strasse. For the next seven years,

the two families were basically neighbors until the Neumanns relocated, first to a small town near the Austrian border, and then, after the Nazi takeover, to Fiesole, in Italy. Even from afar, the bonds of friendship remained unbroken. The Neumanns looked after Mann's daughter Monika when she arrived in Italy to study piano performance. When the Nazis tightened their stranglehold on Europe, the Neumanns were forced to flee again, first to Nice and then to Los Angeles, where Alfred began a new career as a screenwriter. The Neumanns bought a small house at 1527 North Stanley Avenue in West Hollywood, and for the remainder of the war they were once again regular guests in the Mann home.

Neumann was one of the most widely read authors of the Weimar Republic, and his success continued in the United States, where his treatment for the war movie *None Shall Escape* was nominated for an Academy Award in 1944. His fame, however, was transitory. If Mann's novels seem timeless, Neumann's literary works are indelibly tied to the epoch of their creation. With one exception, all are now out of print.

Both writers were undoubtedly aware of this difference in stature. We know very little of their years of friendship during the 1920s, for Mann's diaries of this period are lost and the two men, being neighbors, did not exchange any letters. Once the Neumanns moved away from Munich, the two writers struck up a regular correspondence, in which Alfred often came across as gushing, Thomas Mann as a little aloof. In 1935, Mann turned sixty. As a birthday present, Neumann dedicated his forthcoming novel, *The Gaudy Empire* (*Das Kaiserreich*) to his cherished older friend, and also gifted him the manuscript. When Neumann turned forty only four months later, Mann, preoccupied at this point of his life with his own "immortalization" (*Verewigung*), remembered it only belatedly. His birthday telegram, in which he promised to send the manuscript of a recently published open letter in support of German journalist Carl Ossietzky, arrived three days late. If Neumann was disappointed by this neglect, he did not show it, instead praising the "mighty and good" (*grossmächtiges und liebes*) telegram.

The friendship became more even-handed once everybody was living in Los Angeles. The Neumanns now were frequent guests in Pacific Palisades, and the Manns occasionally also ventured out to West Hollywood. The two men read to each other from their works in progress, and Mann regularly recorded his critical judgments in his diaries, even if they remained distinctly cooler than those that Neumann conveyed in his letters. No doubt Mann was grateful to have such an appreciative but also intellectually qualified interlocutor. His speeches in front of admiring crowds may have bolstered his reputation, but they invariably had to be carried out in English. Survival in exile required emotional sustenance, however, in addition to affirmation in one's native language. The intimate parlors of San Remo Drive and Stanley Avenue provided this.

Alfred and Kitty Neumann returned to Europe in 1951. In September 1952, just a few months after the Manns joined them in Switzerland, Alfred died of a heart attack. Mann wrote a moving obituary in which he referred to Neumann as a "man of dignity and gravity [...] who out of faith and love said 'yes' to

my existence, and who could not keep this affirmation locked up in his heart, instead announcing it to everyone, whether they wanted to hear about it or not." The "Magician" knew what he owed to his most loyal audience member.

LUDWIG HARDT
418 Mount Holyoke Avenue
Sylvia Asmus

Whenever we pass your house over the sea—where we often go for walks—we say to each other, shaking our heads: 'It was a mistake, a mistake!'" wrote Thomas Mann to the German actor Ludwig Hardt on February 21, 1947. This "mistake" was already more than two years in the past. In December 1944, Hardt and his wife, Giulia, had abandoned their home in the Manns' Pacific Palisades neighborhood and moved to Long Island, New York; a momentous decision,

as Mann emphasized to his friend Agnes E. Meyer: "Here in Pacific Palisades he lived with his wife in a nice little house that had cost him almost nothing and, since his wife had some money, could exist poorly. [...] Despite our blatant shaking of heads, the fool sold his little house and moved to New York, where he bought a much more expensive one in Great Neck [...]. With his plans and hopes, of course, he failed completely. [...] The best thing for him would be to go to Berlin or Vienna and starve with the others, but at least he would receive some appreciation of his abilities."

Mann had known Hardt for many years. On April 10, 1920, his diary entry read: "Tea with Bertram, Glöckner and the lecture artist Ludwig Hardt, who afterwards gave excitingly topical poems by Heine [The Rats], something by Walser and finally the Kleiderschrank to the best." The diary revealed that it was Hardt who introduced Mann to the work of Franz Kafka in 1921.

Hardt was one of the most famous reciters of the German language of his time. At his performances, where he recited from a wide variety of texts, he introduced the public to many new writers. These were social events at which one could meet many representatives of the cultural scene. Walter Benjamin, Bertolt Brecht, Veza and Elias Canetti, Kurt Hiller, Kafka, Else Lasker-Schüler, Joseph Roth, Rainer Maria Rilke, Hans Sahl, Gershom Scholem, Kurt Tucholsky, and Mann were among the guests. It was not unusual for them to record their admiration for the "reciter after the heart of the poets" in literary portraits and enthusiastic reviews. Mann dedicated an entire essay to Hardt in 1920.

After the National Socialists seized power, Hardt's public activities were soon limited to the Jewish Cultural Association (Jüdischer Kulturbund). He made his way to the United States via Austria, Czechoslovakia, and France. "The line that deposited him at the New York docks in autumn, 1938, took Germany's best dramatic reader to America. For those who understand the language it will be a great and lasting experience to hear him—but at present only for them. It will take a good time for Hardt to feel at home in another language," Erika and Klaus Mann foresaw in their book *Escape to Life*. Hardt's personal files, in the archive of the Deutsche Akademie im Exil / American Guild for German Cultural Freedom, shows how difficult his life was in the United States. Hardt had approached the aid organization several times with a request for support. When this failed to materialize, he angrily addressed a request for help to Paul Tillich in May 1939, who then approached Eduard Heimann of the Selfhelp for German Émigrés: "Hardt was with me, he is very bitter and desperate. I think it would be best for him to take up some kind of profession, preferably horse training, in which he is obviously a master. Nevertheless, at least once an attempt should be made to give him so much that he can make a lecture tour. I am very pessimistic, but I think it is right to demonstrate the matter to him *ad oculus*."

Hardt received encouragement from Mann. After his immigration and settlement in Pacific Palisades, they paid each other visits and exchanged letters. " At the end of the coming week or the beginning of the next we hope to be able to contact you. I would like to read you the first beginning of the novel [*Doctor Faustus*], which I don't think you know yet," Mann wrote on June 10, 1944, only to note that the meeting took place twelve days later: "For dinner at Hardts. [. . .] Read the first chapters of the novel. Enthusiasm of the little Hardt, who is looking forward to his first performance in English."

On August 6, 1944, Hardt held his first English-language recitation and sent Mann tickets. The evening took place at the Beverly Fairfax Community Center on Beverly Boulevard, about eleven miles from San Remo Drive. It was not a success. "After dinner for Hardt's recitation evening at the Beverly Fairfax Community Center. Dismal mock success with Jewish audience," Mann noted in his diary. He later reported to Meyer: "Yes, poor L. Hardt! [. . .] I took part in an English reading evening of his here as a favor, and it made me so sad that I had to drink a lot afterwards to help myself back on my feet."

Hardt was unsuccessful in translating his career into English and performing for U.S. audiences, so he read again for a German-speaking audience. Hardt suggested that he read from Mann's still-unfinished *Doctor Faustus*, but Mann rejected the suggestion: "it is really not possible, from a book with which I am still in such a struggle and will be for a long time, I do not like to have anything read in public." Mann also rejected Hardt's idea of organizing a recitation for his seventieth birthday. Nevertheless, Hardt was present at a birthday party for Mann, which took place on June 9, 1945, at Times Hall in New York. Among the attendees were Ferdinand Bruckner, Bruno Eisner, the American novelist Christian Gauss, and Erika von Wagner-Stiedry.

On August 30, 1946, *Aufbau* reported in the column *"Wie wir hören"*: "Ludwig Hardt has accepted an invitation to lecture in Germany and Austria." However, this never came to pass. Hardt died in New York on March 4, 1947. "His wish to help to stir up the weary spirits in Vienna has not been fulfilled," the diary states.

UPTON SINCLAIR
464 North Myrtle Avenue · Monrovia
Hans Rudolf Vaget

On April 18, 1938, a quiet but intriguing encounter unfolded in the Los Angeles area: Upton Sinclair, American-born author of *The Jungle* (1906), invited Thomas Mann, German-born author of *The Magic Mountain* (1924) Did these literary greats converse in English, or in German? What did Mann know of Sinclair's work? To what extent can we speak of an affinity?

Mann's diary tells us nothing about their conversations; his command of English at the time was still spotty. It is not clear that he was aware of Sinclair's attempts to get elected to Congress as a Socialist, or, in 1934, to the governorship of California. We learn merely that they spent time in the house and in the garden, that they went for a stroll, and that they enjoyed dinner at a nearby hotel restaurant.

Like many of his American colleagues, Sinclair looked up to his German counterpart and admired him not only for his literary accomplishments but also for his stance against Hitler. In his 1962 autobiography, Sinclair cited with pride what Mann wrote about his series of Lanny Budd novels: "Someday the whole cycle will certainly be recognized as the best founded and best informed description of the political life of our epoch."

The Jungle, of which a German translation appeared shortly after its publication, is a devastating exposure of conditions in the Chicago stockyards. Mann was very much aware of the book's success. In defending himself against the accusation made in a medical journal that his portrayal of the medical profession in *The Magic Mountain* was unflattering and damaging, Mann protested that his novel was no investigative hit job (*Enthüllungsepos*) in the manner of Upton Sinclair, and not at all a counterpart to *The Jungle*. The tone of his reference was strictly professional and by no means disrespectful. He saw Sinclair as the "American Zola," as he would write in his letter on the occasion of Sinclair's sixtieth birthday.

During the years of the Weimar Republic, one of Mann's growing fears concerned the politically motivated miscarriage of justice. We may assume, then, that he duly took note of Sinclair's 1928 novel *Boston,* which addresses the case of Sacco and Vanzetti, two Italian immigrants falsely accused of terrorism and executed in 1927. In 1926, Mann had signed a protest against their sentencing. And in a 1929 preface to an American novel, he stated that it would be obtuse to think that "the case of Sacco and Vanzetti was of concern only to America." By 1937, Mann considered Sinclair to be a friend and ally and felt free to ask him for a contribution to the Thomas Mann Fund, set up to aid German exiles in Prague.

Before that meeting in 1938, for several years

Mann and Sinclair exchanged books and complimentary notes. In particular, Sinclair seems to have appreciated Mann's response to his 1942 novel, *Dragon's Teeth,* about the rise of Hitler. Mann assured his American colleague that nothing in the book was exaggerated.

Another letter, dated June 9, 1944, is of some biographical interest. Puzzled by the delay in his swearing in as an American citizen, Mann asked Sinclair, who was well connected, if he could do something to move the matter along, which, it seems, he did. To assure Sinclair of his loyalty, Mann stated categorically that he would never return to Germany. The poisonous controversy that had been stirred up in his homeland over his return immediately after the war stiffened his decision not to settle in Germany, only to visit. On June 23, in a ceremony at the New Federal Building in Los Angeles, Thomas and Katia Mann became Americans.

The question of the two men's affinity is easy to settle. In terms of style and aesthetics, there is none. But in the political arena, they felt a kind of brotherly colleagueship. Both proclaimed their belief in Socialism in the German sense of Social Democracy. This may explain why their correspondence petered out after 1946. At a time when Mann came under increased scrutiny as a purported "Communist dupe," he may have deemed it prudent not to correspond with a well-known Socialist and notorious critic of capitalism.

Upton Sinclair's house at 464 North Myrtle Avenue still stands. It was listed on the National Register of Historic Places and declared a National Historic Landmark in 1971.

Upton Sinclair broadcasts a speech during his campaign for governor of California, November 4, 1934

ALDOUS HUXLEY
701 Amalfi Drive
Andreas Platthaus

When Thomas Mann and his family rented the house at 740 Amalfi Drive in Pacific Palisades in April 1941, they would be living barely a hundred meters away from Aldous Huxley. The British-born author and his wife, Maria, had resided across the street at 701 Amalfi Drive since April 1939. The closeness between the two writers was, however, mostly geographical: shortly

before Mann was awarded the Nobel Prize for Literature in 1929, Huxley's novel *Point Counter Point* was published, a major work not only of his own oeuvre but also of the entire genre of the psychological novel, to which Mann felt he belonged. In chapter 22 is a passage that must have excited the German novelist. It was a quotation from the fictional notes of the writer Philip Quarle, Huxley's literary alter ego in *Point Counter Point*: "The musicalization of fiction. Not in the symbolist way, by subordinating sense to sound. (*Pleuvent les bleus baisers des astres taciturnes.* Mere glossolalia). But on a large scale, in the construction. Meditate on Beethoven. The changes of moods, the abrupt transitions." This already described the connection between musicality and literature that Mann was

to give shape to in 1943 with *Doctor Faustus*. Critics saw in *Point Counter Point* the English answer to *The Magic Mountain*. No wonder Mann was interested in Huxley.

The two authors had first met in 1933 in Sanary-sur-Mer, France, where Huxley had lived since 1929 and had written *Brave New World*. Mann, in turn, had moved abroad only a few months after Hitler's rise to power. Huxley was one of the international writers who actively supported German literary exile: together with André Gide and Thomas's brother Heinrich, he had just become a patron of the Amsterdam-based journal *Die Sammlung*, which was edited by Thomas's son Klaus. The Briton was a frequent guest of Mann's in Sanary, when the host would read from the then-emerging second part of the Joseph novel. They remained in contact after Huxley arrived in Los Angeles in 1937 on the steamship *Normandie*. Mann happened to be traveling on the same vessel on one of his American lecture tours, as a Nobel Prize winner in first class, while the Huxleys could only afford tourist class. In 1938, Mann finally followed Huxley to the United States, residing temporarily in Brentwood and then the Palisades until his teaching arrangement at Princeton ended.

On Amalfi Drive, both families maintained close relations. In Mann's diaries, there are regular entries about visits to the Huxleys' for dinner and especially tea (obligated by the host's British origins!) as well as return invitations to the Manns'. Again and again, they met on walks on the streets of Riviera Hill, where the Mann family home was under construction, or on the beach in Santa Monica. Huxley had just published *Grey Eminence*, the study of a seventeenth-century Capuchin friar who was a close adviser to Cardinal Richelieu under the name Père Joseph—a fascinating parallel to Mann's own literary work in the Joseph tetralogy. On New Year's Day 1942, the Manns brought flowers to their neighbors, but the following month both families left Amalfi Drive in quick succession: the Huxleys relocated to the desert colony known as Llano del Rio, some seventy miles away, and the Manns moved into their new home at 1550 San Remo Drive, just across Sunset Boulevard, a mere mile and a half from their previous residence. Thomas and Katia hired the Huxleys' former domestic staff.

Thus ended the physical proximity of two of the most famous writers of the twentieth century, but not Mann's interest in Huxley's work. Mann read *Time Must Have a Stop* in Pacific Palisades immediately after its 1944 publication, as well as its successor, *Ape and Essence,* in 1948. In 1950, after *Brave New World* was published in German for the first time since the Nazi era, Mann followed its reception in his former homeland with interest, especially the harsh criticism from Theodor W. Adorno, which had been leaked to him months earlier. Mann's sympathy for Adorno's point of view signaled a shift away from Huxley's perspective. Yet, in July of that year, Mann still felt a literary affinity and had counted Huxley, along with James Joyce and Marcel Proust, among his "bourgeois" and "formalist" relatives. Mann's last word on Huxley, however, was harsh. It came in 1954, after his return to Switzerland from America. On reading *The Doors of Perception*, Huxley's accounts of his experiences with psychedelic drugs, Mann noted in his diary: "Occupation with Huxley's glorification of mescaline. Don't like it and don't like him."

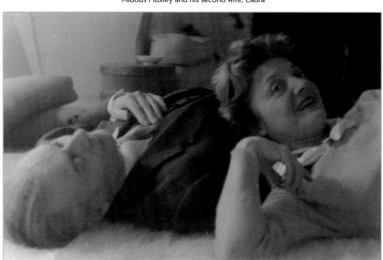
Aldous Huxley and his second wife, Laura

SUSAN SONTAG

Pickwick Books · 6743 Hollywood Boulevard

David D. Kim

On December 21, 1987, Susan Sontag published an autobiographical essay whose self-conscious tone and historical inaccuracy were unusual even for her. "Pilgrimage: Tea with Thomas Mann," which appeared in the *New Yorker*, described in simultaneously religious and secular terms an experience that had morphed over the years into a hidden treasure of complicated childhood memories and feelings. That event involved meeting her idol as a precocious fifteen-year-old college student. In December 1949, she visited Mann—the "god in exile"—with two friends at 1550 San Remo Drive, and came away from the once-in-a-lifetime experience as "an embarrassed, fervid, literature-intoxicated child." In the essay, however, Sontag curiously claimed that she had been in high school when in reality she had just transferred from the University of California, Berkeley, to the University of Chicago. What explained the profound shame she associated with that audacious meeting?

Sontag went on to become a world-renowned American writer, essayist, film and theater director, and political activist. She would belong to the last generation of twentieth-century public intellectuals whose discussions of sensual experiences through art, or of political and public health crises such as the HIV/AIDS epidemic, shaped the transatlantic cultural landscape well beyond the academy. Her intellectual development was deeply indebted to the diverse avant-garde traditions of Europe, but her works engaged in original and provocative ways, posing enduring questions about aesthetic sensibility, visual politics, communal ethics, and the literary canon. *Against Interpretation* (1966), *On Photography* (1977), *Under the Sign of Saturn* (1980), *AIDS and Its Metaphors* (1988), *In America* (1999), and *Regarding the Pain of Others* (2003) were some of her most widely read books tracking the various twists and turns in modern aesthetic and social movements.

Having relocated with her newly expanded family from Arizona to California, Sontag spent some of her most formative teenage years in the San Fernando Valley and attended North Hollywood High School. A voracious reader, after school she would take the trolley into town and could comb through the mountains of books at one of the now-vanished institutions in Los Angeles: Pickwick Books at 6743 Hollywood Boulevard. It was here that Sontag discovered the pioneering works of contemporary American writers and German-Jewish exiles through journals such as *Partisan Review* and *The Saturday Review of Literature*, to which she would later contribute herself. However, Sontag had come across an affordable copy of Mann's *The Magic Mountain* (1924) even before the end of the Second World War. The publisher was the Modern Library, the parent company of Random House, and Helen T. Lowe-Porter—Mann's favorite translator—had made the novel accessible to an English-speaking readership in 1927. Sontag's 1946 edition of *The Magic Mountain* is preserved in the special collections of the Young Research Library at UCLA, which holds all of her papers. By the time Sontag immersed herself in the cultural and literary worlds of Los Angeles during the second half of the 1940s, she was intimately familiar with Mann's "stature of an oracle in Roosevelt's *bien-pensant* America," as well as with the "good Germany" and the "Great Writer" he embodied after World War II.

For Mann, the meeting with the three students from the University of Chicago was just one of several tasks he completed on December 29, 1949. He noted it in his diary matter-of-factly: "In the afternoon interview with three Chicagoan students about the

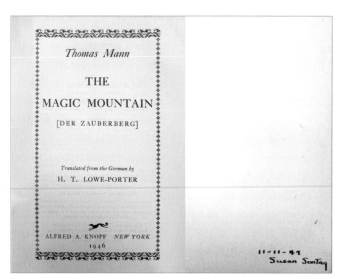

Title page from Susan Sontag's copy of *The Magic Mountain*

'Magic Mountain.'" For Sontag, it was anything but ordinary. Awestruck and filled with thoughts too difficult to capture in words, she felt that she could not live up to Mann's expectations of "American young people, who showed the vigor and health and fundamentally optimistic temper of this country." On the contrary, Mann shared his well-known position on literature's role in fighting against human "barbarity," some anticipatory information about his forthcoming novel *Doctor Faustus*, and his love for *The Magic Mountain*. While sitting "in the very throne room of the world," as Sontag remembered Mann's study, these complex feelings and thoughts became the building blocks of a deeply personal memory that would only come to voice nearly four decades later.

Sontag's essay misrepresented other key historical details of the meeting: she had been accompanied by two friends, whereas the essay mentioned only her high school friend Merrill. These figments of her imagination were integral to the self-fashioning strategies with which Sontag sought to cover up and expose at the same time her shame at the end of the meeting. Although she recognized later in life that there could be a huge "gap between the person and the work," she felt the need, despite her deep knowledge of psychoanalysis, to infantilize herself in order to make sense of her childlike, reverential "admiration," "embarrassment," and "plenitude" in 1949. The essay was a work of pilgrimage whereby Sontag marked a sacred return of sorts to the origin of her writerly life.

CHRISTOPHER ISHERWOOD
145 Adelaide Drive · Santa Monica Canyon
Stefan Schneider

A lucky find: A photo by Carl Maydens for *Life* magazine taken at the Mann residence in Princeton in 1939 shows Christopher Isherwood and W.H. Auden with the Mann family. Isherwood is on the far left, next to Auden. Everybody is smiling, all looking at Isherwood (except Erika). Only Thomas is standing, his glance apparently directed at Christopher. Colm Tóibín writes in *The Magician*, a fictionalized biography of Mann,

that the photographer in Princeton gave some stage directions aimed at getting a more formal photo: all should pose accordingly, only Thomas Mann as the paterfamilias in the center, standing upright. He suggested the family "share a joke" in order to relax. But who told the joke, and what was it? From *The Magician*: "When the reporter asked them what relationship Isherwood had with the family, Erika replied under her breath that he was their pimp." In an interview in 1977 with Louis "Studs" Terkel, Isherwood set the record straight: it was Thomas, not Erika, who had made the joke in reference to the Isherwood-mediated marriage of convenience between Auden and Erika. Said Isherwood, "Uh, Thomas Mann answered in German, which everybody understood except the

photographer. He said, 'He's the family pimp.'"

We find traces of Isherwood in Mann's diaries: *P. P. [Pacific Palisades] Saturday December 1, 1946: (...) In the evening, I am reading Isherwood's 'Prater Violet.'*
P. P. (Pacific Palisades) August 6, 1946 (...) "Isherwood's visit with his boy.

An apt word, "boy." When it comes to Mann's longings, consider the entry dated Friday, July 18, 1936: "Blue, overwarm (...) From there (I went) to the Corso to (see) the Indian dancers. Lovable bodies of the young boys." A wonderful and meaningful entry from Mann in his early diaries on July 20: "I was preoccupied with an elegant young man who had a charming-clueless face of a lad, blond, a refined German type, rather delicate, of whom I had, without question, an impression of the kind I haven't had for a long time. Was he a guest in the club or will I encounter him again? I am ready to admit that an adventure could result out of it." So there was no space for snooty irreverence when "boys" were around in Pacific Palisades.

P. P. Tuesday, March 1, 1949 – "Isherwood (visiting), desperately seeking booze, joined by his flabby and unattractive Bill. Hard to understand.
P. P. Saturday, July 3, 1949 (...) "A very good portrait-style contribution from Isherwood to the Book of Remembrance for Klaus. Moving.
P. P. Tuesday, July 12, 1950 (...) For lunch, Christopher Isherwood with *Bettfreund* [lover] Bill.

In his diaries, Thomas Mann mentions Isherwood rather randomly, *en passant*. There is no detailed character study, and the tone is slightly *von oben herab*, a bit condescending. However, he read Isherwood's books and texts, including *Prater Violet*. By contrast, Isherwood's diaries present a far more sophisticated thumbnail sketch of "the Magician." But do Isherwood's lists of the books he read each year contain some of Mann's works? We know from his diaries that he seems to be quite familiar with *Death in Venice*, *Confessions of Felix Krull*, and *The Magic Mountain*.

But let us return to our *Bildbeschreibung*, our description of the scene:

Isherwood, in his diaries from July 1940:

"At lunch were Thomas and Frau Mann. [...] He looks wonderfully young for his age—perhaps because, as a boy, he was elderly and staid. With careful, deliberate gestures, he chooses a cigar, examines a cognac bottle, opens a furniture catalogue—giving each object his full, serious attention. Yet he isn't in the least pompous. He has great natural dignity. He is a true scholar, a gentlemanly householder, a gracefully ironic pillar of society—solid right through. He would be magnificent at his own trial. Indeed, he has been making the speech for the defense ever since he left Germany."

Christopher Isherwood and W.H. Auden with Thomas Mann in Princeton, N.J., 1939

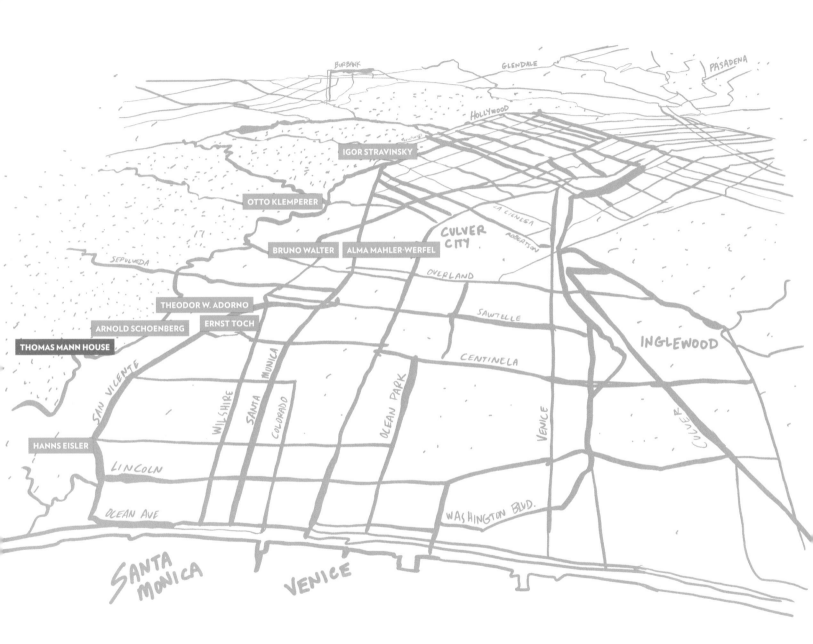

PART 5

IGOR STRAVINSKY

OTTO KLEMPERER

BRUNO WALTER   ALMA MAHLER-WERFEL

CULVER CITY

THEODOR W. ADORNO

ARNOLD SCHOENBERG   ERNST TOCH

THOMAS MANN HOUSE

INGLEWOOD

HANNS EISLER

SEPULVEDA

SAN VICENTE

WILSHIRE

SANTA MONICA

COLORADO

OCEAN PARK

CENTINELA

SAWTELLE

OVERLAND

VENICE

CULVER

LA CIENEGA

ROBERTSON

LINCOLN

OCEAN AVE

WASHINGTON BLVD.

SANTA MONICA

VENICE

BURBANK

GLENDALE

PASADENA

HOLLYWOOD

THE BEGINNINGS OF A NEW MUSIC

Nikolai Blaumer

T he middle way, is the only one that does not lead to Rome," wrote the Austrian-born composer Arnold Schoenberg in the mid-1920s in the preface to his composition *Chorsatiren*. The inventor of the twelve-tone technique was mocking those who "nibble at dissonances, wanting to pass for modern, but who are too cautious to draw the consequences." His commentary pointedly summarized the conflict that would come to dominate musical discourse in Los Angeles several years later.

After Schoenberg lost his professorship at the Prussian Academy of Arts because of his Jewish ancestry, he left Germany for the United States and eventually settled in Los Angeles in 1934, joining other great German-speaking composers of his time, such as Ernst Toch, Erich Wolfgang Korngold, Hanns Eisler, Ernst Krenek, and Eric Zeisl. However, it was his relationship with Igor Stravinsky, the Russian composer of *The Firebird* and *Petrushka*, that set the trend for the development of modern music. These two giants of music lived only a few miles apart, just off Sunset Boulevard.

Stravinsky resided on North Wetherly Drive in Beverly Hills, while Schoenberg lived on North Rockingham Avenue in Brentwood. Both pursued contrasting ideas of music. Schoenberg, approached music primarily from the harmonic side with his twelve-tone method, whereas Stravinsky, the composer of the *Rite of Spring*, focused on rhythm. The sociologist and music theorist Theodor Adorno describes the difference in his *Philosophy of New Music*: "The former has its source in singing; it aims at surmounting time through its fulfillment and, in its supreme manifestations, inverts the heterogeneous movement of time as a force of the musical process. The other type obeys the beat of the drum, intent on the articulation of time through its division into equal quantities that virtually abrogate and spatialize time."

In his work, Adorno left no doubt that he preferred Schoenberg's approach to that of Stravinsky. He derisively wrote off the latter as an ironic imitation of "tootling" and praised Schoenberg's work as revealing the "philosophical truth." For his part, Schoenberg enjoyed cultivating a public persona as an uncompromising avant-gardist who was unwilling to make any concessions to the market, even in his adopted home: "If immigration to America has changed me—I am not aware of it."

In her memoirs, the émigré screenwriter and activist Salka Viertel recounted a meeting between Schoenberg and Irving Thalberg, the influential American-born producer at MGM. The latter wanted to woo Schoenberg for a film project based on the book *The Good Earth*. Thalberg began by saying, "Last Sunday when I heard the lovely music you have written . . ." intending to evoke Schoenberg's *Verklärte Nacht*. Before he could continue, the composer harshly interrupted and snapped, "I don't write 'lovely' music." Despite the incident, both pressed ahead with the idea of a collaboration. Even the incredible $50,000 fee Schoenberg demanded was not a problem for MGM. But Schoenberg wanted full artistic control, with no changes to be made to his score. This eventually derailed the project.

Like other European composers in exile, Schoenberg was torn between tonality and the musical avant-garde, between the claim to artistic validity and the need to be seen, heard, and paid. Whereas in the early twenties Schoenberg confidently proclaimed, "I have made a discovery that will ensure the supremacy of German music for the next 100 years," in the period since his emigration to the United States he felt an "upsurge of desire for tonality." If the invention of twelve-tone music had made him a living legend, it nevertheless limited his sphere of influence to certain cultural elites.

Schoenberg, who first taught at the University of Southern California and later, from 1936, for twelve years at UCLA, complained after his retirement: "Unless I succeed in forcing exploiters of my works, publishers, performers, etc., to pay what they owe me, I would have to live on $29.60 with a wife and 3 small children. It has often enough occurred that I had for months no other income. There remains still the hope that my works might provide for us." Schoenberg stated in frustration that his music was virtually unknown in America and that he wanted to take every opportunity to acquaint the greatest number of people with his work. This need for recognition probably went hand in hand with his willingness to turn to more accessible compositional styles during his years in the United States: "a longing to return to the older style was always vigorous in me, and from time to time I had to yield to that urge."

Thus, in the late 1930s, Schoenberg completed Chamber Symphony no. 2, a work he had begun in 1906, long before he developed the twelve-tone technique. Alex Ross classifies Schoenberg's String Trio of 1946 as the crucial work of his American period: "On its surface, it is a piece of unapologetic difficulty, reminiscent of Schoenberg's wildest early atonal music. The score is full of distortion and noise [. . .]. Yet the contrasting lyrical episode radiates nostalgia for the former tonal world." Schoenberg himself remarked that the composition was a musical description of a severe asthma attack he had recently suffered.

Both Schoenberg and Stravinsky were passionate movie buffs; they moved to California at least in part to seek work in Hollywood. Stravinsky in particular was a gifted networker. During his first year in the United States, he was in talks with Walt Disney about a film adaptation of *The Firebird*. Even though the project fell through and his music appeared instead in the Disney classic *Fantasia*, hardly a day went by without him taking meetings with Hollywood luminaries such as Bette Davis, Greta Garbo, and Alfred Hitchcock. Stravinsky also wrote for jazz musicians of the time, including Benny Goodman and Paul Whiteman. The actor Edward G. Robinson supported his application for American citizenship, and entertainer Danny Kaye

Arnold Schoenberg with his students

is said to have accompanied him to rehearsals and even carried his notes.

A connection soon developed between Stravinsky and Thomas Mann. In 1940, Mann was still complaining about the "very hard and cold conception of music" in Stravinsky's *Petrushka*, noting "characteristic Bert Brecht 20th-century folksiness," a damning verdict. Two years later, however, he devoured Stravinsky's memoirs in just five days. Impressed, he noted in his diary, "Absolute artistry" and "Much that is interesting, timely, and frank about music." In 1943, he and Katia met Stravinsky and his wife, Vera, first at the Werfels' home. This was followed by an invitation for the Stravinskys to visit San Remo Drive along with the legendary pianist Artur Rubinstein. At least four more gatherings occurred, during which the novelist and the composer exchanged ideas not only about Leo Tolstoy and Richard Wagner but also about Arnold Schoenberg.

Mann had already begun work on *Doctor Faustus* at the time. Surrounded by outstanding composers; brilliant interpreters such as Rubinstein, Vladimir Horowitz, and Yehudi Menuhin; and conductors of the caliber of Arturo Toscanini, Bruno Walter, and Otto Klemperer, Mann found the ideal environment from which to draw inspiration. Confessing himself just an "informed amateur," the Nobel Prize winner relied on, above all, the expertise of Theodor Adorno to familiarize himself with various compositional techniques, first and foremost Schoenberg's twelve-tone system.

Doctor Faustus, published in 1947, tells of the life of Adrian Leverkühn, a fictional composer who, possessed by ambition and arrogance, makes a pact with the devil to enable himself to create ingenious works. The book is more than a fictional story: Mann stated that with this work he was returning to his very own theme, the "history of the soul of the German bourgeoisie." In his lecture "Germany and the Germans," delivered at the Library of Congress a few weeks after the end of World War II, he confessed that music was a demonic realm: "Music is calculated order and chaos-breeding irrationality at once, rich in conjuring, incantatory gestures, in magic of numbers, the most unrealistic and yet the most impassioned of arts, mystical and abstract. [. . .] the relation of the German to the world is abstract and mystical, that is musical [. . .]."

From today's perspective, Mann's cultural essentialism and generalizations about "the German soul" may seem disturbing. But to him, music was the key to understanding the monstrosities that German National Socialism had brought upon the world in those years. To his friend and patron Agnes Meyer, he predicted that *Doctor Faustus* would be perhaps his "most daring and sinister work"—"sinister" probably because the novel is a relentless self-examination that not only delves into madness and political seductiveness but also reveals dark secrets about family and one's own desires.

As Mann confessed in his book *The Story of a Novel, Doctor Faustus* incorporated a variety of literary and historical sources as well as Stravinsky's memoirs and Adorno's manuscript on Schoenberg, which would later become part of the latter's *Philosophy of New Music*. Through Adorno, Mann discovered the dark side of Schoenberg's music: "However necessary it may be objectively to subject music to rigorous rational analysis, and however illuminating that may be, the effect is just the converse of rationality. Over the head of the artist, as it were, the art is cast back into a dark, mythological realm. What could fit better into my world of the 'magic square'?"

It is well known with what chutzpah Mann empowered himself in *Doctor Faustus* by using Schoenberg's technique, only to then abandon his fictitious, syphilis-stricken composer to madness. To top it off, Mann sent the composer, with whose family the Manns were on friendly terms, a copy of the novel, which was dedicated to "the real one" (*dem Eigentlichen*). In 2018, E. Randol Schoenberg, the composer's grandson, documented the whole inglorious affair in a remarkable volume, *The "Doctor Faustus" Dossier*.

Arnold Schoenberg was upset and angry. First and foremost, he was concerned that the novel would erase him as the inventor of the twelve-tone technique. Having already seen his work denigrated and banned as "degenerate" in Nazi Germany, it was not far from his mind that posterity would remember Mann, not him, as the system's creator. At the same time, the actual scandal—that his music was placed in the vicinity of fascism by the novel—was not even addressed by Schoenberg.

There is no doubt that the controversy surrounding *Doctor Faustus* is inextricably linked to the circumstances of living in exile: the need for economic survival, the fear of not being heard, the desire not to be forgotten. As Ehrhard Bahr has pointed out, Mann, Adorno, and Schoenberg are very similar in at least one respect: during their exile in Los Angeles, they all tried to resolve the fact that with their radical striving for modernity, their artistic work was increasingly under threat of falling into social obscurity and oblivion. At least *Doctor Faustus*, and the rupture it caused, kept the work of all three legends in the public's mind.

THEODOR W. ADORNO
316 South Kenter Avenue
Alex Ross

Of the German-speaking émigrés who moved to the Los Angeles area during the Nazi era, the philosopher and critic Theodor Wiesengrund Adorno had perhaps the most openly antagonistic relationship with Southern California culture. *Minima Moralia*, the brilliant aphoristic volume that Adorno began writing in 1944, pours scorn upon Hollywood, popular music, the mass media, sports, and the rest. *The Dialectic of Enlightenment*, co-written with Max Horkheimer in the same period, dissects the "culture industry" at withering length. Adorno's critiques placed him at odds not only with the general populace but also with many of the émigrés themselves, who were trying gamely to adapt to their new milieu. Arnold Schoenberg, for one, disliked Adorno's writing and left instructions that, upon his death, that the philosopher should have no access to his legacy.

Yet Adorno's Californian years were by no means unproductive. He may have been intellectually unhappy and financially pressed, but he benefited from close observation of Hollywood culture, regularly attending movie screenings. At Salka Viertel's famous gatherings he got to know Charlie Chaplin, having had the distinction of once being mimicked and mocked by the great comedian. Adorno recounted the episode in a 1964 essay titled "Chaplin in Malibu": "All the laughter he brings about is so near to cruelty; solely in such proximity to cruelty does it find its legitimation and its element of the salvational." Adorno's closest Los Angeles friendship was, perhaps surprisingly, with the émigré Austrian director Fritz Lang, who made some twenty movies in Hollywood and helped to define the genre of film

noir. Although Adorno never made the connection explicit, Lang's bleak visions of human behavior in *Fury, Scarlet Street, The Blue Gardenia*, and *The Big Heat* could be seen as subversive gestures against the compulsory optimism of mass entertainment. There were moments, in fact, when Adorno's world seemed not so distant from the alien planet of Hollywood. The 1943 anti-Nazi film *Hangmen Also Die!* was directed by Lang, co-written by Bertolt Brecht, and scored by Hanns Eisler, with whom Adorno collaborated on the book *Composing for the Film*.

Adorno was in awe of Thomas Mann, and when the opportunity arose to serve as a musical adviser for *Doctor Faustus*, the life of the fictional composer Adrian Leverkühn, the philosopher felt considerable excitement, as letters to his parents show. The two men apparently met at a dinner at Horkheimer's in March 1943, shortly before Mann began writing the novel. Adorno lent the author several books, including his own *Philosophy of New Music*, which Mann read closely and with fascination. Many more meetings took place over the next several years, with Adorno often coming to the house on San Remo Drive, where Mann read aloud from his work-in-progress. One entry in Mann's diary reads: "Visit by the Adornos, with their ape-like dog. In the evening, Parsifal music." Mann also dined at the Adorno home on South Kenter Avenue, in Brentwood. On October 4, 1943, he wrote that Adorno played Beethoven's Sonata op. 111 and read aloud from his writings on the composer, an experience that undoubtedly informed the character Wendell Kretzschmar's lecture about the sonata in *Doctor Faustus*.

As the project proceeded, Adorno became more deeply involved, supplying several provisional descriptions of Leverkühn's visionary later works, which were revised and incorporated into the novel. Mann also absorbed passages from Adorno's writings—most strikingly in the account of the final bars of Leverkühn's final work, *The Lamentation of Doctor Faustus*. In describing Alban Berg's Lyric Suite, Adorno had written: "One instrument after another falls silent. The viola alone remains, and it is not even entitled to expiration, to death. It must play for ever; it is only that we can no longer hear it." From that, Mann converted those sentences into one of the most supremely haunting passages in his fiction: "One instrumental group after another falls back, and what remains as the work dies away is the high G of a cello, the final word, the final disappearing

Adorno at his desk in Los Angeles

sound, slowly dissipating in a *pianissimo fermata*. Then nothing more—silence and night. But the tone that hangs echoing in the silence, which is no more, which only the soul still hears, which was the cadence of sorrow—it is no longer that, it changes its meaning, it abides as a light in the night."

After *Faustus* was published, Mann felt uneasy about this unusual collaboration, and in *The Story of a Novel* gave Adorno a degree of credit for his contributions. Later, in the 1960s, Adorno was crestfallen to read a slighting remark in Mann's posthumously published correspondence, to the effect that the philosopher "puffs himself up in a not entirely pleasant way, so that it looks a little bit as if he had actually written *Faustus*." This was unfair: although Adorno was proud of his contributions to the work, he would never have presumed to claim authorship. He retained the ambiguous but ultimately lofty "honor" of having been depicted in *Faustus* as none other than the Devil himself, in the guise of a bow-tie-wearing musical philosopher "who writes of art, of music, for vulgar newspapers, a theorist and critic, who is himself a composer, insofar as thinking allows." And, in an ironically sentimental cryptogram, the German word for "meadowland" appears in Kretzschmar's discussion of Beethoven's op. 111 as a mnemonic for the Arietta theme: "*Wie-sengrund.*"

ARNOLD SCHOENBERG

116 North Rockingham Avenue

Jeffrey L. High and Glen Gray

Thomas Mann's relationship with the Austrian-born composer, music theorist, and painter Arnold Schoenberg began with an exchange of letters in 1930 and ended just prior to Schoenberg's death. Schoenberg was active in the Expressionist movement, was the founder of the Second Viennese School, and is considered to be one of the most innovative composers and theorists of the twentieth century. Unfortunately, in contrast to Mann's broad literary resonance, Schoenberg's music garnered neither popular nor critical acclaim beyond his own composition students, among them Alban Berg, Anton Webern, Hanns Eisler, and Otto Klemperer. In literary circles today, Schoenberg is arguably best known as the model for the eponymous character in Mann's 1947 novel *Doctor Faustus*, a fate he predicted shortly after its publication.

Both Mann and Schoenberg left Europe in 1933. Schoenberg, persecuted by the Nazis as a Jewish artist and singled out for his "degenerate" music, fled to the United States shortly after the Nazi book burnings on May 10, 1933. Schoenberg found work as an instructor at the Malkin Conservatory in Brookline, Massachusetts, before making the move to Los Angeles, where he served as a professor of composition at UCLA. Mann and Schoenberg regularly encountered each other and their fellow exiles at the Pacific Palisades homes of the Austrian composer and author Alma Mahler-Werfel, Austrian actress and screenwriter Salka Viertel, and author Lion Feuchtwanger. They also often socialized at each other's homes; notably, they shared dinner at Schoenberg's house on May 8 and August 27, 1943, just as Mann was initially outlining *Doctor Faustus*. After Mann's first recorded meeting with Schoenberg in 1938, his diaries indicate an interest in what he refers to as the "crisis of music." Mann sought musical advice from Schoenberg as well as from the philosopher Theodor Adorno, whose essay on Beethoven was reworked in *Doctor Faustus*. Despite Mann's engagement with the work of living composers, including Schoenberg's *Verklärte Nacht* (Transfigured Night, 1899), he admits a preference for "romantic kitsch," concluding on February 22, 1948, that he would "happily swap [the] entire output of Schoenberg, Berg, Krenek, and Leverkühn" for one passage of the Rhinemaidens, the water nymphs of Richard Wagner's opera cycle Der Ring des Nibelungen.

Mann and Schoenberg became inextricably linked in literary history with the publication of *Doctor Faustus*, which follows the rise and fall of the fictional composer Adrian Leverkühn, who possesses the traits of, among others, the German theologian Martin Luther and philosopher Friedrich Nietzsche, but whose music bears the most obvious similarity to that of Schoenberg. After contracting syphilis, Leverkühn enters a pact with the Devil, agreeing to deny himself love in any form in exchange for twenty-four years of musical genius. At the performance of his final masterpiece in 1930,

Leverkühn collapses and descends into madness. The compositional approach, form, content, and possessed-composer protagonist are reminiscent of ideas prominent in Mann's 1945 lecture, "Deutschland und die Deutschen" (Germany

Arnold Schoenberg plays ping-pong at his house on 116 North Rockingham Avenue

and the Germans), in which he attributes the fate of Germany to the country's national character—one marked by subjectivity, introspection, indifference toward politics, and simultaneous love of mathematical order and irrational attraction to music. Mann concludes, "Music is a demonic realm." The attraction to music is thus a "politically suspicious" trait; this was already featured in Mann's 1924 novel, *The Magic Mountain*, which ends in a mystical-hypnotic call to reject reason and embrace the self-destruction of World War I.

On January 15, 1948, Mann sent Schoenberg a copy of the novel bearing the dedication "For Arnold Schoenberg, the real one" ("dem Eigentlichen"). Due to his failing eyesight, the composer had to be informed of the novel's content by others, including his assistant Richard Hoffmann and his friend Alma Werfel. Schoenberg's letters reveal his concern that the novel would inevitably result in misunderstandings of his ideas and personal character, as expressed in his satirical musicological remark dated 2048, which states that Thomas Mann, not

Schoenberg, is credited as the inventor of dodecaphony—the twelve-tone scale. Schoenberg was particularly displeased with the notion that his music could be described as that of a syphilitic madman: "Leverkühn is depicted, from the beginning to end, as a lunatic. I am now seventy-four and I am not yet insane, and I have never acquired the disease from which this insanity stems. I consider this an insult, and I might have to draw consequences." On February 24, 1948, Mann agreed to Schoenberg's request to add a note to the novel attributing intellectual property of the twelve-tone system to Schoenberg. Initially Mann was hesitant based on his creative principle of montage, which held that details about the lives and ideas of historical figures should appear without citation for the sake of the novel's "spherical, self-contained nature."

Throughout their private and public exchanges, Mann's conciliatory gestures stand in contrast to Schoenberg's combative tone, as indicated in Mann's final letter to him, dated December 19, 1949, and written in response to the composer's article in the London journal *Music Survey*: "You are striking out at a bugbear from your imagination, not at me," Mann declared. "Thus, I have no desire for revenge. If, by all means, you want to be my enemy—you will not succeed in making me yours."

IGOR STRAVINSKY
1260 North Wetherly Drive
David Kaplan

After performing Beethoven's last piano sonata—discussed so extensively in Thomas Mann's *Doctor Faustus*—on Mann's own piano, in Mann's own living room, the pianist Igor Levit was asked if he felt any special aura, any ghostly communion, with the instrument's former owner. "In a word . . . No," he blurted. Not everyone, however, manages such rational indifference to the spirits lingering within objects and dwellings. The Finnish conductor Esa-Pekka Salonen was sensitive enough to the memory of another early twentieth-century titan, Igor Stravinsky, that he demurred from buying Stravinsky's Beverly Hills home at 1260 North Wetherly Drive in the late 1990s.

Stravinsky lived on North Wetherly Drive after he first arrived in America in 1942, but it wasn't the outdated kitchen or the lack of south-facing windows that gave Salonen pause. For the young maestro, the dealbreaker was the carpet—specifically, the three unmistakable indentations where a grand piano had only recently stood. On this piano, the composer of *The Rite of Spring* and *Petrushka* had written all his major Los Angeles works: the turbulent and chromatic *Symphony in Three Movements*, the angular Concerto in D for String Orchestra, the English-language opera *The Rake's Progress*, the luminously neoclassical Mass, and the aridly spare ballets composed for George Balanchine, *Orpheus* in 1948 and *Agon* in 1953.

For Salonen, even the absence of a piano might stifle his creativity. Stravinsky, after all, had loomed large in his life and career: *Rite of Spring* was the featured work on his debut recording with the Los Angeles Philharmonic and had become his calling card; Salonen's first major tour with the orchestra, for an extensive festival in Paris in 1996, centered on Stravinsky's music. About the *Rite*, Salonen once mused, "The miracle of the piece is the eternality of it. It's so fresh, it still kicks ass." If too much "eternality" remained at 1260 North Wetherly Drive, Salonen might have had trouble getting work done.

Like Salonen, Mann fully understood the significance of place and the power it possessed in shaping people and their stories: the decline of the titular family in *Buddenbrooks* is framed by the acquisition and sale of their proud mansion, itself an allusion to Mann's own family home; the Alpine sanatorium atop the magic mountain is the physical and figurative trap that ensnares Hans Castorp in a yearslong spell, a *passacaglia* of peace before the outbreak of the First World War; and an entire city lures and ultimately engulfs Aschenbach in a feverish demise at the end of *Death in Venice*. Throughout his oeuvre, physical place is as active a player as the characters themselves.

A special confluence of setting, character, and action must therefore have been palpable when Mann resided on San Remo Drive in the midst of researching and writing *Doctor Faustus*, as a constant flow of musical luminaries streamed through the house not only to socialize but also to consult the author on his new novel. Centering on a fictitious composer madly inventing a new musical language, the book unsurprisingly appropriates numerous aspects of the life, work, and ideas of many of these visitors. In fact, as he worked on *Faustus* in 1943, Mann articulated the difficulty of "the fictitiously convincing placement of a musician (composer) of importance within contemporary music history, whose roles and places are already occupied: there is Schoenberg, there Bartok, there Alban Berg, there Stravinsky, there Krenek etc."

Between 1943 and his return to Europe, Mann met Stravinsky several times, both at San Remo Drive and at the homes of others, including Franz Werfel and Alma Mahler-Werfel. Even if Mann had found Stravinsky "personally so attractive," as he described him following a 1944 meeting that also included Schoenberg, his appreciation of the composer's music was not immediate. One wonders what was responsible for the shift in attitude toward the iconic *Petrushka*, which he first characterized as "anti-romantic" and representing a "hard and cold conception of music," but which he later praised as "humorous, picturesque music" and as "worldly and accessible in comparison with the German innovators."

Some of Mann's initial aversion was consistent with his general distrust of musical modernism. Like another great German writer before him, Johann Wolfgang von Goethe, Mann's musical taste was highly cultivated but skeptical of the latest innovations. Just as Goethe was cool toward Beethoven's audacious musical inventions, instead preferring Mozart and his imitators, Mann preferred Wagner, Vivaldi, the now sanctified Beethoven, Schubert

(whose B-flat Major Piano Trio was a favorite work), and Verdi to the efforts of his contemporaries, including the imaginary works of Adrian Leverkühn, the protagonist of *Faustus*. Listening to the song of the Rhinemaidens from Wagner's Ring cycle, Mann wagered that he would "sacrifice all Schoenberg, Berg, Krenek, and Leverkühn for that passage."

But Stravinsky's music, heard in the context of Stravinsky the man, might have been more palatable to the helpless romantic. Mann gulped down Stravinsky's 1937 memoirs over a period of just a few days in 1942, after which he acquired some respect for the "purely musical" viewpoint of the composer. Once the two men became further acquainted, Mann's descriptions of Stravinsky's music, even when critical, seemed unable to resist the latter's personal charm and charisma of Stravinsky's personality: Mann found the music by turns "amusing," "witty," "artful," "grandiose," and "parodistic."

Most of all, it must have been the technicolor anecdote in Stravinsky's memoir describing his own childhood introduction to music that won Mann over, since he appropriated it directly into Leverkühn's musical genesis. In *Faustus*, Stravinsky's "first sonic impressions" of a singing peasant became Leverkühn's memory of the "singing of the women from the neighboring village," which had a bewitching effect on both their real-life and their fictional young listeners.

So, on San Remo and North Wetherly Drives, plenty of ghostly aura must remain for those inclined to perceive it, whether it lies buried deep in Stravinsky's carpet, or resonates in the spruce of Mann's piano.

HANNS EISLER

689 Amalfi Drive

Nikolai Blaumer

The word 'friend' is a bit too intimate, but one can almost call it a paternal affection," the composer Hanns Eisler said in looking back on his relationship with Thomas Mann, who was twenty years his senior. After fleeing Berlin and working as a visiting professor at the New School for Social Research in New York, Hanns and his wife, Lou, had settled in Los Angeles in 1942.

Two years later, he and Mann met for the first time at a dinner at the home of Arnold Schoenberg in Brentwood. The evening was dominated by conversations surrounding Richard Wagner. A Wagner aficionado, Mann bantered with Eisler about the opera *Parsifal* and discussed harmonics and unresolved dissonances. "So badly composed!" was how Eisler critiqued the monumental, romantic work. At the end of the evening, the composer asked Mann for his autograph, which the latter mentioned in his diary.

Though the Eislers had lived in poor conditions in New York for several years, the success of Fritz Lang's anti-Nazi film *Hangmen Also Die!*, for which Eisler wrote the score, had unexpectedly allowed them to purchase a home on Amalfi Drive in Pacific Palisades, near the Mann family's home. The Eislers' residence became a popular meeting place among European émigrés. Theodor W. Adorno, Bertolt Brecht, Charlie Chaplin, Fritz Kortner, Lion and Marta Feuchtwanger, and the Manns were frequent guests. The prudent Eisler also acted as a mediator between quarreling personalities. Brecht, his longtime friend and colleague, with whom Eisler collaborated on outstanding works such as *Life of Galileo* and the *Hollywood Songbook*, could not stand Mann and mocked the Nobel Prize winner as a "short story writer." Thomas Mann retaliated by speaking of the "unfortunately gifted Brecht." Nevertheless, Eisler did not shy away from inviting both of them to his home together.

As early as 1943, Eisler was under surveillance by the FBI. Tragically, his sister, the publicist Ruth Fischer, set the wheels in motion for his indictment by the House Un-American Activities Committee (HUAC). She testified not only against Hanns but also against another brother, Gerhart, who lived in New York. Ruth called Hanns a "communist in the philosophical sense," even though he had never been—and was never proven to have been—a member of the Communist Party. A few weeks before the committee's interrogation, on October 11, 1947, Mann noted in his diary: "Towards evening visit from Eislers. Nervousness of persecution and depression are noticeable in him. Consultation, assisted by Erika, on petition to Czech government for admission there to facilitate voluntary departure from here." Mann publicly condemned the Eisler brothers' charge. Together with W.E.B. Du Bois, Dorothy Parker, and Arthur Miller, he launched appeals in which he called HUAC's actions undemocratic.

Concerts in support of Eisler were organized in Los Angeles and New York by Ernst Toch, Igor

Stravinsky, and Leonard Bernstein, and despite further public expressions of solidarity, Eisler's formal expulsion from the United States was handed down in February 1948. Before his departure, he said: "I leave this country not without bitterness and infuriation. I could well understand it when in 1933 the Hitler bandits put a price on my head and drove me out. They were the evil of the period; I was proud at being driven out. But I feel heart-broken over being driven out of this beautiful country in this ridiculous way."

Eisler returned to Berlin via Vienna, where in 1949 he wrote the music for the new national anthem, *Auferstanden aus Ruinen* (Risen from Ruins) of the German Democratic Republic, and helped build the Hochschule für Musik, one of Europe's foremost schools of music, which today bears his name.

Hanns Eisler denies that he is a Communist before the House Un-American Activities Committee in Washington, September 24, 1947

ALMA MAHLER-WERFEL

610 North Bedford Drive · Beverly Hills

Lily E. Hirsch

Alma Mahler-Werfel, née Schindler, was a prominent figure in Viennese artistic circles during the early 1900s. Daughter of the landscape painter Emil Schindler, in 1902 she famously married the composer Gustav Mahler, who insisted that she give up her own career ambitions. Alma was a progressive woman in some respects, having studied music and composition and taken lessons from the Austrian conductor and composer Alexander von Zemlinsky. However, she agreed to Gustav's demands, vowing in her diary to "live only for him." Only when their marriage was in crisis did Gustav help Alma publish her first set of songs, *Fünf Lieder*, in 1910. Her second set of songs, *Vier Lieder*, was published in 1915 after Gustav's death. That same year she married the German-born architect Walter Gropius, a union that lasted five years. In 1924, she published her third set of songs, *Fünf Gesänge*, which included "Der Erkennende," set to a poem by Franz Werfel, who would become her third husband in 1929.

When Alma Mahler and Franz Werfel emigrated from Europe, Mann was already living in the United States. Part of the couple's journey included a trek across the Pyrenees with Thomas's brother Heinrich and his wife, Nelly, and Thomas's son Golo.

On October 13, 1940, the group arrived safely in New York, where Thomas and Katia, were there at the pier to welcome and collect their family. Mann had not yet made the decision to move across the country, but the Werfels were ready. On December 30, 1940, they settled in the Hollywood Hills, at 6900 Los Tilos Road, though they would soon purchase a home in Beverly Hills, at 610 North Bedford Drive, close to Arnold and Gertrud Schoenberg, who had been corresponding with Alma.

When Mann moved to Los Angeles in 1942, he joined an already thriving émigré community. The Werfels, Mann, and Schoenberg often dined together, conversing about culture and history, both easy points of connection and correspondence. What Mahler-Werfel and Schoenberg did not yet know was that Mann had begun work on a new novel: *Doctor Faustus: The Life of the German Composer Adrian Leverkühn*, as Told by a Friend. In it, the system of composition used by the fictional protagonist was modeled on that of Schoenberg without explicit citation or a note crediting Leverkühn's real-life inspiration. Mahler-Werfel has often been named as the first to inform Schoenberg of this (in part because the composer suggested as much in an article in the *Saturday Review of Literature*). Though she did know of it before Schoenberg did, Mahler-Werfel would insist she wasn't the one who incited the conflict between Schoenberg and Mann: "I did not draw Schoenberg's attention to the fact (as he writes in the *Saturday Review of Literature*) that his theory takes up a long passage in Thomas Mann's book. Here there must be some error of memory on Schoenberg's part. On the contrary, they both told me that Mrs. Schoenberg had read aloud for her husband the many pages relevant to this matter." However, she did take on the role of mediator, at least according to her own memoirs, speaking separately to Mann and Schoenberg on the other's behalf, in an attempt to help avoid a lawsuit. In his diaries, Mann recorded the back-and-forth, writing on February 21, 1948: "Spoke to Alma Mahler on the phone about Schoenberg. . . . He wants a note indicating that the twelve-tone system is his intellectual property. How to proceed?" Subsequently, frustrated that such a clarification did not appear as he thought it would, Schoenberg publicized his infamous take on the perceived wrong in the *Saturday Review of Literature*, published on November 13, 1948. About a month later, on December 9, Mann vented in his diary, upset by Schoenberg's "wretched, insulting" account, with Mahler-Werfel cast as "intermediary."

Biographers have depicted Mahler-Werfel's role in a less than flattering light, contributing to the broader negative view of her. In Karen Monson's description, "Alma, a friend of Schoenberg and Mann, was happy to find herself in the middle." To some, she was a meddler who reveled in the drama. In a passage you might expect to find in a Mahler-Werfel biography titled *Malevolent Muse*, Oliver Hilmes opens with similar disdain: "this is where Alma's dubious role begins," though he does give her credit for recognizing Schoenberg's compositional framework in Mann's book. "Alma was informed of the content of the novel through a number of private readings, and as a musician, she knew for certain that Adrian Leverkühn was a practitioner of Schoenberg's compositional theory." In her own account, she

maintained, "I wanted nothing but good—and justice. That it now looks bad and unjust I cannot help."

In *Passionate Spirit*, a more recent examination of Mahler-Werfel's life, Cate Haste points out that any tension between Thomas and Alma over the Faustus affair would eventually dissipate. Even in the middle of the conflict, on Alma's sixty-ninth birthday, Mann sent a note: "To Alma, the personality, on her birthday, August 31, 1948, from an old friend and admirer." After the death of Franz Werfel, he would refer to Alma as "la grande veuve" (the grand widow). The two had a relationship long before *Doctor Faustus*, and that bond would endure. Mann enjoyed Mahler-Werfel's company for a host of reasons, some of them quite simple. As he once said, "She gives me partridges to eat, and I like them." To Mann, Alma Mahler-Werfel would remain significant despite those bent on casting her, a particularly strong woman, in a negative light, both during her lifetime and well after.

ERNST TOCH
811 Franklin Street · Santa Monica

Lawrence Weschler

Two dachshunds meet on the palisade in Santa Monica—or so goes the story with which the European émigrés in flight from the fascist gyre engulfing their homelands used regularly to regale themselves on balmy evenings there along the arcing bay, back during the thirties and forties of the last century—and the one says to the other, "Here, it's true, I'm a dachshund, but back in the old country, I was a St. Bernard!"

When it came to the Viennese-born Weimar-era composer Ernst Toch, the jest always seemed particularly bittersweet, in part because he had owned a succession of dachshunds himself (each called Peter, and each somehow more cherished than the one before). But mainly because back in the Old Country, Toch really had been a St. Bernard: one of the principal stars of the Neue Sachlichkeit movement alongside Paul Hindemith, with whom he shared a major *New York Times* spread on the latest modernist trends in German music in 1930); an avid participant in all sorts of experimental festivals (including by way of his invention of the *Geographical Fugue* for spoken chorus, "perhaps the world's first instance of rap music," as his friend the Russian lexicographer and pianist Nicolas Slonimsky used to say). And he was the model for the profession of

"Composer" in the photographer August Sander's legendary survey *People of the Twentieth Century*—not surprisingly, since his dozens of chamber, orchestral, and operatic pieces were regularly programmed and performed across the 1920s and early 1930s by the likes of Furtwängler and Klemperer and Steinberg and Emanuel Feuermann and Walter Gieseking (who performed the Toch First Piano Concerto dozens of times all over Europe before Hitler's ascension to power, following which, alas, he immediately pulled it from his repertoire, summarily canceling an impending London performance).

For his own part, an otherwise not particularly political Toch immediately took the measure of the new reality in the weeks immediately following the Nazi seizure of power and took advantage of the fact that he'd previously been chosen to represent Germany, alongside Richard Strauss, at an upcoming musicological conference in Florence to plot his escape. Instead of returning home he fled first to Paris (from where he cabled his wife, Lilly, back in Berlin, "I have my pencil," the prearranged signal indicating that she was to come join him with their then-five-year-old daughter Franzi) and from there on to London (where he scored the Bertolt Viertel-directed film *Little Friend*, based on a screenplay by Christopher Isherwood, the project upon which the latter would subsequently base his novella *Prater Violet*) and thence onward to New York (where Toch was appointed founding professor of composition in Alvin Johnson's University in Exile at the New School) and finally on to Pacific Palisades, where the Tochs arrived in 1935. (The Palisades were a different sort of place in those days: I've seen the envelope of a letter addressed "Professor Ernst Toch, Pacific Palisades, USA," that clearly must have arrived.)

Alas, once re-settled, Toch fell victim to the benign indifference and "echolessness of the vast American expanses" (in the coinage of his émigré compatriot Ernst Krenek): performances of his music fell off sharply, as presently did his own composing, as he shifted his energies toward the desperate need to rake in money so as to be able to file support affidavits on behalf of dozens of his friends and family members stranded back home. He taught at USC and composed for Paramount, where his modernist stylings were deemed perfect for chase scenes (as in Shirley Temple's *Heidi*, 1937) and horror effects (as in the "Hallelujah Chorus" in Charles Laughton's *Hunchback of Notre Dame*, 1939). It's not that he went entirely without recognition (he eventually netted three Academy Award nominations) but for all that his income was relatively modest and it was never quite clear how he and Lilly were able to afford the extraordinary property upon which they came to build their home at 811 Franklin Street in Santa Monica.

Part of the answer, perhaps (and this applied to many of the émigrés in those days) is that back then (before the advent of the Santa Monica and San Diego Freeways) the coastal communities on the west side really constituted a sort of boondocks (a good hour's drive, for example, from the opera or concert hall downtown) and were hence less highly priced than other parts of the city. And then, too, there were the particular financial blandishments afforded by the Federal Housing Administration in those final years of the Depression (in which context the emigres counted as "white" as opposed to all the indigenous communities of color that were being systematically excluded from such subsidies). But there was also something special about that particular hill, the only such promontory between the cliffs along the coast and the Santa Monica Mountains further inland—and a promontory regarding which most people weren't even aware. Driving down Wilshire Boulevard toward the coast, one could easily miss its existence, just a couple hundred yards to the right of where the boulevard crossed the West L.A./Santa Monica divide. But there it was, capped by a water tower that serviced much of the surrounding area. And in 1940, or so Lilly used to say, that water tower was thought to be one of the most likely, breachable targets should a war ever break out between the United States and Japan (and its associated axis powers). So there was a marked hesitancy on the part of potential buyers for empty lots on that hill. But Ernst and Lilly were damned if, after having succeeded in fleeing the far more tangible threats posed by Hitler, they were going to spend any time worrying about such an unlikely prospect.

Next time you're in the neighborhood, do turn north off Wilshire at Franklin Street and head up the slope: the view up top (the tower has in the meantime been taken down and the water facilities buried beneath ground) is Getty-level breathtaking. (And since the war the hill has indeed been thoroughly built up with the sorts of luxury mansions you might expect, so many of them lapped up by psychiatrists that for a long time the promontory was being referred to as Pill Hill). But the lot the Tochs secured was on the far other side of the saddle, with their view facing east toward the mountains rather than west toward the more conventionally prized vistas of the arcing bay. However, owing to the intervening existence down below of the eucalyptus-and-palm strewn greens of the Brentwood Country Club (indeed the Santa Monica-Brentwood divide coursed right through the Toch's dining room), the view (only a block and a half from busily surging Wilshire) was a serene Da Vinci-backdrop pastorale.

Ultimately deciding against going with their friend Richard Neutra (owing to the notoriously exacting demands the master builder was known to impose ever after on his hapless clients), Lilly instead secured the services of a female Bauhaus-trained architect, Lianne Zimbler, in developing a home that would thereafter be featured in the likes of *Architectural Forum*: boxy, modest, with clean efficient lines, the two-story living quarters bunched to one side, with a lateral hall leading to Ernst's one-story teaching and composing studio off to the other.

The noise from the living side was muffled by the presence of the intervening dining room just beyond the lateral entry hall (for that matter, the whole living side of the house could be walled off during Ernst's private sessions with the likes of the young Andre Previn). Extraneous sounds were further muffled by a wall-long bookshelf on the studio side, featuring a forty-volume edition of the complete scores of Mozart that Toch had had privately bound early in his career. Those had made it across the ocean from Berlin, along with his Blüthner baby grand piano (it's worth noting how relatively lucky many of the artists and writers and composers had it during those years, in that Hitler, himself a resentful would-be conventional painter, had from the very start gone after such "degenerate" cultural types, long before he began his concerted campaigns against the Jews, for example, per se—such that many of the culturally canceled were still able to get away, and often with their furnishings and the like, whereas most of the latter masses would not prove as fortunate later on.)

In 1948, as Toch was preparing to release a summary exposition of his views on, as the book's title had it, *The Shaping Forces in Music*, he sent an advance copy to his friend and fellow émigré Thomas Mann in the hopes of soliciting an endorsement. The Tochs and Manns had long been occasional guests at each other's homes and would frequently intersect at such other regular émigré gatherings as the salons at the homes of Salka Viertel and Lion and Marta Feuchtwanger. (In later years, Lilly and Marta would both regale interviewers with tales of Mann off in the corner at successive Viertel Sunday salons engaged in earnestly intense colloquies, over glasses of orange juice, with none other than Johnny "Tarzan" Weissmuller.) At any rate, Mann presently wrote Toch back a remarkably effusive letter in which he averred that while he'd found Toch's book, in which he'd been "engrossed very intensively over the last few days" to be "the most amiable book of instruction and perception in the field of music that has ever come to my attention," for reasons he couldn't go into in any detail, outside complications (obviously the simultaneously unfolding contretemps surrounding the then recent publication of his own novel *Doctor Faustus*, regarding which Arnold Schoenberg had taken such righteous umbrage) were going to prevent him from setting such convictions to print at the present time. Still, he used the occasion to pass along a signed copy of his own *Faustus* novel, slyly dedicating it, "To Ernst Toch, who wouldn't need the Devil, with neighborly greetings." (Both letter and book now reside at the Ernst Toch Archive at UCLA, and decades later, after all those involved had passed on, the Mann letter was included in full by way of preface to all subsequent editions of Toch's *Shaping Forces* book, which remains in print to this day.)

In some ways, Toch's writing of the *Shaping Forces* book had prefigured a major change in his life. Increasingly exhausted by his teaching and Hollywood duties, in lingering despair over the outcome of the war (across which he had proved incapable of rescuing fully half of his sixty-four cousins) and bedeviled by a seemingly intractable blockage with regard to his own work, he was approaching a climactic crisis, and indeed, by the end of the year, he had been felled by a catastrophic and near-fatal heart attack. On the far side of that experience, he resolved to give up both teaching and film scoring and to henceforth devote himself exclusively to his own muse, and there ensued a remarkable resurgence of that capacity. Across the remaining fifteen years of his life, he produced seven symphonies, a major opera and countless new chamber pieces, much of it composed at the desk of his Franklin Street studio, wedged up against a wide bay window giving out onto a view of that sublime green panorama, Mount St. Mary's College gleaming like a Tuscan village on the distant slopes. At one point during his last year in 1964, a reporter visiting him in that studio exclaimed: "No wonder you can compose with a view like that!" To which Toch, sitting at his desk, the most recent and last of the Peters snuggled in his lap, mildly replied: "Whenever I am composing, I always close the curtains."

Ernst Toch's house

BRUNO WALTER
608 Bedford Drive · Beverly Hills
William Kinderman

The friendship between Thomas Mann and the German-born conductor Bruno Walter spanned two continents and four decades, from Munich to Los Angeles, from the First World War to the 1950s. When Walter was appointed music director of the Bavarian State Opera in 1913, he took up residence in the Munich district of Bogenhausen, near Mann's home on Poschinger Strasse. His daughters soon became friends with Mann's children. But the deep bond between musician and writer had roots in their shared commitment to an artistic legacy that reached its pinnacle during the years before the outbreak of the war in 1914.

Two figures who brought them together were Richard Wagner and Gustav Mahler. At the age of eighteen, in 1894, Walter first encountered Mahler, who was conducting his First Symphony at Weimar; Walter later was a coach under Mahler in Hamburg and served as Mahler's assistant during his tenure at the Vienna State Opera. Wagner loomed large for Mahler as he did for Bruno Walter. *Lohengrin*, the Ring cycle, *Tristan und Isolde, Die Meistersinger*—these works also had a strong influence on Mann. Mann told of the impact of Wagner's music on his own writing, observing that "the novel was always a symphony for me," with "leading motives [*Leitmotiv*] carried into the narrative . . . in the symbolic representation of music." Wagner's final drama, *Parsifal*, was

at the time mainly confined to performances at the Bayreuth Festival, where Mann saw it in 1911, but Bruno Walter later conducted *Parsifal* in Munich. After one such performance, the novelist confessed in his diary that "it hopelessly hits home," recognizing its affinity to his own major work in progress: "It is precisely *Zauberberg* [*The Magic Mountain*]."

Mann's friendship with Walter marks the period of the novelist's evolving political convictions, as he defended Walter against the anti-Semitic attacks that led to the conductor's departure from Munich in 1922. Ominously, Walter was replaced by Hans Knappertsbusch, a staunch anti-Semite and later ringleader of the disgraceful petition issued against Mann in 1933, which forced the Nobel Prize winner into exile. The petition was a crude ambush, published in response to Mann's probing lecture "The Sufferings and Greatness of Richard Wagner," delivered at the University of Munich in February of that year. A poster from the time depicted Hitler as a redeemer figure modeled on the title character from the end of Wagner's *Parsifal*.

Recalling his 1912 novella *Death in Venice*, Mann related how he borrowed the first name and placed the "mask" of Mahler on his artist protagonist, Gustav von Aschenbach, modeling his visual description of the character on a photo of Mahler he found in a newspaper obituary of the composer. In 1910, Mann had attended the premiere of Mahler's Eighth Symphony in Munich, shortly before his own visit to the fabled city of canals and lagoons. Venice similarly entranced Wagner, who wrote parts of *Tristan und Isolde* in that city and who died at Venice in 1883. Even today, the theme of *Death in*

Seated from left, Thomas Mann, Lotte Lehmann, Bruno Walter, Elsa Walter; (standing) Klaus Mann and Erika Mann, in Santa Barbara, c. July 1942

Venice remains both fascinating and timely, not least because of its depiction of a cholera epidemic, which parallels the COVID-19 pandemic that has gripped the world.

In view of all these correspondences, it is remarkable that Walter and Mann resumed their long-standing personal and professional friendship in Los Angeles. Walter conducted the Los Angeles Philharmonic Orchestra many times beginning in 1939. In 1942, he settled at 608 Bedford Drive in Beverly Hills, next to Alma Mahler-Werfel and Franz Werfel, who lived at 610 Bedford Drive. That same year, Mann moved into his home at 1550 San Remo Drive, Pacific Palisades.

Reunited, Mann and Walter witnessed the turning point of the war, as the Nazi nightmare began to recede by 1943, revealing appalling atrocities and devastation in its wake. Already in *The Magic Mountain*, completed in 1924, Mann had closed his narrative by bidding farewell to his protagonist Hans Castorp in the dismal trenches of World War I, in a "worldwide festival of death." In borrowing generously from *Parsifal*, the novelist ironically inverted its overall narrative, negating Wagner's transcendent ending as "ideologically suspect" and concluding instead with a grim antiwar message. Two decades later, Mann began *Doctor Faustus*, his major work written entirely in Pacific Palisades, which ironically blended fictional and actual events. Mann places his narrator, Serenus Zeitblom, in Germany and describes him as writing in secret starting in 1943, Mann's own precise time of writing the novel. In chapter 36, Walter is inserted into the story as conductor of the *Cosmic Symphony* written by the Faustian protagonist Adrian Leverkühn. At the end of *Doctor Faustus*, Mann returns to the subject of war. The narrator, Zeitblom, describes how Germany, in 1940, "a hectic flush on its cheeks, was reeling at the height of its savage triumphs, about to win the world on the strength of the one pact that it intended to keep and had signed with its blood."

A few years later, Germany found itself "in the embrace of demons, a hand over one eye, the other staring into the horror, plummet[ing] from despair to despair." Works like *Doctor Faustus* and the recordings of Bruno Walter carry a conviction that moves us on account of their artistic integrity, passionate gravity, and an openness or vulnerability to external conditions in the world. Of Mann, Walter wrote, "his talent becomes like that of Proteus; heart and imagination, flooded by 'the other,' generate a kind of fusion." The achievements of these friends in exile illustrate the power of such artistic fusion while reminding us of the precarious relation of culture to political conditions.

OTTO KLEMPERER
924 Bel Air Road
Nikolai Blaumer

"There are deaths where you can't even condole," conductor Otto Klemperer recalled of Berlin's Kroll Opera House. He had served as its director until its forced closure in 1931. The opera house was an important venue for artistic experimentation in the Weimar Republic. Thomas Mann defended it against nationalist forces: "it stands at the crossroads of social and cultural interests and is

a thorn in the eye of . . . obscurantism. If opera today is still or has once again become an intellectual issue and a subject of intellectual discussion, that is in the first place the merit of this institution."

After a two-year interlude as general music director of Berlin's Staatsoper Unter den Linden, Klemperer, who was of Jewish descent, was banned from performing in Nazi Germany. He accepted the position of music director of the fourteen-years-young Los Angeles Philharmonic. "He won by musicianship, authority and well-nigh ideal control over the resources of the orchestra," raved the *Los Angeles Times* of the imposing, towering Otto Klemperer's first concert, in October 1933. "He triumphed unquestionably, but he made no popular concessions in doing it."

On their first trip to California, in 1938, Thomas and Katia Mann and Klemperer were reunited

in Vicki Baum's garden. Klemperer had been connected to the Mann family in various ways for years. Katia's twin brother, Klaus Pringsheim, and Klemperer had been friends since their time under Gustav Mahler at the Vienna Court Opera—Klemperer as choir director, Pringsheim as *répétiteur*—and their families were acquainted. Once Mann had permanently relocated to L.A., the fellow exiles began building on their acquaintance, visiting each other regularly, often accompanied by Otto's wife, the singer Johanna Geissler, and daughter Lotte, and attending each other's concerts and lectures.

Even though Klemperer stepped down as music director following brain surgery in 1940, he continued to conduct the Philharmonic's concerts on a regular basis. The performances were sometimes held at UCLA's Royce Hall or Pasadena's Civic Auditorium, but most took place at the Philharmonic Auditorium downtown (427 West 5th Street).

Mann held the great conductor in high esteem, both personally and as an artist. His diaries regularly speak of his wonderful evening concerts ("euphonious"), even if the featured soloists in the performances ("bad piano music") were not always of the desired standard. Grateful for their friendship, Mann immortalized Klemperer in his monumental work *Doctor Faustus* as the conductor of the world premiere of the work *Apokalypse* by the book's protagonist Adrian Leverkühn.

After the end of World War II, Klemperer took positions as chief conductor of the State Opera in Budapest, the Montreal Symphony Orchestra, and the Philharmonia Orchestra in London before eventually settling in Zurich. A convert to Catholicism at a younger age, he returned to his Jewish roots in his final years and regularly attended temple. In 1970, he became an Israeli citizen. Klemperer died in 1973 in Switzerland.

Otto Klemperer with his family in Santa Monica

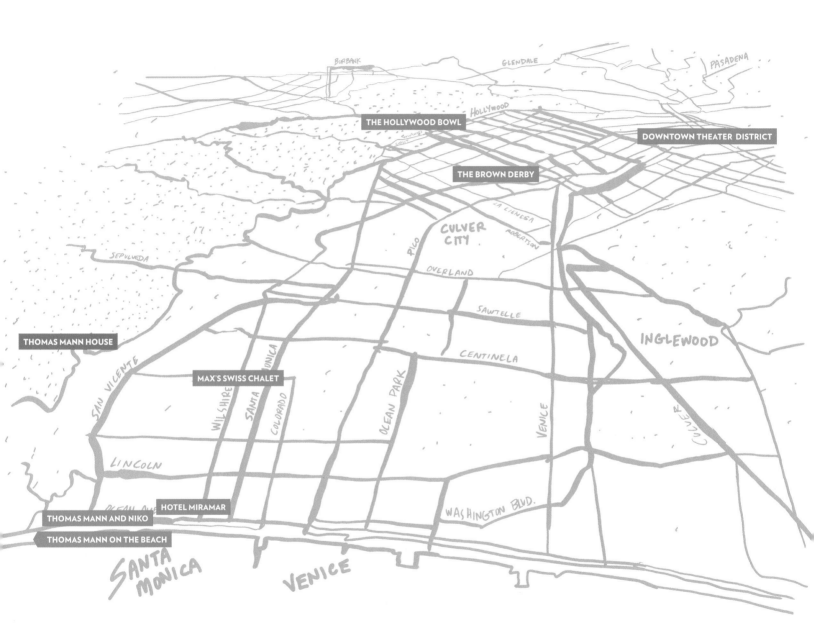

PART 6

THE HOLLYWOOD BOWL

DOWNTOWN THEATER DISTRICT

THE BROWN DERBY

THOMAS MANN HOUSE

MAX'S SWISS CHALET

HOTEL MIRAMAR

THOMAS MANN AND NIKO

THOMAS MANN ON THE BEACH

LEISURE UNDER THE PALM TREES
Benno Herz

The music video for Randy Newman's hit single "I Love L.A." (1983) seems as far removed as it's possible to be from the world of Thomas Mann. While Newman sings about L.A.'s mountains, trees, and endless palm-lined boulevards, he offers sightseeing tour in a classic convertible, showing a slideshow of all there is to love about the city: sunny beaches and dreaming tourists, skimpy swimsuits and retirees in hot tubs, cinemas, theaters, soul food restaurants and Burrito King, Santa Monica Bay Club and Mermaid Café, Disneyland and powerlines, high rises and residential houses, freeways along the dried-up L.A. river and the Pacific Coast Highway in Malibu. While the song instantly became an evergreen ode to the charms of Los Angeles, these aren't the first images of the city that one expects to find in Mann's diary.

Yet they're not altogether different, either. Far from ignoring the city's popular culture, Mann's daily entries include details about long afternoons at the beach, American fast food, and a deep passion for a black poodle named Niko (a passionate dog-owner-relationship that is still a very "L.A. thing"). A full picture of Mann shows aspects beyond the serious, austere novelist—the disciplined German writer with "the reserved politeness of a diplomat on official duty," as Salka Viertel put it in her memoir. Looking at his private life in Los Angeles reveals a more casual side of this "Greatest Living Man of Letters," and how he immersed himself in the culture of his new home. His appreciation for L.A.'s climate and vegetation, his erotic observations during long sunset walks on the beach, and his vivid descriptions of the heavenly smell of eucalyptus could have easily made it into Newman's ode to the city.

Time for leisure and tourism have long been overlooked and misunderstood as hours squeezed in between the time one devotes to life's serious occupations. A pause that one takes in between achieving goals and reaching one's accomplishments— vacations, sports, hobbies, and travel occur separately from one's character-defining career. But upon reading Mann's diaries more closely, it is obvious that he spent a lot of time enjoying life's simple pleasures with his friends and family. The contributions in this chapter interpret the meaning of these activities and explore the question of if, and how, they affected his work. These activities also made Mann more familiar with American culture, urban life, and the many treats of L.A. While working on *Joseph the Provider* in the summer of 1940, Mann often mentioned afternoon trips to the beach as a welcome break and source of inspiration, or the many daily walks down San Remo Drive with his dog Niko, which gave him the opportunity to let his thoughts roam away from an otherwise highly structured writing routine. These outings show another idyllic slideshow of L.A., this time from the 1940s, such as when Thomas and Katia Mann took their new Buick for a ride on October 26, 1949: "Favored by beautiful weather, we took a trip in the new Buick to San Diego via Laguna Beach, where we had lunch at the wonderfully located Victor Hugo Inn." What is more iconic for Southern California than lazy days on the beach and road trips down the Pacific Coast Highway?

With its countless beaches in Venice, Santa Monica, and Malibu; miles of hiking trails in the canyons and hills of Hollywood and Topanga; mountains, skiing areas, lakes, and rivers all in close proximity; and year-round sunny weather, L.A. always has been a paradise and a recreational hub. But its cultural richness, diverse restaurant scene, and the musical venues and theaters are also a trademark. Mann immersed himself in all these offerings and described many of them in his diaries. Among the landmark restaurants he frequented were the Swiss Chalet and the Brown Derby. From concerts at the iconic Hollywood Bowl to the historic theater district downtown, Mann and his family indulged in a number of leisure activities that made his time in exile more enjoyable.

Santa Monica Beach, crowded with sunbathers, 1945

Thomas Mann with daughter Elisabeth in their garden, Pacific Palisades, c. 1946

THOMAS MANN & NIKO
Palisades Park · Santa Monica
Rembert Hüser

am I because my little dog knows me" was said not by Thomas Mann but by the American poet and novelist Gertrude Stein. But just as Stein attempted to navigate Paris in 1936 by leaving questions of identity and agency to her dog, Mann, after many years spent in the United States, would have been completely at sea without his poodle, Niko.

Mann's first night under his newly built roof at

1550 San Remo Drive went "pretty well," according to Mann's diary, because the man of the house had made certain to bring along his personal protection: "my own silken blanket." Once the second skin of the blanket is peeled off, Day One at his future home starts with leaving, right away, what is still under construction and exposing himself

to his surroundings outside. "Walked up San Remo Dr with the poodle after getting dressed, had breakfast, and singled out some auxiliary books from the wilderness of the studio. The weather was slightly cloudy." As the house was still a construction site, with shelves being transported to the library, his

family sorting through the books, and swarms of strangers, "workers in the house and in the garden," Mann had no choice but to withdraw to his bedroom and set up an auxiliary desk. "Wrote a little bit." All he required was a few books, some kind of desk, and a dog that pulled him away—no need for excuses.

Walking Niko up San Remo Drive, in between dreaming and writing, was much more than a routine. Mann had already considered this type of reset—the chance encounters and moments of undecidedness that blossom while walking and dreaming with Niko—at another turning point in history almost a quarter of a century prior. After the end of World War I in 1918, between writing *Reflections of a Nonpolitical Man*—which still considered a democracy in Germany to be "stupid and un-German"—and resuming work on *The Magic Mountain*, Mann had written a novella about how dogs address their owners and how this interferes with the writing process.

To better understand why owning a dog, which starts as a fantasy of control, can cause one to project about what is known and impossible to know, one has to see the underlying Hegelian dialectics in the German title of Mann's book, which, literally translated, is "Master and Dog," not "A Man and His Dog," or *Bauschan and I*, as it was titled in English. Mann's day begins by greeting Niko, who takes his master out of the house and on the precious morning stroll, delaying the working hours of the day and helping Mann's mind drift between philosophy and triviality, out beyond the pleasure principle, from death drive to San Remo Drive, when even the sentimental choice of a street name might magically conjure up memories of a famous Italian spa of the

Belle Epoque, or the orientalism of La Pigna—both the present and past, America and Europe, mingling together. Although Mann was a man obsessed with control, his walks with Niko replaced control with happenstance, and opened him up to new possibilities of thought and experience.

At home, still under the influence of the weather outside, Mann witnessed what for him was a highly symbolic ritual: "A 25 year old olive tree is ingrafted." Twelve years ago, in his book *The Trees in the Garden*, Mann had identified the olive tree as representing the powerful masculine principle that is characteristic of Eastern myth. He called it "the tree of the sun," symbolizing day, masculinity, spirit, reason, liberty, and future—all this in opposition to the fig tree, "the tree of the moon," symbolizing night, sensuality, the feminine principle, soul, irrationality, bondage, and the past and the love of it. The fig tree does not make it to Mann's garden.

Spending time outdoors with Niko isolates Mann's experience of spiritual and intellectual unsettlement in the first half of this special day. Right after the tree's symbolic reinstallment, walking the dog is mentioned for the second time in this brief, nineteen-sentence-long diary entry of Thomas Mann's first day in Pacific Palisades. "Walked with the dog in the close proximity of here." The repetition of drawing the second circle of his walk closer to the promise of his desk is noteworthy for Mann.

If one searches for "Niko" in the author's diaries, one will find more than a hundred entries; if one searches for "poodle," more than two hundred entries. The big black dog drew Thomas Mann out of his mind and onto the page, day by day, whether they stayed closer to home or out in Santa Monica's Palisades Park.

To reassure oneself with a blanket, a dog, and a tree of one's own seems to be particularly important in a situation of exile when, in the particular historical moment of February 6, 1942, when the precise status of German refugees in the U.S. is still up in the air. While the afternoon in the House of Mann is left to reading and politics, reading his son's published journal (*Decisions*), and walking with his wife ("Walked a little bit with K."), the airspace above—the other element, besides the water of the ocean, that connected Mann to his former home—occupied his thoughts on the very same day. "Refusal of the idea of a dedication of fighter jets through the enemy aliens." Affirming the technical term that President Franklin Delano Roosevelt had used on December 8, 1941 to classify all unnaturalized Germans and Italians over age fourteen, Mann refuses to participate in the dedication. Acting as nose art for bomber jets is not an option for refugee immigrants.

No, there is no elephant in Thomas Mann's room, but there is a large poodle.

THOMAS MANN ON THE BEACH
Along the Pacific Coast Highway
Benno Herz

In his very first diary entry made in Los Angeles, Thomas Mann highlighted the beach and the ocean, key Southern California elements that would become an important part of his daily routine. On March 24, 1938, of his first visit to the Santa Monica Pier, he noted, "Promenade over the sea. Everything wide, bright and new. Beautiful beach." And the next morning: "The day is blue and fresh like yesterday. Smell of eucalyptus mixed with sea air." He described more than a hundred excursions to beaches in the greater L.A. area: "one of the further ones," "the small one," "the one surrounded by cliffs," "the closer one," and so on.

The Los Angeles County coastline consists of over twenty-five miles of sandy beaches. From Malibu to Santa Monica, from Venice to Rancho Palos Verdes, like some of the most popular beaches in the world, attracting over fifty million visitors each year. Even though Mann did not refer to his favorite beaches by name, he most likely spent much of his time at what is known today as Will Rogers State Beach in Santa Monica, just a few minutes' drive from Pacific Palisades. In the early 1930s, Will Rogers was one of the biggest actors in Hollywood. Rogers was actually more than an actor: he was a vaudeville performer, a cowboy, a columnist, and a philosopher and reporter. After becoming friends with the aviation pioneer Charles Lindbergh, he became interested in aviation, which ultimately cost him his life in a plane crash in 1935.

During the 1920s, Rogers acquired land in Santa Monica on which he built a ranch with his wife, Betty. At one point, he owned more than three hundred acres overlooking the Pacific Ocean in what is now Pacific Palisades. After his death, Betty donated all of the land to the state of California, which turned it into Will Rogers State Historic Park and the Will Rogers State Beach.

Mann mentions morning walks with Katia at the Will Rogers Ranch in his diaries. But on some days, the Manns were drawn farther west: "Drove Sunset Blvd. with K. all the way to the far beach," he wrote on August 2, 1940. It is likely that they drove the thirty minutes to Zuma Beach or Point Dume in Malibu. Just like today, the beaches in Santa Monica could be crowded on the weekends, so it was worth the trip for a little more peace and quiet. Mann enjoyed strolling the beach with Katia, his poodle, Niko, and his children, grandchildren, and friends. Most notable perhaps is a walk at the beach in Rancho Palos Verdes with his fellow novelist and friend Aldous Huxley and his wife: "walked quite far at low tide at the blue-white illuminated sea. On the beach numerous condoms. I did not see them, but Madame Huxley pointed them out to K.," read the entry on April 14, 1938. The excursions had their occasional unpleasant moments, depending on the weather and one's mood. After long walks in the sun, Mann commented "headache" (September 27, 1940), "lost my little smoking pipe at the beach" (June 18, 1941), and even "beach trip: never again" (September 14, 1945).

But most of the time, these trips had a positive and inspiring effect, especially on days that were less hot, even a bit foggy. On May 7, 1941, Mann even noted his "intention of joining a beach club." He would take his walks around lunch or the early afternoon as a welcome break between writing sessions. For example, while living in Brentwood and working on *Joseph the Provider* in the summer of 1940, he often mentioned afternoon trips to the beach as a break and a source of inspiration. On the weekends, the family often spent afternoons picnicking at the beach.

But you would be wrong to picture Mann in swim trunks. Even for a casual walk, he always dressed up in a chic white suit and stylish beach shoes, with the appropriate accessory: "To Santa Monica, buying beach shoes and cigars," he wrote on May 31, 1941.

Thomas Mann and family on the beach

THE HOLLYWOOD BOWL
2301 North Highland Avenue
Benno Herz

After visiting the Hollywood Bowl, Thomas Mann described this quintessential L.A. venue in the Hollywood Hills: "Concert in the huge rondel of the 'Bowl'. With Walters and Pinza in the box. We listened to the 4th Symphony by Brahms," read his entry of July 12, 1940. His experience sounds very familiar to anyone who has attended a summer concert there: "Terrible traffic. Huge crowd. In Walter's box. (. . .) Schubert, Strauss and Beethoven. Often immersed in the music. During the intermission, colorful lighting effects. Walter was very celebrated" (August 30, 1940). One of the reasons Mann frequented the Bowl was certainly his love for classical music; another might be the fact that the conductor and composer Bruno Walter, one of his closest friends in L.A., led the Los Angeles Philharmonic on a regular basis and invited Mann to many concerts and exclusive rehearsals at the d Bowl. Among the programs Mann saw were symphonies by Brahms, Beethoven, Friedrich Smetana, Dvořák, Schubert, Strauss, and Debussy. Between 1940 and 1948, Mann visited the Bowl more than twenty times, often accompanied by Katia or one of his children, stopping for snacks and beer at the Walters' home after the show.

Set against the backdrop of the iconic Hollywood sign, the Hollywood Bowl has been a landmark in Los Angeles ever since it opened in 1922. Hosting concerts by legendary artists from Billie Holiday to the Beatles to Yo-Yo Ma, the concentric-arched band shell has a long and storied history. In 1919, the Theatre Arts Alliance Inc. purchased the land, then a popular picnic spot in the Cahuenga Pass. Over the next few years, the first wooden stages, boxes, and bench-seating sections were built. In July 1922, Alfred Hertz, "the father of the Bowl," conducted the Philharmonic's inaugural concert. The stage underwent many changes and phases, with different designs by renowned architects such as Lloyd Wright in 1927 and Frank Gehry in the 1980s. The Hollywood Bowl is still a popular venue and a must-see for every music fan visiting Los Angeles. Make sure to leave enough time, though, for the *schrecklicher Traffic* ("horrible traffic") and the "long and dangerous drive home" (August 1, 1941). And even in the 1940s, he struggled to find parking, a challenge that continues to confront visitors. On July 29th, 1943, After listening to pieces by Tschaikovsky and Wagner, Mann wrote "problems parking and driving."

On days when the traffic and driving proved too much for him, Mann often tuned in to concerts from the Bowl via radio. The Philharmonic started broadcasting entire concerts in January 1929, making it the first orchestra in the United States to send their concerts into people's living rooms. The broadcasts were much appreciated by Mann. On July 7, 1943, after visiting the Bowl to see Walter conduct a Beethoven symphony, Mann's car, nicknamed "the green," ran out of gas: "7.30 p.m. snack. Drive to Beverly Hills to see Walters, who took us to the Bowl. 1. Beethoven Symphony. 2. Dances of Dvořák. There is a boldness to the symphony, reminiscent of Mahler. The dances seem like upscale folklore. Got stuck on the drive home with 'the green' out of gasoline. Brought home by friendly people (after many rejections). Chocolate."

Still, Mann never tired of the venue. He last mentions the Bowl in his diaries on September 2, 1948, when he and Golo went to a dress rehearsal of conductor Eugene Ormandy's production of Giacomo Puccini's opera *Madama Butterfly*.

Bruno Walter with the Hollywood Bowl Orchestra

DOWNTOWN THEATER DISTRICT
520 West 5th Street
Anthony Caldwell

Brentwood, Wednesday 21.VIII.40 (...) Drove to Franks ... and had dinner there. Then to Los Angeles with Mr. and Mrs. Massary to the Biltmore Theatre: 'Ladies in Retirement,' well done mystery play with Englishwoman Robson, an actress of atmosphere. Well entertained. Brought home by Frank."

The theater Thomas Mann writes of was just one of many that dotted the landscape of downtown Los Angeles in the 1940s. The Biltmore Theatre opened in March of 1924. Designed by the New York architecture firm of Schultze and Weaver, the million-dollar structure represented the latest in theater construction and audience comfort. The brick and terra-cotta style was similar to that of the adjacent, recently built Biltmore Hotel, also designed by Schultze and Weaver. Collectively, the hotel and theater created a complete experience in which one could arrive downtown, park in an enclosed garage, walk to the hotel for a fine dinner, and stroll over to the theater for the evening's entertainment.

The play Mann attended that August evening, *Ladies in Retirement*, starred Flora Robson, a leading English actress of the time. The play had come to Los Angeles directly from a successful season in New York, receiving good reviews. Written by two English writers, Edward Percy and Reginald Denham, the play was a murder mystery. In a review that appeared in the *Los Angeles Times* dated August 16, 1940, it was described as a modern-style thriller: "There are no guns or bloody knives, no mysteriously appearing hands or blood-curdling moans. In fact, there is only one shriek in the play, but that is so well placed and timed that it is much more effective than a dozen of the old-fashioned melodramatic kind." We do not know where Mann sat—perhaps it was in the balcony or some other prime location.

Downtown Los Angeles in 1940 was still very much the city center. Broadway, a major commercial boulevard, hosted an array of department stores with names familiar to longtime Angelenos: May Company, Broadway, and Bullock's, as well as specialty stores like Desmond's, Blackstone's, and Harris & Frank. Broadway was also home to many theaters: the Arcade, the Los Angeles, the Million Dollar, the Palace, and the Orpheum, to name a few. The avenue would have been ablaze at night from the large marquees and signs. Angels Flight, the funicular connecting the communities on top of Bunker Hill to the central commercial district below, was still in its original location alongside the Third Street tunnel. Streetcars known as Yellow Cars streamed up and down the main streets of downtown. Along with Pacific Electric's Red Car system, Los Angeles had an extensive local and interurban rail system in the early twentieth century.

The Biltmore Hotel, still located on the west side of Pershing Square, remains mostly as it was in August 1940. Although not directly on the square, the Biltmore Theatre was part of a group of theaters located on the streets around the park: the Biltmore, the Philharmonic Auditorium, and the Metropolitan/Paramount—the largest theater ever constructed in the downtown district. In 1940, Pershing Square would have been filled with lush trees and tropical-looking plants and shrubs. The square was crisscrossed with paths and had a central three-tier fountain. The park was considered the heart of downtown—a popular place for military ceremonies, military recruiting, and political rallies.

After World War II, there was a population shift to the suburbs, leaving the city's core in decline. The decline had actually started many years earlier but only accelerated during the postwar period. Many old buildings were demolished to make way for parking lots to satisfy the never-ending demands of the automobile. This collection of lost buildings sadly included the Biltmore Theatre, demolished in 1964. In the early 1950s, Pershing Square was completely redesigned. The park had all of its foliage and paths, as well as its great fountain, removed and replaced by an underground parking structure, leaving a large, open grassy area bordered by new trees. In 1992, the square was once again redesigned.

The downtown Los Angeles Mann knew is still there if you look. Many of the buildings, including the Biltmore Hotel, are still standing. Beginning around 2000, the area began to experience a renaissance. Development of the historic core district with its historic office buildings, hotels, and theaters has led to a new future. Broadway hosts the largest district of surviving landmark theaters in the United States. Angels Flight has been reassembled in a new location and returned to service. A new, greener, pedestrian-friendly vision for Pershing Square is under development, promising a better connection between the park and the surrounding city.

Walking in downtown Los Angeles, it is still possible to glimpse the Los Angeles of that August evening in 1940. The skyline of the historic core looks essentially as it did during Mann's time. One can almost hear the Yellow Cars, their bells ringing out and the sound of their steel wheels on rails, the horns of cars as they whiz by, and the voices of pedestrians long gone but forever captured in our imaginations.

Crowds of people lined the street to enter the Biltmore Theatre, March 4, 1924

THE BROWN DERBY
3377 Wilshire Boulevard
Benno Herz

There is something intriguing about the idea of Thomas and Katia Mann walking into a restaurant shaped like a giant brown hat and ordering pancakes and ice cream alongside the philosopher Max Horkheimer and his wife, Maidon. But this was a common part of Mann's everyday life in Los Angeles. It is fair to say that the Brown Derby restaurant was one of Mann's favorite lunch spots in the city. With several locations close to downtown, Hollywood, and Beverly Hills, there was always one close enough for a quick bite. The first Derby was opened in 1926 by the playwright and entrepreneur Wilson Minzer, film producer Herbert K. Somborn, and chef Robert H. Cobb. Mann's acquaintance Jack L. Warner fronted the money for the rather odd architectural endeavor.

The original restaurant was at 3427 Wilshire Boulevard but in 1936 relocated to a larger building, with another derby, of course, at 3377 Wilshire. The first time Mann mentions the second location is on March 7, 1942. After he accompanied Bruno and Liesl Frank to their immigration hearing, they enjoyed lunch "at the Brown Derby on Wilshire" together.

In Disney's 1947 animated film *Fun and Fancy Free*, Willie the Giant can be seen walking around Los Angeles, picking up the Brown Derby and looking for Mickey Mouse under the dome. Chances are he would have found Mann instead, for the Wilshire location became Mann's most visited Derby. He would dine there after attending the commemoration of the theater director Max Reinhardt at the Wilshire Ebell Theatre, with the philosopher Ludwig Marcuse after his passport examination, and

after his many visits at his doctor Rachelle Seletz's medical practice downtown.

The Derby's other locations were at 1628 North Vine Street in the heart of Hollywood, opened in 1929, and at 9537 Wilshire Boulevard in Beverly Hills, opened in 1931, though neither featured the iconic Brown Derby dome. In his diaries, Mann would indicate which of the Derbies he visited, distinguishing between the "Derby on Wilshire," Beverly Hills, and the "Hollywood Derby." The latter was especially convenient for a lunch stopover after recording his speeches for *Listen, Germany!* at the NBC studios on Vine, and after visiting his dentist Dr. Joseph Cooper on Hollywood Boulevard, even if this meant he could only partake of certain foods: "To Cooper for the very bothersome jaw tumor. Some grinding of the denture. Lunch at Brown Derby: onion soup and ice cream" (March 24, 1949).

The Hollywood location was the most glamorous. Frequented by movie stars, film producers, and gossip columnists Louella Parsons and Hedda Hopper, it was a convenient lunch place for many people working in the studios nearby. Legends and myths surround the Derby in Hollywood: the nonalcoholic cocktail dubbed the Shirley Temple was created upon the actress's request, and one of the first episodes of the classic TV show *I Love Lucy* is set there. The Hollywood location is also famous for another invention: the Cobb Salad. One version of the story suggests that cofounder and owner Robert H. Cobb, looking for a late-night meal and finding nothing left in the kitchen but leftovers, diced everything up and tossed it with a little French dressing. *Voilà*! Cobb invented the Cobb Salad that night.

The Beverly Hills Derby was actually the closest to Mann's home in the Palisades. It was where he learned about "Chaplin's acquittal in the absurd trial" from his friends the Singers over pancakes and coffee on April 5, 1944. Mann was dining there after arriving at Union Station from a trip to Chicago. Chaplin had been accused of transporting two women across state lines, but the allegations were fabricated to harass the actor-director for his leftist political views. The case was personally instigated by FBI director J.

Edgar Hoover, who had called Chaplin one of Hollywood's "parlor Bolsheviks."

In his diaries, Mann recounted more than twenty visits to the restaurants, but we know there were countless others. "Surprisingly good lunch at the Brown Derby!," Mann noted in February 1945. After all, Mann's appreciation for filtered coffee, pancakes, ice cream, and onion soup shows how immersed he was in the culture of his new city. Unfortunately, none of the Brown Derby locations are extant. The Hollywood location closed in 1985 and the building was demolished after the 1994 Northridge earthquake. The Beverly Hills Derby was closed and demolished in 1982. The last remnant of this iconic gathering place is from the original Wilshire location. It closed in 1980, but the derby-shaped dome was placed on top of a newly constructed parking lot. In 1985, the Brown Derby Plaza Shopping Mall opened; the original dome can still be seen inside the mall on the third floor.

The original Brown Derby restaurant on Wilshire Boulevard, 1956

HOTEL MIRAMAR
101 Wilshire Boulevard · Santa Monica
Nikolai Blaumer

The Fairmont Miramar Hotel and its restaurant have been among L.A.'s most upscale addresses since Thomas Mann lived in the city. The property originally belonged to Senator John Percival Jones, who had become wealthy from silver mining. It was Jones who gave the site its name, Miramar, and built a Shingle-style mansion here, with magnificent views of the Pacific Ocean and Santa Monica Bay. After several sales, including one to businessman King C. Gillette, the mansion was converted into a hotel in 1921, and a wing was added soon after.

When Thomas and Katia first visited the Miramar in 1938, the hotel was again undergoing a major remodel, and the old mansion was demolished. In its place, bungalows and a swimming pool were built. During his years in Los Angeles, Mann was a guest numerous times. These visits had to fit into Mann's tightly regulated daily schedule. His mornings were reserved for writing, followed by a walk in Pacific Palisades or on the Ocean Avenue Promenade, to which Thomas had himself driven by car. For lunch, the Miramar was a fixed point of call. The visits were so regular that Mann recorded in his diaries when they had to eat at home "instead of at the Miramar."

The style-conscious novelist was attracted to the Hotel Miramar not only because of its fantastic view and pleasant ambience but also because of the food. His notes contain positive comments, from "Lunch at the Miramar, delightful," to "Lunch at the Miramar. (Light attraction)," to "Lunch at Hotel Miramar. Heavily eaten."

Usually Mann was accompanied by Katia or his children and grandchildren. When he came alone, he read letters or newspapers. He would also come to socialize with friends who were staying at the hotel's bungalows, including the diplomat and art collector Robert Woods Bliss and his wife, Mildred, and Mann's patron and admirer Agnes E. Meyer. Mann noted in his diary on March 30, 1942: "At Meyer's in the Bungalow. Conversation with her, about her work, her condition, about 'us'; then reading of a part of 'Thamar.' Lunch with her, which I relished."

The Miramar has been a center of attraction for celebrities from culture and politics since its early days. During the Jones era, illustrious guests such as Mark Twain or the women's rights activist Susan B. Anthony visited the house. Later, Greta Garbo stayed at the hotel for several years when she first came to the United States from Sweden. Eleanor Roosevelt, Cary Grant, Marilyn Monroe, and John F. and Jackie Kennedy were also guests.

In the late 1950s, a tower with more apartments was added, which dominates the site to this day. At the turn of the millennium, it passed into the hands of Fairmont Hotels and Resorts, which gave the hotel its current name, the Fairmont Miramar Hotel.

Hotel Miramar in Santa Monica

MAX'S SWISS CHALET
2201 Wilshire Boulevard · Santa Monica
Nikolai Blaumer

Max's Swiss Chalet in Santa Monica is one of those forgotten places of European exile whose history can only be vaguely reconstructed today. And yet, Thomas Mann visited hardly any other place more frequently during his time in California. In his diaries, we find a whole fifty-six entries mentioning lunch at the establishment, located at 2201 Wilshire Boulevard.

Pictured on an old postcard for the restaurant is a traditional wooden house with a flat gabled roof and a balcony all around, as is still commonly seen in the Alpine regions. Next to it are two large conifers that remind the viewer of Zermatt or Lake Lucerne in Switzerland. Menus from the period reveal the culinary merits of the restaurant. In addition to American classics and fish dishes, "Salad ala Swiss" and "Wiener Schnitzel Horlstein" [*sic*] were served. Mann seems to have enjoyed the food very much, praising it as either "good" or "very good" and regularly reporting "good appetite" and great hunger.

In addition to the cuisine, homesickness for Europe undoubtedly also brought Mann to the Swiss Chalet. One can assume that Max Naef, the eponymous host, was himself from Switzerland. The Manns sent him regards from there when they traveled to Lugano in the early summer of 1950, where they met, among others, their friend and fellow writer Hermann Hesse. Over the years, a cordial relationship seems to have developed with Naef, who often provided food for Mann's beloved poodle, Niko, which Mann attentively recorded.

At his restaurant, Naef cultivated the spirit of the old European world. He advertised his restaurant with the slogan "You will find it 'Different'

here." Some of his employees were likely also Swiss. For example, Mann noted in January 1951: "Lunch at Swiss Chalet. Waitress from Zurich who almost forgot to bring soup because of excitement." Meeting other Europeans, especially Nobel Prize winners, was not an everyday event, even in Los Angeles in the 1950s.

In October 1948, Thomas Mann noticed a large poster that read "We are for Dewey and Warren" at the Chalet. The presidential election between Harry S. Truman and Alben W. Barkley and their Republican opponents Thomas E. Dewey and Earl Warren was coming up. That was the basis for a political disagreement between Mann and his host, since Mann, a proud American citizen for three years, felt committed to the Democratic Party. But the poster in no way prevented him from continuing to be a regular guest.

In June 1951, Naef told Mann that he planned to sell the restaurant and retire. A year later, Mann wrote, "Walked with K. and ate at the Chalet. Change of owner." A few months later, the Manns themselves emigrated to Switzerland. The Swiss Chalet had been a piece of home on the distant Pacific for over a decade.

Swiss Chalet restaurant interior with tables, chairs with heart-shaped backs, cuckoo clock, and carved bear, 1939

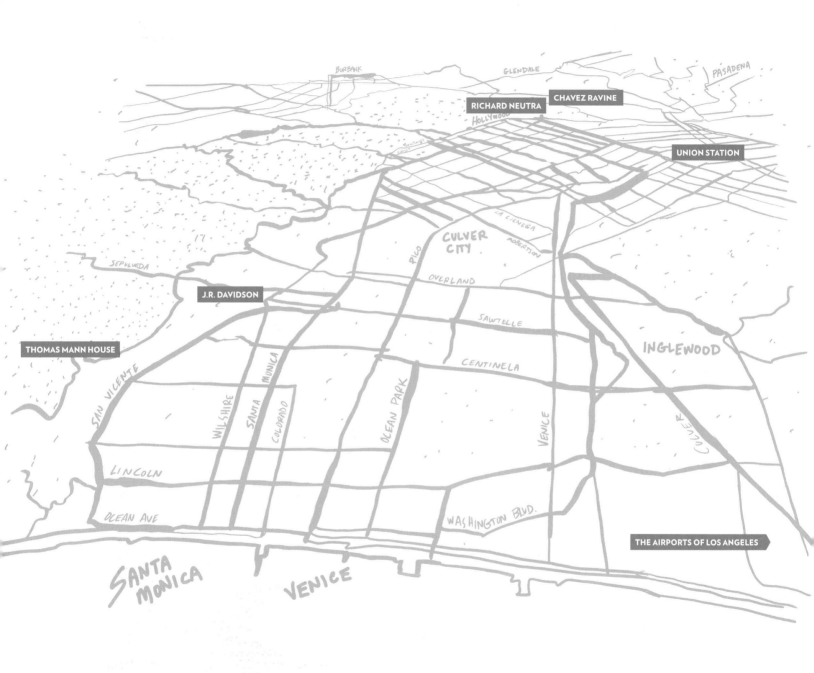

PART 7

BURBANK

GLENDALE

PASADENA

RICHARD NEUTRA

CHAVEZ RAVINE

UNION STATION

HOLLYWOOD

LA CIENEGA

CULVER CITY

17

SEPULVEDA

PICO

ROBERTSON

OVERLAND

J.R. DAVIDSON

SAWTELLE

THOMAS MANN HOUSE

CENTINELA

INGLEWOOD

SAN VICENTE

WILSHIRE

SANTA MONICA

COLORADO

OCEAN PARK

VENICE

CULVER

LINCOLN

OCEAN AVE

WASHINGTON BLVD.

THE AIRPORTS OF LOS ANGELES

SANTA MONICA

VENICE

A CITY IN TRANSITION

Benno Herz

Between Thomas Mann's first visit in 1938 and his departure to Switzerland in 1952, Los Angeles underwent major changes. Mann's time in L.A. was marked by massive structural urban change, the effects and the aftermath of World War II, and the unleashing of new industrial sectors that conflicted with an abundance of progressive ideas. With the aviation industry on the rise, a massive influx of wartime workers, and the Cold War on the horizon, the era was predestined for social tensions as well as infrastructural and political decisions that continue to impact the city.

The United States's entry in World War II in 1941 had made the greater L.A. area a hub for aircraft and ship manufacturing, given the proximity to the Pacific Ocean and the existing harbors. With many military facilities opening up, new industrial factories arising, and the booming Hollywood film industry, which proceeded full force into the production of anti-Nazi propaganda films, the Golden State emerged from the war as a major economic player. But this was at the cost of an especially paranoid atmosphere during the war, given the proximity of California's coast to Japan. After the attack on Pearl Harbor, many feared that an attack on California could be next. Prejudices, suspicion, and fear of Japanese, Germans, and Italians led to new repressions. The attack on Pearl Harbor was followed by an Executive Order 9066, which granted the U.S. War Department the right to "remove" people who were considered a danger in areas close to military facilities. The order laid the legal groundwork for the internment of thousands

Department of Justice notice directed towards aliens of German, Italian, and Japanese origin to apply for a certificate of identification

UNITED STATES DEPARTMENT OF JUSTICE

★

NOTICE TO ALIENS OF ENEMY NATIONALITIES

★ The United States Government requires all aliens of German, Italian, or Japanese nationality to apply at post offices nearest to their place of residence for a Certificate of Identification. Applications must be filed between the period February 9 through February 28, 1942. *Go to your postmaster today for printed directions.*

EARL G. HARRISON,
Special Assistant to the Attorney General.

FRANCIS BIDDLE,
Attorney General.

AVVISO

Il Governo degli Stati Uniti ordina a tutti gli stranieri di nazionalità Tedesca, Italiana e Giapponese di fare richiesta all' Ufficio Postale più prossimo al loro luogo di residenza per ottenere un Certificato d'Identità. Le richieste devono essere fatte entro il periodo che decorre tra il 9 Febbraio e il 28 Febbraio, 1942.
Andate oggi dal vostro Capo d'Ufficio Postale (Postmaster) per ricevere le istruzioni scritte.

BEKANNTMACHUNG

Die Regierung der Vereinigten Staaten von Amerika fordert alle Auslaender deutscher, italienischer und japanischer Staatsangehoerigkeit auf, sich auf das ihrem Wohnorte naheliegende Postamt zu begeben, um einen Personalausweis zu beantragen. Das Gesuch muss zwischen dem 9. und 28. Februar 1942 eingereicht werden.
Gehen Sie noch heute zu Ihrem Postmeister und verschaffen Sie sich die gedruckten Vorschriften.

敵國外人注意

日獨伊諸國ノ國籍ヲ有スル在留外人ハ
二月九日ヨリ二月二十八日マデノ間ニ其居所ニ近キ郵便局ニ行キ身分證明書ヲ申込ムベシ
合眾國政府ハ行李ス可シ
右證明書ヲ願フ様願フ尤モ

of people of mostly Japanese descent in desert camps such as Manzanar, two hundred miles north of Los Angeles, where more than 120,000 innocent Japanese Americans were incarcerated from March 1942 to November 1945. German and Italian exiles had to register as enemy aliens. They faced new curfews, and the already difficult process of acquiring visas and work permits became even harder. For German-Jewish refugees, this development was a slap in the face. Having escaped the death camps of Nazi Germany, they once again found themselves exposed to new exclusions and ostracized in a country that they considered a safe haven.

At the same time, people from all over the country were coming to California to find work in the booming war industry. Most of them settled and brought their families, leading to what some refer to as the "Second Gold Rush." The aviation industry, in particular, expanded its output with modern mass-production techniques, employing more than 280,000 workers by 1944 and producing airplanes faster than ever. The aviation industry had a major impact on L.A.'s architecture and geography, influencing the new architectural forms like the space age Googie style that became so iconic to the city. At the Los Angeles International Airport, the 1961 Theme Building, often compared to a four-legged flying saucer, remains one of the most popular examples of futuristic midcentury modern architecture. Entire neighborhoods such as Inglewood, Burbank, and Hawthorne emerged around the factories of aviation heavyweights like Douglas, Lockheed, and Northrop. Disney even designed fake rooftops to make factories look like suburban communities from the sky so that potential Japanese bombers couldn't recognize them from above. With many working-age men serving overseas in the war, many of these new jobs were occupied by women, which changed the economic fabric of California and transformed traditional gender roles. In just

Lockheed planes in front of their plant

two years, the number of female workers in California rose from 45,600 in 1941 to 182,800 in 1943.

As a German refugee and political thinker, Mann closely followed the war and California's involvement in it. In his diaries, he commented on military maneuvers and strategic decisions. Mann even played a small role in the war effort by helping advertise war bonds, which were used by the government to borrow money to bankroll military efforts. People could make loans to the government and, in exchange, were offered a return below the market rate. The promotion of these bonds was strongly linked to patriotic notions and the idea of defending democracy itself. Many of the exiles supported them. Albert Einstein donated the original manuscript of his theory of relativity for a war bond auction. Mann sold his manuscript of his lecture "The Coming Victory of Democracy" to raise money. On February 2, 1944, *Aufbau*, the newspaper for German-Jewish immigrants, reported: "$100,000 in War Bonds for Thomas Mann Manuscript. At the handing over of Thomas Mann's manuscript for 'The Coming Victory of Democracy' to the New York Public Library, in a small, impromptu ceremony outside the main entrance of the building, Marc van Doren, Orville Prescott (the *New York Times* book critic), Konrad Heiden, Erika Mann, and Stanley Isaacs, among others. An anonymous donor had subscribed $100,000 in War Bonds for the manuscript, which had been given to the 'Immigrants Victory Council' by the poet for auction." A text in support of war bonds titled *On War Saving Bonds* by son Golo was even printed on the back of the dust jacket of Mann's *Order of Day*: *Political Essays and Speeches of Two Decades* for the 1942 publication by Knopf.

In 1940s Los Angeles, the burgeoning Hollywood entertainment industry, aviation industry, and exploding real estate market worked together to create a new perception of the city that resonates to this day. But with the end of the war in 1945, L.A. was facing plenty of problems with infrastructure that came with a huge increase in population, the return of thousands of veterans, and an exponentially expanding economy. While the united efforts and patriotic ideologies of the war helped to hold together an urban society drifting apart, many of these problems rose to the surface in the late 1940s and early 1950s. City planners were thinking about how to design a city for an increasingly dense population, while at the same time building structural racism into the very fabric of the city, a system that divided and excluded nonwhite communities through the layout of highways and bridges. The Arroyo Seco Parkway opened in December 1940, connecting downtown Los Angeles with Pasadena, and while the massive highway development promised convenient car travel, it already heralded the end of L.A.'s comprehensive net of public transportation, the Pacific Electric Railway's famous Red Cars, in the 1950s. And while the developers still ceremoniously declared that the Santa Monica freeway would move commuters "from downtown to the beach in twenty minutes," Mann was already complaining about the terrible traffic in his diaries, and anyone who ever visited Los Angeles knows what he was talking about.

By the end of the 1940s, reactionary and progressive currents were at odds, sparked by ideas of unleashed, ever-increasing growth and the need for progressive solutions to the problems created by these very same developments in postwar L.A. Social housing initiatives, unions, and antiracist civil movements were in conflict with real estate developers and conservative business moguls who had different plans for the city. In anticipation of a housing crisis, architects such as the Austrian Richard Neutra pushed for social housing initiatives at Chavez Ravine and other locations, trying to apply the ideas of the Bauhaus, Adolf Loos's concept of modern design, and Frank Lloyd Wright's organic architecture to the brittle vegetation and vast geography of Southern California. Involved in many public housing projects throughout the 1930s and 1940s, L.A. was among the country's most progressive cities, with more than 4,250 social housing units built between 1940 and 1945. Neutra alone was involved in three different housing projects and built eight schools. He was especially interested in public buildings: the Corona Avenue School in Bell, in southeast L.A., revolutionized the design of public schools in 1934 and became the model for schools in Southern California. Dark, heavy brick buildings were replaced by open, L-shaped structures with classrooms connected by an outdoor hallway through glass sliding doors. Neutra and his fellow California modernists understood the problems associated with growing urban density and envisioned new concepts of urban living. Neutra was convinced that "high-density design could succeed in a fully human way." By combining and reconfiguring these ideas, they stripped the city's architecture of abundant ornaments and succeeded in creating the ideal of L.A. architecture in the hillsides of Hollywood and Beverly Hills: California modernism. But where they succeeded creatively, they failed politically: the fears stoked by McCarthyism in the late 1940s and early 1950s and the lobbying of private real estate ended most of the public housing projects. Groups like Citizens against Social Housing and the Lobby of California Real Estate Business attacked the projects, and most of the units were demolished to make room for private residential housing.

Even if Mann and Neutra had ideological disagreements, and Mann passed on Neutra's cubic "glass box style" for his own residence, it is fair to say that they were aligned on social democratic concepts. Neutra, his fellow Austrian Rudolph Schindler, and the German-Jewish architect J.R. Davidson had already landed in California by the 1920s, more than a decade before the great wave of émigrés arrived. Unlike the exiles, these California modernists were not mourning their home countries but were instead interested in becoming Californians themselves. Embracing their new home, Neutra and Davidson created an architectural style that has become synonymous with the state, and while the architects became more like California, in many ways California became like them; what we think of as California living would not be what it is today without the contributions of these European-born architects.

With the end of World War II came another massive cultural change: the so-called red scare and the beginning of McCarthyism. Once again, many of the same refugees who escaped Nazi Germany ten years earlier found themselves accused of being Communists by the government and anti-Communist propaganda groups. The steady increase of political repression over the late 1940s and the persecution of left-leaning authors, directors, actors, and intellectuals culminated early on in the process against the "Hollywood Ten"

Screenwriter and novelist Dalton Trumbo sits at HUAC hearing with his wife Cleo, as Bertolt Brecht looks on from behind, 1947

in 1947. The House Un-American Activities Committee (HUAC) accused seventy-nine individuals working in the film industry of inserting Communist propaganda into their films. Many did not prevail against the accusations and threats. Bertolt Brecht, accused by HUAC of being a member of the Communist Party on October 30, 1947, left for Paris the next morning. The philosopher and Frankfurt School founder Max Horkheimer found himself under FBI surveillance. Charlie Chaplin was denied reentry into the United States after promoting his film *Limelight* in London. He left L.A. for Switzerland in 1952. That same year the Manns decided they could no longer endure the atmosphere of fear and suspicion. Even though Mann never considered himself a Communist, his support for social democracy and humanitarian values as a public intellectual brought him dangerously close to those no longer welcome in the City of Angels.

All of these issues were of primary importance to Mann. Although living at a distance from many of these problems in the sheltered and somewhat detached suburb of Pacific Palisades, he was still involved and engaged in the city's affairs, and regularly participated in the infrastructure of a city in transition.

LOS ANGELES FREEWAYS
Los Angeles County
Josh Widera

It may be surprising to find Thomas Mann, the eminent representative of German language and culture, sliding into Anglicism in his own diaries. In fact, the journals of his American years are sprinkled with English words and phrases. Considering that he continued to produce fiction and essayistic work of the highest quality in German and never neglected his native language, these are probably not merely inadvertent lapses into colloquialism. They are literary *amuse-bouches*. Thomas Mann relished the delectations of a foreign tongue.

There are two words in particular that the author of *Buddenbrooks* Anglicizes during his time in Los Angeles: *traffic* and *highway*. Both terms can be found in German in his diaries (*Verkehr* and *Autobahn*, respectively) on numerous occasions, but only during the Manns' time in California are they referred to in English. On Friday, August 30, 1940, Mann wrote: "Then drove to the Bowl concert with Eva Hermann. Horrible Traffic (*Schrecklicher Traffic*)." It seems that this reference to traffic, heightened by the capital letter that is ordinary grammar for German nouns, shines a light on how he thought of traffic in Los Angeles as a phenomenon. It is not simply *schrecklicher Verkehr* but explicitly "Traffic," something exalted to the level of an institution, an event, a particular. Despite traveling widely throughout the United States, he used these loanwords only when discussing Los Angeles. This suggests that there is something special about it, characteristic of and exclusive to the city. Most Angelenos today would probably still share this sentiment. After all, their preoccupation with traffic is both renowned and ridiculed across the nation. The identification of Los Angeles with severe congestion and commuting times culminates in the city's local soccer derby, games between the L.A. Galaxy and Los Angeles Football Club that are nicknamed *El Tráfico,* a play on the *El Clásico* rivalry between the Real Madrid and Barcelona soccer clubs.

The second word Thomas Mann borrows from English is "highway." Having been invited to a dinner party at the director William Dieterle's on September 13, 1941, the Manns drove with Bruno and Liesl Frank "via the new Highway." Back then, freeways were a novelty: the Arroyo Seco Parkway, the oldest freeway in the United States, opened in December 1940, connecting downtown with the city of Pasadena. The second oldest, the Hollywood Freeway, was already being constructed, and its first section, the Cahuenga Pass Parkway, preceded Arroyo Seco with an opening ceremony on June 15, 1940. As the Franks were living in Beverly Hills and the Dieterles near the Hollywood Reservoir, Mann was undoubtedly referring to this section of road, passing the Hollywood Bowl and climbing the Cahuenga Pass into the San Fernando Valley.

Mann's admiration for this new type of infrastructure shines through in his diaries. In October 1948, he noted: "Frido is proud of his accurate (hair) parting, straight as a highway." Clearly, the novelist held some amount of awe for this new type of road and the feat of civil engineering behind it, praising its almost mathematical attributes and linearity as an aesthetic achievement that he compares to his favorite grandson's haircut. Mann's interest was not unwarranted. In 1940, the freeway project was a massive achievement: to construct the two-mile stretch of the Cahuenga freeway cost one and a half million dollars, equal to almost thirty million in 2022. These projects were a response to the city's rapidly increasing population, sprawling growth, and soft spot for the automobile. The idea of the freeway was heavily promoted by the Automobile Club of Southern California in its 1937 "Traffic Survey." The idea to have roads exclusively for cars was radical and strange. Public pushback was immense. In fact, the Hollywood Anti-Parkway League called the proposed freeways in 1940 "un-American." Nothing could seem more far-fetched from today's vantage point.

Though public protest and concern were somewhat successful in the case of the Hollywood Freeway, where mostly white, wealthy, and influential homeowners succeeded in wrestling concessions from the city when it came to route planning, relocation, and noise concerns in their neighborhoods, other constituents were not as lucky. In the three decades that followed, freeways in Los Angeles routinely split communities in half, lowered living standards and home values, and demolished entire neighborhoods. Working-class and nonwhite areas on the eastside suffered most, where local objections did not prevent the building of more than half a dozen highways until the 1960s. These three decades of freeway construction saw the city of Los Angeles displace over 250,000 of its citizens.

When Mann witnessed the construction of the Hollywood Freeway in the 1940s, these developments were only just beginning. The Cahuenga Pass still featured train tracks for the streetcars of the Pacific Electric Railway, marking its role as a waypoint in L.A.'s development. But use of the Red Cars, which had formed the largest electric railway system in the world just twenty years earlier, was already on the decline, and no other motorways were incorporating them. Today, only the metal bolts in Barnham Bridge—just a few yards away from Dieterle's former home on Knoll Drive—serve as reminders of the public railway that once shared the Hollywood Freeway with automobiles. They anchored the trolleys' overhead guiding lines more than seventy years ago. The tracks were out of service by the 1950s and removed in 1952 as a new era of urban mobility began in Los Angeles. The era we know today: unthinkable without its highways and its traffic.

HOUSING CRISIS
Chavez Ravine
Nikolai Blaumer

The need for social housing concepts and solutions is an ever-present issue for the city of Los Angeles. On May 20, 1952, Thomas Mann noted in his diary: "'Daily News' publication on the scandalous slum housing in Los Angeles. Houses occupied by large families with children, living in one room for $45 a month. The owner lives in Hollywood. Huge cash outlays for armaments and external power while bills for housing improvements are voted down." The entry refers to the "Public Housing War," which took place in Los Angeles in 1952 and 1953.

During World War II, tens of thousands of families, many of them African American, had moved to Los Angeles to work in ports and in the defense industry. Historians Richard Rothstein, Don Parson, and others point out that the city built public housing primarily in white-dominated neighborhoods. At the time, the Housing Authority chairman stated bluntly, "the Authority selects its residents by following the previous racial pattern of the neighborhoods in which [projects] are located." In the postwar years, though, the authorities changed their approach and instead exercised a nondiscrimination policy. But this did not last long. Public housing became part of the political culture war at the height of the McCarthy era. The real estate lobby mobilized supporters and warned of the alleged Communist dangers of public housing.

A racially integrated project in centrally located Chavez Ravine became the litmus test. Until the postwar years, this was home to generations of Mexican Americans. The Federal Housing Act of 1949, part of President Harry Truman's so-called Fair Deal, motivated Los Angeles city officials to build thousands of affordable housing units in Chavez Ravine. Legal scholar Matt Parlow and others have described how virtually the entire neighborhood was displaced by eminent domain in 1952 and 1953. In its place was to emerge a project designed by the famous Austrian architect Richard Neutra—an acquaintance of Mann's—called Elysian Park Heights. Shortly before construction was to begin, the city council convened a meeting and halted the project. When the California Supreme Court overturned that decision, the city council organized a referendum. Voters overwhelmingly rejected public housing. The already prepared, depopulated land was sold to build Dodger Stadium.

The problems of non-affordable accommodation, eviction brought on by gentrification, and a lack of social housing persist and are even worse today. The Skid Row district, close to L.A.'s downtown, has become a symbol of the rampant growth of homelessness in the city dating back to the 1930s. Skid Row contains one of the largest stable populations of people experiencing homelessness in the United States. Its long history of structural racism, police raids, targeted city initiatives, and advocacy makes it one of the most notable districts in the city.

But there are also positive examples that endure. One of the first housing projects in the city was Ramona Gardens, which broke ground in 1939. Acclaimed architects including Frank Lloyd Wright formed Housing Architects Associated, which was responsible for the design of this first public housing development, located in the Boyle Heights neighborhood. From its beginnings, the project gave shelter to families from diverse backgrounds. Jewish residents started the racially and economically integrated Heights Cooperative Nursery School for Ramona Gardens children in 1949. It was situated nearby at the Jewish Cultural Center in City Terrace until the widening of Interstate 10 required it to be moved in 1969. The project still serves as a home for mostly Latino families today.

Ramona Gardens, Los Angeles, 1941

RICHARD NEUTRA
2300 Silver Lake Boulevard
Heike Catherina Mertens

Ten years before Thomas Mann moved into his newly built home on San Remo Drive, in 1932, the renowned architect Richard Neutra celebrated the completion of his spectacular residential and office building on Silver Lake Boulevard, which was to make architectural history as the "VDL Research House."

Neutra, born in Vienna in 1892 as the son of

assimilated Jews whose friends included Sigmund and Martha Freud and the composer Arnold Schoenberg, studied architecture at the Technical University of Vienna from 1911 to 1918—interrupted by his military service as an artillery lieutenant in Albania and Serbia. It is said that he was only eight years old when he decided to become an architect upon seeing the subway stations designed by Otto Wagner. He admired Adolf Loos and his ideal of leaving out everything superfluous and using undecorated materials. As early as 1914, Neutra familiarized himself with the groundbreaking work of Frank Lloyd Wright, for whom he would work for three months in Chicago in 1924.

Even more than his architectural idols, Neutra's views of life and of the interplay between man, architecture, and nature were influenced by Wilhelm Wundt, the cofounder of the field of experimental psychology. Neutra studied Wundt's *Grundzüge der physiologischen Psychologie* (*Principles of Physiological Psychology*, published in 1874) and became interested in research on physical sensations and "the physical foundations of the life of the soul." Equally formative was his first employment in 1919 with Gustav Ammann, an important Swiss garden and landscape architect whose approach involved extending architecture into the surrounding space. It was here that Neutra gained knowledge of plants, trees, and garden design, and it was here that the foundation was laid for his relationship to nature, which he would later call "biorealism," the "inherent and inseparable relationship between man and nature."

After working in the municipal planning and building office in Luckenwalde and with the architect Erich Mendelsohn in Berlin, Neutra and his wife, Dione, immigrated to the United States in 1923. After stints in New York and Chicago, the Neutras in 1925 moved cross-country and into a separate apartment in Rudolf and Pauline Schindler's house on North Kings Road in Los Angeles. The two architects successfully collaborated for five years until rivalries led to their separation. Between 1927 and 1929, Neutra built Lovell Health House, the first American residential home with a steel frame, and in 1932 he was the only architect from the West Coast to be invited to the legendary exhibition *Modern Architecture: International Exhibition* at the Museum of Modern Art in New York. The same year, he opened his own office on Silver Lake Boulevard in Los Angeles, which to this day is open to architecture students as a research and workshop center.

Neutra and Mann probably met at a soiree at the home of the Austrian novelist Vicki Baum on April 6, 1938. Mann must have enjoyed the evening, for he noted in his diary: "Almost only German-speaking guests. The architect Neutra, the comedian, musician, actor, Dr. Klemperer, Schoenberg etc. Long conversation before dinner. Buffet dinner. Finally Bali film with male youths in ritual trance. Twitchings.—The beautiful young Indian dancer."

While Neutra, the conductor Otto Klemperer, and Schoenberg had already gained a firm foothold in Los Angeles, the Manns had yet to "immigrate." In the days that followed, they planned the necessary steps and explored the city. In his diaries, Mann noted that he was impressed by the beautiful coastal road and the richly furnished homes of the who's who to which he and Katia were invited. He enjoyed Easter Sunday evening with "plenty of champagne" in the company of the Hollywood star Madeleine Carroll and the theater luminary Max Reinhardt at the villa of the director Ernst Lubitsch, who had been making successful Hollywood movies since 1923. Whether Neutra was among the guests courting Mann's favor remains uncertain. But on April 18, 1938, a "warm summer day," the Manns went on a late morning excursion with Dione and Richard, as Mann noted: "I wrote rather easily but not for long, since we had to go out with the architect Neutra and his wife to see houses. Cubic glass box style, unpleasant."

Quite obviously, the excursion was not entirely voluntary. At this point, the Manns did not have any plans to move or to build a house in Los Angeles. The desire to relocate from Princeton to the West Coast did not arise until the "palm summer" of 1940, when there was a downright éclat between Neutra and Mann. During another party at Baum's, the writer is said to have exclaimed: "Get that Neutra off my back!"

How did this clash of giants arise? If one considers their headstrong characters—one arguably the most important German writer of the twentieth century, the other perhaps the most important representative and cofounder of American modernism—it is not surprising that these two alpha males did not warm to each other. Unlike J.R. Davidson, who was to receive the commission for Mann's house in Pacific Palisades one year later, the highly confident Neutra would hardly have allowed any meddling in his designs. More important, perhaps, is the fact that Neutra's concept of a translucent architecture, where interior and exterior spaces flow into each other and where the rooms are proportioned in relation to the human figure, did not at all correspond to Mann's idea of a domestic domicile that was both representative of and isolated from the outside world. It is easy to picture Mann wrinkling his nose as he entered Neutra's residential and office building on Silver Lake Boulevard, finding himself in front of a narrow staircase leading upward instead of a spacious foyer. Typical of Neutra, the rooms are conceived as a series of rather small, nested minimalist boxes and equipped with numerous built-in closets made of waxed fiberboard without any handles. The furniture is rectilinear, and folding glass doors and floor-to-ceiling mirrors extend the view into the garden and onto the lake, which in 1938 still touched the property, so that the water surfaces were reflected in the glass walls. This ostentatiously open architectural language was a far cry from the traditional brick aesthetic of the villa that the Manns had built in 1913 in Munich's Bogenhausen neighborhood. Despite biographical parallels and their shared *Bildungsbürger* (middle-class) background, the aesthetic preferences of the two could not have been more different.

For all their successes in the 1930s, Neutra and Mann had a pecuniary commonality: Neutra was only able to build his residential and office building with the help of a no-interest loan from the Dutch philanthropist and psychiatrist Cornelis Hendrik van der Leeuw (Neutra thanked him by choosing van der Leeuw's initials, "VDL," as the name for his house). In 1941, the Manns were able to build on San Remo Drive because Thomas's patron Agnes E. Meyer, the wife of the owner of the Washington Post, guaranteed the mortgage.

Even though the two did not get along personally, Mann appreciated the master architect, at least intellectually. In 1954, he read Neutra's manuscript "Survival through Design." But the fact that Neutra, through his furniture, has found his way into Mann's fully refurbished home in Pacific Palisades, which since 2018 has been used as a residency center of the Federal Republic of Germany, would probably not have pleased the Magician.

Neutra VDL Studio, August 2018

J.R. DAVIDSON
548 South Barrington Avenue
Lilian Pfaff

Thomas and Katia Mann commissioned the architect J.R. Davidson to design their San Remo home in the Pacific Palisades, most likely because his quiet and considerate demeanor was in sharp contrast to the two other renowned European émigré architects of the moment, Richard Neutra and Rudolf Schindler. The Manns wanted a collaborative process, something that seemed possible with Davidson—not with Schindler, and definitely not with Neutra. A modernist of note, by the time he met the Manns Davidson already had made a name for himself renovating movie star haunts such as the Cocoanut Grove nightclub at the Ambassador Hotel and the fire-ravaged Sardi's restaurant. He understood the world of celebrities as well as what it meant to be an exile living in Los Angeles. He was a match for Thomas and Katia Mann.

Julius Ralph Davidson was born in Berlin to a Jewish family—a British father and German mother—who raised him to speak both English and German. After the death of his parents, he moved to Posen, in what is now Poland, and constantly drew his surroundings. Chastised for sketching a Polish soldier, he was suspended from school and eventually left without graduating, a story he told on several occasions. Though he dreamed of becoming an artist, his uncle encouraged him to work as an apprentice for a furniture maker, Moritz Hirschler. That experience helped him earn a living while he studied independently in Berlin. He later traveled to London and Paris, where he worked for interior designers, furniture makers, and architects. Every job influenced his future work; he learned the nuances of architecture, style, and color. He had followed his future wife, Grete, to Paris, where she was offered a job at the House of Lanvin and he was surrounded by fashion and art deco. After World War I, Davidson opened his first architecture office, designing building renovations for other architects of note, including Bruno Paul. In 1919, while he and Grete lived in the attic apartment of the home of the famed German publisher Ernst Wasmuth, he redesigned its interior in the Biedermeier mode.

Postwar inflation convinced the Davidsons it was time to move to the United States. They arrived in Los Angeles in 1923. Davidson immediately contacted Kem Weber, a colleague from Bruno Paul's office, who was working in the city as an architect and interior designer. The thirty-six-year-old Davidson then met the celebrated architect Robert D. Farquhar, with whom he worked for several months, and also got jobs doing film sets for various film studios.

Four years after reaching the West Coast, Davidson opened his own office on West 7th Street. His work on several art deco storefronts, plus his trendsetting indirect-light installations and elegant store-window designs, attracted the attention of the architectural press, which led to the Cocoanut Grove and Sardi's projects, as well as numerous single-family home commissions for Hollywood clientele, including the home of composer Herbert Stothart. By 1930, he was one of the leading representatives of California modernism. His work was included in two important exhibitions that focused on California architecture, one at Los Angeles's Academy of Modern Art in 1929 and Pauline Schindler's exhibition the following year, *Creative Architecture in California*.

For two years during the Great Depression, J.R. and Grete sheltered their seven-year-old son Tom with Kem Weber and his family in Ojai while they worked on hotel and bar renovations in Chicago. Once the Davidsons returned to Los Angeles, Weber introduced them to the Schindlers and Neutras, resulting in a lifelong friendship between Grete and Dione Neutra.

The architect formed many client relationships with the Jewish and European émigré communities; the connection to Mann came through either Scheyer or Heinrich Mann, whom Davidson apparently already had met. After Thomas hired Davidson, Neutra erupted in anger: "Why settle for less—when you can get the best?," a comment that undoubtedly confirmed for Mann that he'd made the right decision. Davidson, whose work was always overshadowed by his highly publicized "friend," had been the architect that many would-be Neutra clients turned to when rejected by "the best." The Joseph Kingsley House was one of the best examples of a Neutra reject turned Davidson masterpiece.

Davidson and Mann had a harmonious collaboration. In his diary, Mann wrote: "At noon, drove to the architect Davidson, who behaved sympathetically and reasonably" (April 18, 1941). Although their friend Paul Huldschinsky was responsible for the interior design, Davidson, accompanied by contractor Ernest Schlesinger, and Mann discussed the color of the floors, walls, and ceilings extensively as well as the lighting, which Mann called the *"neumodische Esszimmer-Licht"*—new fashion dining room light (February 10, 1942). Mann especially appreciated the little stair from his study to his spacious bedroom. Grete and J.R. were invited to tea on many occasions, and even if there was much debate about the costs of the building, their connection to Mann was always cordial.

After completing the house on San Remo, Davidson designed three Case Study Houses for the famed project of *Arts and Architecture* magazine. His were Case Study Houses No. 1, No. 11, and No. 15, though they were not completed in that order. Davidson's vision for No. 1, with its open floor plan and multipurpose rooms, became a hallmark for most of the Case Study Houses that followed. In all, Davidson created more than fifty houses in Los Angeles and Ojai either on his own or with the help of his son Tom.

Later in life, Davidson rarely mentioned the Mann house, possibly to maintain the privacy of the famous writer or perhaps because he did not approve of Huldschinsky's interior design. Though at the time Davidson was always mentioned alongside Neutra and Schindler, his work long went unnoticed, as Davidson was not one to promote himself. Finally, he received his due when Esther McCoy included him in her book *The Second Generation* with Gregory Ain and Raphael Soriano, though his age, education, and architectural background actually placed him within the "first generation" of modernists.

UNION STATION
800 North Alameda Street
Nikolai Blaumer

In the first years of his American exile, Thomas Mann was constantly on the move. From New York to Ottawa, to Austin, Minneapolis, Seattle, and Los Angeles, all in all, he gave ninety lectures across North America. The aim was to convince Americans to form a united front against Nazi Germany.

In April 1939, before the Manns moved to Los Angeles, *Life* magazine ran an eclectically illustrated piece on the German writer and his lecture tours: "His new home in exile is this fine rented house in Princeton, N.J. But he is away lecturing two months of the year." The article not only mentions the preparation for his speeches and his fight against National Socialism but also details of the Manns' life as travelers: "Nine walking sticks help him enjoy his only exercise. (...) After their meals on lecture tours, the Manns enjoy a scotch and soda or apricot brandy. Mrs. Mann lays the drinks out on the dresser, alongside Dr. Mann's slippers."

Mann traveled often by train, accompanied mostly by Katia and daughter Erika. In one of his earlier literary works, *Railway Accident*, he confessed, "I like to travel in comfort, especially when I'm paid." This was all the more true because the family struggled with the distances in the United States. The Manns, of course, traveled first class, preferably on the best trains of the time, those luxurious long-distance trains that ran between the West Coast and Chicago and bore illustrious names like "The Streamliner," "Heart of Gold" or "Super Chief."

Mann had a special soft spot for the "City of Los Angeles" train, a kind of luxury hotel on wheels. The train ran from 1936 to 1971 between Chicago and

L.A.. It was outfitted for weight and aerodynamics, with a massive grilled nose. Since only one train was available for the route, service was initially limited to one trip per week. In the following years, additional streamliners were purchased so that the line could run every third day. With eighteen cars, the train was the longest in the Union Pacific fleet. The highlight of the train was the "dome diner" offering a panoramic view under a glass dome. There were also observation cars with their own attendants.

Despite all these amenities, the "*Reiserei*" (traveling) was quite arduous. Sometimes Mann only had a few hours between arrival and departure. On March 27, 1941, he wrote in his diary about his arrival at Union Station: "Yesterday evening, 6 p.m. arrival in Los Angeles in a very damaged condition. No one at the station. Taxi to luxury Hotel Ambassador." Mann, Katia, and his brother Heinrich made their way to the sold-out Wilshire Ebell Theatre. After Mann's lecture, the reception, and five hours of sleep, they continued on to the next stop on the tour, San Francisco.

The iconic Union Station building was the linchpin for many of Mann's travels. It was completed in 1939, a year before the Manns moved to Los Angeles. Built in a mix of Spanish Colonial and art deco, it is one of the last major train stations to be built in the United States. Even though Mann began traveling less often in 1944, Union Station remained central to his and Katia's lives. Above all, it remained the hub for the numerous visits of friends and family.

On May 24, 1945, the joyfully received news of the death of Reichsführer SS Heinrich Himmler reached Mann in the garden of Union Station. As described in his diaries, Mann allowed himself a small celebration in the station shortly before boarding his beloved streamliner to Chicago.

The "City of Los Angeles," 1936

THE AIRPORTS OF LOS ANGELES

Benno Herz

On August 18, 1939, Thomas Mann made an entry in his diary about a flight from Zurich to London:

Woke up today at 3.47 a.m. in Zurich. Heavy fog. Tea for breakfast and got ready. Golo escorted us. Took a cab to train station, then Swiss Air omnibus. Visitations. Farewell to Golo. By bus to the airport. Long wait there. Takeoff in the large aluminum apparatus with 3/4 hour delay. Ascent at 3/4 10 o'clock. Flight to Basel, layover. Then to high altitude, over the fogs, 2,500 meters. White-soft cloudscape under the light blue. Above calm, fast ride. Efficient Swiss stewardess. 12 o'clock lunch: bouillon and ham sandwich. Cigarettes. Just a touch of excitement in my heart. Over the channel, small steam boats on it, the English coast as geographic relief. Arrival in London, bumping down through the cloud layer. Landing. Moni with Lanyi waving from the terrace.

Mann's poetic description is just one of many accounts of his devotion to the little details in aviation, and may call to mind the work of the French pilot and author Antoine de Saint-Exupéry. These and other anecdotes from Mann's diaries hint at his ambivalent fascination with aviation. During his time in the United States, Mann and his family flew frequently. For many of their trips, lecture tours, and visits, they chose planes over trains to cover the vast distances of the country.

In the 1940s, there were already three major airports in Los Angeles County connecting the growing city with the world: Hollywood Burbank Airport, then known as Lockheed Air Terminal; Grand Central Airport, in Glendale; and today's Los Angeles International Airport (LAX). The story of

LAX began in the mid-1920s, when the Los Angeles City Council and the Chamber of Commerce understood that L.A. needed its own airport due to the rapidly growing aviation industry. A 640-acre piece of land in the neighborhood of Westchester, known as Mines Field and formerly used to grow wheat and beans, was leased by the city and the Department of Airports in August 1928. On October 1, 1928, the airport officially opened. The first building on the new airfield, Hangar No. 1, is still in use today. Soon the sand runways were replaced with granite, and more hangars, restaurants, and a tower were built. By 1930, the airport was known as the Los Angeles Municipal Airport. Though the city was hoping to make it the main hub for the greater Los Angeles area, the airlines had yet to be convinced. At that time the airport in Burbank was more established, and most of the major airlines were operating from there or Glendale's Central Airport. Commercial civil aviation slowed during World War II, and by 1942 the military was in charge of the municipal airport. Flying schools for pilots and the production of aircraft were in high demand. After the war, commercial airlines services increased in December 1946, and in 1949 the airport was renamed Los Angeles International Airport. Further developments followed, and by the 1960s the airport already had eight passenger terminals.

Mann did not mention airports by name in his diaries, so it is hard to determine which one he used most frequently. Los Angeles Municipal Airport was probably among them, but it is also very likely that he departed from Burbank or Glendale, since Burbank was the biggest hub at the time; by 1939, sixteen airlines a day were departing from there. Historic accounts of this airport can be confusing, as it underwent many name changes: United Airport (1930–1934), Union Air Terminal (1934–1940), Lockheed Air Terminal (1940–1967), Hollywood Burbank Airport (1967–1978), Burbank-Glendale-Pasadena Airport (1978–2003), and finally Bob Hope Airport starting in 2003. In 2017, it was renamed Hollywood Burbank Airport.

Built in 1920, the Grand Central Airport in Glendale also played an important role in L.A.'s aviation history. The terminal was designed by the architect Henry L. Gogerty, who envisioned it as a train station by combining art deco and Spanish Colonial revival influences. The airfield closed in 1959 and was sold to the Walt Disney Company in 1997. The terminal is now listed on the National Register of Historic Places and is home to Disney's Grand Central Creative Campus.

Air travel in Mann's time was not nearly as safe as it was just a few decades later. This might explain why the Nobel Prize winner had a bit of a dark interest in the dangers of aviation. On January 13, 1947, he noted, "Cool, half sunny weather. — Always new airplane disasters and hotel fires." Reading his diaries, one cannot help but find a macabre fascination with airplane crashes; he commented on many accidents that he heard about in the media. One

could almost read some kind of obsession into these entries, which oddly always began with a benign description of the weather before leading up to a horrible remark about a plane crash. "Half overcast, cool / Murders and dismemberments accumulate like airplane disasters. Newspapers, crudely sensationalized, arouse the image of neglect. — Began to write on Nietzsche" (February 17, 1947). "Very warm weather. Flies. (...) Walked Amalfi Drive all the way down. Depressed by inactivity, suffering. (...) Radio: plane wrecked in Atlantic at high seas with many passengers, small children. Rescue ships damaged. 2/3 of the victims rescued so far." Perhaps Mann was reading too much Nietzsche? Interestingly, the German word for flies, *Fliegen*, meaning the insect, which Mann uses in this entry from August 14, 1947, also means "flying." Remarks like "Overcast, cool. Terrible plane accident, engine fire, emergency landing, explosion, death of over 40 people" (June 18, 1948) make it hard to believe that Mann actually enjoyed flying himself, but he did. His diaries are filled with descriptions of beautiful cloud formations, beer and ham sandwiches heartily eaten in the sky, and friendly flight attendants.

Among his typical flight routes were the connections between L.A. and Berkeley, Oakland, and Chicago. For his trips to Europe, Mann still relied on ships—even though he complained incessantly about the uncomfortable accommodations on the trips. Transatlantic flights had been available since the late 1930s, but broader civil aviation was interrupted by World War II. Postwar, more runways became available and carriers such as TWA, Trans Canada Airlines, and Pan Am started offering frequent transatlantic flights to civilian passengers, with layovers in Gander, Newfoundland, or Shannon, Ireland. By 1946, Pan Am was flying from New York's LaGuardia to London's Hurn (now known as Bournemouth Airport) five days a week. The average length of an Atlantic crossing was about eighteen hours, and the equipment was usually Douglas's DC-4 or Lockheed's Constellation model. Mann's first mention of a transatlantic flight was on October 1, 1951, returning from Europe. He flew Swiss Airlines from Zurich to Geneva with layovers in Shannon and Gander, terminating in New York. It is remarkable how much his descriptions mirror modern-day air travel:

> Departure. Rain. Excellent care. Feeling of confidence. The stewardess was a famous yodeler. Descent in Geneva. Evening in Shannon, Ireland. Tea & port wine. In the plane good dinner with beer and coffee.
> 8 hours to Newfoundland, which passed quickly, since I was able to sleep in the chair almost excellently. There, in the well-known Gander, about 9 o'clock breakfast, oat meal and coffee. After an hour, onward flight. Desolated swamp and pool landscapes, empty and useless (...). In Gander very cold. The day brightened blue. Flew over illuminated sea of clouds. Four hours to go. Resetting of the clocks. On the plane a second breakfast with coffee. Arrival at New York airport. There most unpleasant hours of rapid journeys: Overcrowding of the customs office, scattering of luggage, dragging, waiting. The boarder [sic] control was harmless.

Los Angeles Municipal Airport, 1930

ABOUT THE AUTHORS

Nikolai Blaumer was program director at the Thomas Mann House, Los Angeles, from its opening in 2018 until May 2022. He studied at Ludwig Maximilian University of Munich (LMU) and Hebrew University of Jerusalem. Blaumer earned a doctorate in philosophy from LMU with his dissertation, *Korrektive Gerechtigkeit. Über die Entschädigung historischen Unrechts* (Campus Verlag, 2015), and has taught at Ludwig Maximilian University, Bauhaus University Weimar as well as at University of California, Los Angeles. Since 2014, he has been working for the Goethe-Institut's Department of Culture. He is coeditor of the book *Teilen und Tauschen* (S. Fischer Verlag, 2017).

Benno Herz is project manager at the Thomas Mann House, Los Angeles, and was named interim program director in the spring of 2022. Prior to this, he studied theater, film, and media at Goethe University Frankfurt, where completed his M.A. with a focus on digital aesthetics and interface theory. Since 2009, he has been creatively engaged in several music and film projects as a writer and instrumentalist. He is lead singer of the band Okta Logue, which has played with Neil Young & Crazy Horse and Portugal. The Man, and has performed at international festivals such as SXSW. In 2021 and 2022, Herz taught a digital humanities class on European exile at University of California, Los Angeles.

ABOUT THE CONTRIBUTORS

Helmut K. Anheier is a senior professor of sociology at the Hertie School, Berlin, and a member of UCLA''s Luskin School of Public Affairs. He has published widely and received various international awards for his scholarship. He is currently working on governance and cultural affairs, and is founding editor-in-chief of the journal *Global Perspectives*.

Sylvia Asmus is the head of the German Exile Archive 1933–1945 at the German National Library. She is an exhibition curator and has published on German exiles, including German-speaking exiles in Brazil, Soma Morgenstern and Joseph Roth. Asmus is also a member of the scientific advisory boards of the Society for Exile Research and the International Joseph Roth Society.

Tobias Boes is the chair of the Department of German and Russian Languages and Literatures at the University of Notre Dame. His research focuses on the circulation of German culture in the world, and on the question of how German national identity is shaped by global forces. In his most recent and critically acclaimed book *Thomas Mann's War: Literature, Politics, and the World Republic of Letters*, he traces how Thomas Mann became one of America's most prominent anti-Fascists.

Anthony Caldwell is an artist, photographer, and the associate director of the Digital Research Consortium at the University of California, Los Angeles. His work focuses on architecture and architectural history, as well as architectural communication and visualization. Caldwell partners with organizations to preserve the historic theater district in downtown Los Angeles.

Adrian Daub is a critic and professor of comparative literature and German studies at Stanford University. He has published on the intersection of literature, music, philosophy, and social norms in the nineteenth century, including works such as on Richard Wagner, early feminism, Charlie Chaplin, and literary scandals. He wrote the introduction to the book *The "Doctor Faustus" Dossier: Arnold Schoenberg, Thomas Mann, and Their Contemporaries, 1930–1951* and is also the co-host of the podcast *The Feminist Present*.

Heinrich Detering is a poet, professor, and chair of modern German and comparative literary studies at the University of Göttingen. He heads the Thomas Mann Research Center in Göttingen and is the co-editor of the *Große kommentierte Frankfurter Ausgabe*, a compilation of the works, letters, and diaries of Thomas Mann. He is the author of the book *Thomas Mann's American Religion: Theology, Politics and Literature in California Exile*. Detering was a Fellow at the Thomas Mann House, Los Angeles, in 2018.

Jaimey Fisher is the director of the Davis Humanities Institute and a professor of German, and cinema and digital media at the University of California, Davis. He has published on German cinema, politics, and culture after the Second World War. He most recently published his book *German Ways of War: The Affective Geographies and Generic Transformations of German War Films* (Rutgers, 2022).

Claudia Suhr Gordon holds a PhD in Egyptology from the University of Göttingen. She served as director of Villa Aurora from 2002 to 2007 and resumed the position in 2020. In this capacity, she has organized a variety of programs designed to keep the exiles' spirit of cultural interchange alive and commemorate their significant contributions to American culture.

Glen Gray is a PhD candidate in the German program at Johns Hopkins University. He researches the relationship between music and literature from the eighteenth to the twentieth century, with an emphasis on Schiller, Kleist, Mozart, Richard Wagner, and Arnold Schoenberg.

Jeffrey L. High is a professor and section chair of German Studies at California State University, Long Beach. His research focuses on literary, philosophical, and theoretical texts from the eighteenth through the twentieth century as well as their precursors and legacies.

Lily E. Hirsch is a musicologist, writer, and visiting scholar at California State University, Bakersfield. She has published on music during the Nazi era as well as music in criminal law. Most recently she published the book *Weird Al: Seriously*, an examination of the music of the American entertainer "'Weird Al'" Yankovic.

Morten Høi Jensen is a literary critic and the author of *A Difficult Death: The Life and Work of Jens Peter Jacobsen*. His reviews have appeared in such publications, such as the *New York Review of Books*, the *Los Angeles Review of Books*, and the *Wall Street Journal*. He is currently working on a book about Thomas Mann's *The Magic Mountain*.

Jan-Christopher Horak is the retired director of the UCLA Film and Television Archive, and a former UCLA professor of film studies. He is an adjunct professor at Chapman University. His publications focus on German exile Cinema and avant-garde cinema, including such figures as Saul Bass and Helmar Lerski. Horak's text "The Palm Trees Were Gently Swaying: German Refugees from Hitler in Hollywood" is among his seminal publications about German-Jewish émigrés in Hollywood.

Rembert Hüser is a professor of media studies at Goethe University, Frankfurt. His work focuses on film and media studies, the history of science, cultural studies, and contemporary art and architecture, including architectural models and the reenactment of found photographs in the artist Mike Kelley's work *Educational Complex* (1995). He is particularly interested in the rhetoric of scholarly writing.

Noah Isenberg is a professor and chair of the Department of Radio-Television-Film at the University of Texas at Austin. His research focuses on Weimar cinema and exile directors such as Edgar G. Ulmer and Billy Wilder. His most recent book *We'll Always Have "'Casablanca'": The Life, Legend, and Afterlife of Hollywood's Most Beloved Movie* was a *Los Angeles Times* bestseller.

David Jenemann is a professor and dean of the Honors College at the University of Vermont. He has published widely on intellectual and cultural history and the history of the mass media. He is the author of the books *Adorno in America* and *Simply Adorno*, as well as a cultural history of baseball gloves.

David Kaplan is assistant professor of piano performance and music at the University of California, Los Angeles. He has appeared as a soloist with numerous orchestras, including the Britten Sinfonia and the Sinfonie Orchester Berlin. Kaplan has performed recitals at the Ravinia Festival, Highland Park, Illinois; the Sarasota Opera House, Florida; the National Gallery of Art, Washington, D.C.; and Strathmore music center, in Baltimore.

Stefan Keppler-Tasaki is a professor of modern German literature at the University of Tokyo. He has published on German émigré writers in Zurich, Paris, and Los Angeles and their engagement with film and radio. His work focuses on German writing on Hollywood and on the transpacific relations between China, Japan, and the United States. In 2019, he was a Fellow at the Thomas Mann House, Los Angeles.

David D. Kim is a professor in the Department of European Languages and Transcultural Studies and the associate vice provost of the International Institute at UCLA. His latest publications include, among others, *Reframing Postcolonial Studies: Concepts, Methodologies, Scholarly Activisms* (Palgrave Macmillan, 2021) and *Globalgeschichten der deutschen Literatur* (J. B. Metzler Verlag, 2022).

William Kinderman is a professor and chair of performance studies at the University of California, Los Angeles. He is a concert pianist, a chamber musician, and an international expert on Ludwig van Beethoven. His publications include books on Mozart, Richard Wagner, and the creative process in music. He most recently published *Beethoven: A Political Artist in Revolutionary Times* for the 250th anniversary of Beethoven's birthday.

Alexis Landau is a Los Angeles-based author who focuses on historical fiction set during the twentieth century. She has written the novels *The Empire of the Senses* and most recently, *Those Who Are Saved*, the latter of which is inspired by the émigré community in L.A.

Kaltërina Latifi is a research fellow at the Centre for Anglo-German Cultural Relations at the Queen Mary University of London, and is an associate researcher at the University of Göttingen. She has published on the work of E.T.A. Hoffmann and August Wilhelm Schlegel's translation of Shakespeare's *Hamlet*. She is currently working on a book titled *The Aesthetics of the Fragment*.

Steven D. Lavine, after teaching literature at the University of Michigan and building international and intercultural programs at the Rockefeller Foundation, became President of the California Institute of the Arts in 1988. Shortly after stepping down at CalArts in 2017 he was appointed interim Founding Director of the Thomas Mann House and currently serves as Chair of its American Advisory Council.

Irmela von der Lühe is an author, editor, and professor emeritus in the Department of Philosophy and Humanities at Freie Universität Berlin. Her work focuses on modernist women writers, German-Jewish literature in the twentieth century, exile literature, and Holocaust literature. Her books on the life of Erika Mann are among the seminal publications on this topic.

Friedhelm Marx holds the chair of modern German literature at the University of Bamberg. His publications focus on modern and contemporary German-language literature, especially the work of Thomas Mann. He is currently working on how European the perspectives and visions of exiled European writers who fled to California from the Nazis changed in the face of U.S. political reality. In 2021, Marx was a Fellow at the Thomas Mann House in Los Angeles.

Heike Catherina Mertens is Executive Director of Villa Aurora and of Thomas Mann House and appointed Executive Director of the Alfried Krupp von Bohlen und Halbach Foundation, in Essen, Germany. She also founded Stadtkunstprojekte, a Berlin-based association for the promotion of urban public art.

Kalani Michell is assistant professor of European languages and transcultural studies at the University of California Los Angeles. She has published on a variety of art, film, and media topics, including installation art and 16mm film (in *Re-Animationen*), paintings in pornographic set design (in *CineAction*), performance art in computer games (in *kultuR-Revolution*), comics and filmic shot composition (in *Storyboarding*), and podcasts (in *Format Matters*).

Verena Mund is the coordinator of the research training group Configurations of Film at the Goethe University Frankfurt. She has published on the roles of women in the workforce by analyzing places of the everyday in visual culture, films, and texts. She is the author of the book *Bridge, Switchboard, Bar / Lunch Counter—Working Girls on Location*.

Lilian Pfaff is an architectural historian, critic, and lecturer of architecture at Otis College of Art and Design, California State Polytechnic University, Pomona, and Woodbury University. She has published extensively on architecture. Her most recent book is *J.R. Davidson: A European Contribution to California Modernism*. She is also a real estate agent for the brokerage firm at Suprstructur, which specializes in architecturally significant houses.

Andreas Platthaus is the head of the Literature and Literary Life Department at the German daily *Frankfurter Allgemeine Zeitung*. He has published on Alfred Herrhausen, Lyonel Feininger, and Walt Disney. In 2019, he was a Fellow at the Thomas Mann House, in Los Angeles. In his book *On the Palisades: An American Diary* (Rowohlt, 2020), Platthaus writes about his four-year experience living at the Mann home on San Remo Drive.

Donna Rifkind is a book critic and author. She has published reviews in the *Wall Street Journal* and the *Washington Post*. Her critically acclaimed book *The Sun and Her Stars: Salka Viertel and Hitler's Exiles in the Golden Age of Hollywood* tells the little-known story of the screenwriter Salka Viertel and was a National Jewish Book Award finalist.

Alex Ross has been the music critic for the *New Yorker* since 1996. His first book, *The Rest Is Noise: Listening to the Twentieth Century*, won a National Book Critics Circle Award and was a finalist for the Pulitzer Prize. His second book, *Listen to This*, is a collection of essays. His latest workbook is *Wagnerism: Art and Politics in the Shadow of Music*, an account of Richard Wagner's vast cultural impact. He has written often about Thomas Mann and the émigré community in Los Angeles for the *New Yorker*.

Martin Sauter received an M.A. with distinction from Bath University and a PhD from Warwick University. He is the author of the book *Liesl Frank and Charlotte Dieterle and the European Film Fund: Coming into Their Own—How Exile Changed the Traditional Role Assigned to Women*. In his book, Sauter draws attention to the role of women in exile and refugee organizations that sprang up as a result of Hitler's rise to power.

Friedel Schmoranzer studied German Philology and Sociology at the University of Konstanz (BA) and holds a Master in studies in editing from the FU Berlin. In 2011 she joined the team at Villa Aurora Los Angeles where she has served as Head of Fellowship Programs since 2020.

Stefan Schneider started his diplomatic career in 1987, and his many assignments have taken him all over the world. Before being posted to Los Angeles as consul general of the Federal Republic of Germany, he held various positions in a variety of different fields at the German Foreign Office and in Bangkok, Sofia, Miami, Paris, and Rome, as well as in Izmir, where he served as consul general. He is a lawyer and has studied French literature.

Friederike von Schwerin-High is a professor of German and chair of the Department of German and Russian at Pomona College. A former co-editor of the journal *Pacific Coast Philology,* her publications include work on Shakespeare reception, translation studies, narrative theory, blank verse, Lessing, Goethe, Thomas Mann, Christa Wolf, Jenny Erpenbeck, and on novels that act like biographies of friends.

Kai Sina holds a Lichtenberg Professorship for Modern German Literature and Comparative Studies at the University of Münster. He has published on literature of the open society in the modern age, as well as the work of Susan Sontag, Johann Wolfgang von Goethe, Ralph Waldo Emerson, and Walt Whitman, and on Thomas Mann's transatlantic understanding of democracy.

Diane Sippl is an arts and culture critic who writes and publishes articles on contemporary world cinema. In addition to lecturing in Southern California, she has served as a program advisor for the International Film Festival Mannheim-Heidelberg in Germany, as well as a festival planner, panelist, and jury member for the Locarno International Film Festival in Switzerland.

Michaela Ullmann is exile studies librarian and instruction coordinator in Special Collections at the University of Southern California. She oversees the Feuchtwanger Memorial Library, which houses over 30,000 volumes of rare books and the papers from exiled German-speaking intellectuals and artists.

Hans Rudolf Vaget is professor emeritus of German studies at Smith College. He is cofounder and former president of the Goethe Society of North America and one of the chief editors of the works, letters, and diaries of Thomas Mann. He has published widely on Goethe and Wagner, including a groundbreaking study of Mann's American years, *Thomas Mann, der Amerikaner. Leben und Werk im amerikanischen Exil, 1938–1952* (S. Fischer Verlag, 2001).

David Wallace is the author of nine books, several dealing with the golden age of Hollywood. The *New York Times* hailed *Lost Hollywood* as "(an) inspired concept," and *Capital of the World: A Portrait of New York City in the 1920s* as "compelling...(an) engaging recounting of the era." He is also the author of the book *Exiles in Hollywood.*

Lawrence Weschler, grandson of Ernst Toch, was a longtime staff writer at the *New Yorker* and is a widely published author, with over twenty books ranging from politics through the arts. His article "Paradise: The Southern California Idyll of Hitler's Cultural Exiles" is among the seminal publications on the exile community in L.A. and can be found at his website, www.lawrenceweschler.com."

Josh Widera thinks and writes about the city, theater, aesthetics and political philosophy. In 2021, he published his first book, *Sign and Return*, about the life and work of bicycle messengers. He is currently completing a PhD in Communication Studies at the USC Annenberg School of Communication.

BIBLIOGRAPHY

**PREFACE: THE MANN FAMILY
AND THEIR PATH TO CALIFORNIA**

Bahr, Erhard. *Weimar on the Pacific, German Exile Culture in Los Angeles and the Crisis of Modernism*. Berkeley: Univ. of California Press, 2007.

Boes, Tobias. *Thomas Mann's War*. Ithaca, NY: Cornell Univ. Press, 2019.

Flanner, Janet. "Goethe in Hollywood—1" and "…—2" *The New Yorker*. Dec 5, 1941 and Dec 12, 1941.

Hayman, Ronald. *Thomas Mann: A Biography*. New York: Scribner, 1995.

Heilbut, Anthony. *Exile in Paradise, German Refugee Artists and Intellectuals in America from the 1930s to the Present*. Berkeley: Univ. of California Press, 1983.

Lahme, Tilmann. *Die Manns: Die Geschichte einer Familie*. Frankfurt: S. Fischer Verlag, 2017.

Mann, Thomas. *Tagebücher 1933–1943*. Edited by Peter de Mendelssohn. Frankfurt: S. Fischer Verlag, 1977–1995.

——. *Tagebücher 1944–1955*. Edited by Inge Jens. Frankfurt: S. Fischer Verlag, 1977–1995.

Mann, Thomas, and Agnes E. Meyer. *Briefwechsel 1937–1955*. Edited by H.R. Vaget. Frankfurt: S. Fischer Verlag, 1992.

Prater, Donald. *Thomas Mann: A Life*. Oxford: Oxford Univ. Press, 1995.

Raulff, Ulrich, and Ellen Strittmatter. *Thomas Mann in Amerika*. Marbach am Neckar: Deutsche Schillergesellschaft, 2018.

Reich-Ranicki, Marcel. *Thomas Mann and His Family*. New York: HarperCollins, 1989.

Vaget, Hans Rudolf. *Thomas Mann, der Amerikamer*. Frankfurt: S. Fischer Verlag, 2011.

INTRODUCTION: THE THOMAS MANN HOUSE

Assman, Michael, ed. *Thomas Mann / Erich von Kahler. Briefwechsel 1931–1955*. Munich: Luchterhand, 1993.

Bright, William. *1500 California Place Names: Their Origin and Meaning, a revised version of 100 California Place Names by Erwin G. Gudde*. Berkeley: Univ. of California Press, 1998.

Detering, Heinrich. "Deutschland erwirbt das 'Weiße Haus des Exils.'" *Nordwest Zeitung*. Nov 19, 2016.

Loomis, Jan. *Pacific Palisades*. Mount Pleasant, S.C.: Arcadia Publishing, 2009.

Mann, Erika. *Mein Vater, der Zauberer*. Hamburg: Rowohlt, 1998.

Mann, Katia. Interview. *Los Angeles Times*, Dec 19, 1948.

Jens, Inge, and Peter de Mendelssohn, ed. *Thomas Mann, Tagebücher in zehn Bänden*. Frankfurt: S. Fischer Verlag, 1995.

Pfaff, Lilian. *J.R. Davidson—A Contribution to California Modernism*. Basel: Birkhäuser Verlag, 2019.

Vaget, Hans Rudolf. *Thomas Mann, der Amerikaner: Leben und Werk im amerikanischen Exil, 1938–1952*. Frankfurt: S. Fischer, 2011.

Vaget, Hans Rudolf, ed. *Thomas Mann / Agnes E. Meyer. Briefwechsel 1937–1955*. Frankfurt: S. Fischer Verlag, 1992.

Wefing, Heinrich. "We Are at Home Were the Desk Stands: Thomas Mann's Residence in Pacific Palisades." In *Building Paradise: Exile Architecture in California*, edited by Mechthild Borries. Berlin: Kreis der Freunde und Förderer der Villa Aurora e.V., 2004.

PART 1: THE MANNS AS PUBLIC INTELLECTUALS

Bitterli, Urs. *Golo Mann: Instanz und Außenseiter*. Munich: Kindler, 2004.

Boes, Tobias. *Thomas Mann's War. Literature, Politics, and the World Republic of Letters*. Cornell Univ. Press, 2019.

Coulson, Jonathan, Paul Roberts, and Isabelle Taylor. *University Planning and Architecture: The Search for Perfection*. London: Routledge, 2015.

Detering, Heinrich. *Thomas Manns amerikanische Religion*. Frankfurt: S. Fischer Verlag, 2012.

Dundjerski, Marina. *UCLA: The First Century*. Los Angeles: Third Millennium Pub. Ltd., 2011.

Green Renée. *Other Planes of There: Selected Writings*. Durham, N.C.: Duke Univ. Press, 2014.

Lahme, Tilman. G*olo Mann: Biographie*. Frankfurt: S. Fischer Verlag, 2009.

Mann, Erika. Edited by Irmela von der Lühe and Uwe Naumann. *Blitze überm Ozean. Aufsätze, Reden, Reportagen*. Hamburg: Rowohlt Taschenbuch Verlag, 2000, 2001.

——. *Briefe und Antworten*, vol I, ed. by A.Z. Prestel, dtv Verlagsgesellschaft, 1984.

Mann, Erika and Klaus Mann. *Rundherum*. Frankfurt: S. Fischer Verlag, 1929.

Mann, Klaus. *The Turning Point*. New York: L.B. Fischer, 1942.

Mann, Thomas. *The Coming Victory of Democracy*. New York: Alfred A. Knopf, 1938.

——. *Listen, Germany! Twenty-Five Radio Messages to the German People over BBC*. New York: Alfred A. Knopf, 1943.

——. "Speech at the Hollywood Peace Group." May 31, 1948.

——. *The Story of a Novel. The Genesis of Doctor Faustus*. New York: Alfred A. Knopf, 1961.

——. Edited by Peter de Mendelssohn. *Tagebücher 1933–1943*. Frankfurt: S. Fischer Verlag, 1977–1997.

——. Edited by Inge Jens. *Tagebücher 1944–1955*. 10 vols. Frankfurt: S. Fischer Verlag, 1986–*1989*.

Marcus, Kenneth. *Schoenberg and Hollywood Modernism*. Cambridge: Cambridge Univ. Press, 2015.

Mund, Verena. "Access." Presentation at the Annual Conference of the Graduiertenkolleg "Configurations of Film." Kloster Eberbach, Eltville, Jun 27, 2019.

Shriners International. Al Malaikah Shriners. "History of Shriners International." https://amshriners.com/history/.

Sonderling, Jacob. "The Jews Are Changing Their Music." *Los Angeles Times*, Oct 2, 1938.

——. "The Thomas Mann Controversy." *Aufbau*, Mar 2, 1945.

Spalek, John M. and Joseph Strelka. *Deutsche Exilliteratur seit 1933, Band I: Kalifornien*. Munich: Francke Verlag, 1976.

Stephan, Alexander. *Communazis: FBI Surveillance of German Émigré Writers*. New Haven, Conn.: Yale Univ. Press, 2000.

University of California. *War Relocation Authority Photographs of Japanese-American Evacuation and Resettlement. Online Archive of California*. Berkeley: Bancroft Library, May 29, 1945. http://www.oac.cdlib.org/ark:/13030/ft3w1004r0/?order=2&brand=oac4.

Vaget, Hans Rudolf. Th*omas Mann, der Amerikaner: Leben und Werk im amerikanischen Exil, 1938–1952*. Frankfurt: S. Fischer Verlag, 2011.

Valentin, Sonja. *Steiner in Hitlers Fenster: Thomas Manns Radiosendungen Deutsche Hörer! 1940–1945*. Göttingen, Germany: Wallstein Verlag, 2015.

Winston, Richard, and Clara Winston, trans. *Letters of Thomas Mann 1889–1955*. New York: Random House, 1975.

PART 2: THOUGHT & ACTION: REFUGEES, SUPPORTERS, AND THE NEW LEFT

Anders, Günther. *Der Emigrant*. Munich: C.H. Beck, 2021.

——. *Die Antiquiertheit des Menschen. Band I: Über die Seele im Zeitalter der zweiten industriellen Revolution*. Munich: C.H. Beck, 1956.

Arendt, Hannah. "We Refugees." *Menorah Journal*, vol. 31, no. 1, 1943: 69–77.

Bahr, Erhard: *Weimar on the Pacific: German Exile Culture in Los Angeles and the Crisis of Modernism*. Univ. of California Press, 2008.

Baum, Vicki. *It Was All Quite Different*. New York: Funk & Wagnalls, 1964.

Brecht, Bertolt. Edited and translated by Tom Kuhn and David Constantine. *The Collected Poems of Bertolt Brecht*. New York: Liveright, 2018.

Dell, R.E. "After Evian." *Manchester Guardian*, Jul 16, 1938.

Detering, Heinrich. *Thomas Manns amerikanische Religion*. Frankfurt: S. Fischer Verlag, 2012.

Horkheimer, Max, and Theodor W. Adorno. *Dialectic of Enlightenment*. Freiburg, Germany: Herder & Herder, 1972.

Jeffries, Stuart. *Grand Hotel Abyss: The Lives of the Frankfurt School*. New York: Verso, 2016.

Jenemann, David. *Adorno in America*. Minneapolis: Univ. of Minnesota Press, 2007.

Kellen, Kondrad. Edited by Manfred Flügge and Christian Ter-Nedden. *Mein Boss, der Zauberer: Thomas Mann's Sekretär erzählt*. Hamburg: Rowolht, 2011.

Kirchner, Sascha. *Der Bürger als Künstler: Bruno Frank (1887–1945)*. Düsseldorf: Grupello Verlag, 2008.

Kobal, John. *Marlene Dietrich*. London: Studio Vista; Dutton, 1968.

Lahme, Tilmann. *Die Manns: Geschichte einer Familie*. Frankfurt: S. Fischer Verlag, 2015.

Mann, Erika, and Klaus Mann. *Escape to Life: German Culture in Exile*. Boston: Houghton Mifflin Co., 1939.

Mann, Klaus. *The Turning Point*. Frankfurt: Büchergilde Gutenberg, 1976.

Mann, Thomas. *Doktor Faustus*. Frankfurt: S. Fischer Verlag, 1990.

Marcuse, Ludwig. "Philosophen auf Wanderschaft." *Aufbau*, Dec 12, 1944.

Nenik, Francis and Sebastian Stumpf. *Seven Palms. The Thomas Mann House in Pacific Palisades, Los Angeles*. Leipzig: Spector Books, 2021.

Palmier, J.M. *Weimar in Exile*. Paris: Payot, 1988.

Reich-Ranicki, Marcel. "Fragwürdige Figur mit etwas Seltenem: Format." *Frankfurter Allgemeine Zeitung*, Sep 13, 2007.

Sauter, Martin. *Liesl Frank, Charlotte Dieterle and the European Film Fund*. Berlin: Berlin Epubli, 2012.

Seghers, Anna. Margot Bettauer Dembo, trans. *Transit*. New York: New York Review Books, 2013.

Stern, Carola. *Die Sache, die man Liebe nennt das Leben der Fritzi Massary*. Berlin: Rowolht Berlin, 1998.

Subak, Susan Elisabeth. *Rescue and Flight: American Relief Workers Who Defied the Nazis*. Lincoln: Univ. of Nebraska Press, 2010.

Taylor, J.R. *Strangers in Paradise*. Frankfurt: Ullstein, 1987.

Vaget, Hans Rudolf. Th*omas Mann, der Amerikaner: Leben und Werk im amerikanischen Exil, 1938-1952*. Frankfurt: S. Fischer Verlag, 2011.

Wysling, H. *The Letters of Thomas and Heinrich Mann, 1900–1949*. Berkeley: Univ. of California Press, 1998.

PART 3: FILM IN EXILE IN HOLLYWOOD

Counter, Bill. "Westwood and Brentwood Theatres." Los Angeles Theatres Blogspot.

Dick, Bernhard. *City of Dreams: The Making and Remaking of Universal Pictures*. Lexington: Univ. of Kentucky Press, 1997.

Doherty, Thomas. *Hollywood and Hitler, 1933–1939*. New York: Columbia Univ. Press, 2013.

Eyman, Scott. *Ernst Lubitsch: Laughter in Paradise*. New York: Simon & Schuster, 2015.

Friedländer, Saul. *A City of Nets: A Portrait of Hollywood in the 1940s*. New York: HarperCollins, 1986.

Gomery, Douglas. *The Hollywood Studio System: A History*. London: BFI: Palgrave, 2019.

Gregor-Dellin, Martin ed. *Klaus Mann: Briefe und Antworten 1922–1944*. Hamburg: Rowohlt Verlag, 1991.

Horak, Jan-Christopher. *The Palm Trees Were Gently Swaying: German Refugees from Hitler in Hollywood. Image* 19802.

Jenemann, David. *Adorno in America*. Minneapolis: Univ. of Minnesota Press, 2007.

Jens, Inge, and Peter de Mendelssohn ed. *Thomas Mann, Tagebücher in zehn Bänden*. Frankfurt: S. Fischer Verlag, 1995.

Mann, Thomas. *"Gedenkrede auf Max Reinhardt."* Speech, New York, 1943.

Marx, Friedhelm. "Durchleuchtung der Probleme: Film und Photographie in Thomas Mann's Zauberberg,'" in *Thomas Mann Jahrbuch 22*. Frankfurt: Vittorio Klostermann Verlag, 2009.

Philips, Gene D. *Exiles in Hollywood: Major European Film Directors in America*. Bethlehem, Penn.: Lehigh Univ. Press, 1998.

Polgar, Alfred. "Fritzi Massary." In *Kleine Schriften,* vol. 6, *Theater II*. Hamburg: 1986.

Rifkind, Donna. *The Sun and Her Stars: Salka Viertel and Hitler's Exiles in the Golden Age of Hollywood*. New York: Other Press, 2021.

Schneidereit, Otto. *Fritzi Massary: Versuch eines Porträts,* Berlin: VEB Lied der Zeit Musikverlag, 1970.

Stern, Carola. *Die Sache, die man Liebe nennt das Leben der Fritzi Massary*. Berlin: Rowohlt Berlin, 2001.

Tucholsky, Kurt. "Massary." In *Gesamtausgabe Texte Und Briefe 1907-1913*, vol. 1. Edited by Bärbel Boldt, Dirk Grathoff, and Michael Hepp. Hamburg: Rowohlt, 1997.

Vaget, Hans Rudolf. *Thomas Mann, der Amerikamer*. Frankfurt: S. Fischer Verlag, 2011.

Wallace, David, *Exiles in Hollywood*. Lanham, Md.: Limelight Editions, 2006.

PART 4: LOS ANGELES'S LITERARY RADIANCE

Bahr, Erhard. *Weimar on the Pacific: German Exile Culture in Los Angeles and the Crisis of Modernism*. Berkeley: Univ. of California Press, 2008.

Baum, Vicki. *It Was All Quite Different*. New York: Funk & Wagnalls, 1964.

Boes, Tobias, *Thomas Mann's War: Literature, Politics, and the World Republic of Letters*. Ithaca, N.Y.: Cornell Univ. Press, 2019

Feuchtwanger, Lion. Edited by Tyson Gaskill, Friedel Schmoranzer-Johnson, Marje Schuetze Coburn, and Michaela Ullmann. *A Festschrift for Lion Feuchtwanger. Excerpts from his 60th Birthday Book*. Los Angeles: Univ. of Southern California Libraries; Villa Aurora, 2014.

——. Letter dated Aug 6, 1951. In *Lion Feuchtwanger. Briefwechsel mit Freunden,* vol. 1, edited by Harold von Hofe. Berlin: Aufbau Verlag 1991.

——. *Moskau 1937.* Berlin: Aufbau Verlag, 1937.

Feuchtwanger, Marta. *An émigré life oral history transcript: Munich, Berlin, Sanary, Pacific Palisades.* By Lawrence Weschler. Los Angeles: Oral History Program, Univ. of California, Los Angeles, 1976.

Feuchtwanger Memorial Library. "Marta Feuchtwanger Papers." Collection. Special Collections, Univ. of Southern California Library, Los Angeles.

Fittko, Lisa. *Escape Through the Pyrenees.* Evanston, Ill.: *Northwestern Univ. Press, 1991*

Flügge, Manfred. *Die vier Leben der Marta Feuchtwanger.* Berlin: Aufbau Verlag, 2009.

Heilbut, Anthony. *Exiled in Paradise: German Refugee Artists and Intellectuals in America from the 1930s to the Present.* Berkeley: Univ. of California Press, 2018.

Heusler, Andreas. *Lion Feuchtwanger. Münchner-Emigrant-Weltbürger.* Salzburg: Residenz Verlag, 2014.

Horowitz, Joseph. *Artists in Exile: How Refugees from Twentieth-Century War and Revolution Transformed the American Performing Arts.* New York: Harper Perennial, 2008.

Isherwood, Christopher. *Christopher Isherwood Diaries 1939–1960.* New York: HarperCollins, 1997.

Krispyn, Egbert, *Anti-Nazi Writers in Exile*, The Univ. of Georgia Press, Athens 1978

Mann, Erika, and Klaus Mann. *Escape to Life.* Boston: Houghton Mifflin Co., 1939.

Mann, Thomas, and Alfred Neumann. *Briefwechsel.* Berlin: Verlag Lambert Schneider, 1977.

——. "Freund Feuchtwanger." In *Lion Feuchtwanger zum 70. Geburtstag. Worte seiner Freunde.* Berlin: Aufbau Verlag, 1954.

——. *Tagebücher 1937–1939.* Frankfurt: S. Fischer Verlag, 1979.

——. Edited by Inge Jens. *Tagebücher 1944–1.4.1946.* Frankfurt: S. Fischer Verlag, 1988.

——. Edited by Inge Jens. *Tagebücher 1949–1950.* Frankfurt: S. Fischer Verlag, 2003.

——. Thomas Mann to Ludwig Hardt, Deutsches Exilarchiv 1933–1945 der Deutschen Nationalbibliothek,

Thomas Mann to Ludwig Hardt, Pacific Palisades, April 10, 1944, German Exile Archive 1933-1945 of the German National Library, EB autograph 844, on permanent loan from the Adolf and Luisa Haeuser Foundation for the Preservation of Art and Culture."

——. Thomas Mann to Otto Basler, Sep 23, 1946. In *Briefe II, 1937–1947,* edited by Erika Mann. Frankfurt: S. Fischer Verlag, 1962.

——. "Für Alfred Neumann." In *Gesammelte Werke.* Frankfurt: S. Fischer Verlag, 1990.

Mann, Thomas, and Alfred Neumann. *Briefwechsel.* Berlin: Verlag Lambert Schneider, 1977.

Skierka, Volker. *Lion Feuchtwanger. Eine Biographie.* Berlin: Aufbau Verlag, 1984.

Sontag, Susan. "Pilgrimage: Tea with Thomas Mann." *The New Yorker.* Dec 21, 1987.

Stern, Guy. *Literature and Culture in Exile—Collected Essays on the German-Speaking Emigration after 1933.* Dresden, Munich: Dresden Univ. Press, 1998

Tóibín, Colm, *The Magician.* New York: Scribner, 2021.

Vaget, Hans Rudolf. *Thomas Mann, der Amerikamer.* Frankfurt: S. Fischer Verlag, 2011.

Vaget, Hans Rudolf, Thomas Mann and Agnes Meyer (edited by Vaget) *Thomas Mann/Agnes E. Meyer: Briefwechsel 1937–1955*. Frankfurt: S. Fischer Verlag, 1992.

PART 5: THE BEGINNINGS OF A NEW MUSIC

Adorno, Theodor W. *Philosophie der neuen Musik*. Berlin: Suhrkamp Verlag, 1978.

Adorno, Theodor W., and Thomas Mann. *Briefwechsel. 1943–1955*. Berlin: Suhrkamp Verlag, 2002.

Bahr, Erhard. *Weimar on the Pacific: German Exile Culture in Los Angeles and the Crisis of Modernism*. Berkeley: Univ. of California Press, 2008.

Betz, Albrecht. *Hanns Eisler Political Musician*. Cambridge: Cambridge Univ. Press, 1982.

Eckert, Nora. *Von der Oper zum Musiktheater: Wegbereiter und Regisseure*. Leipzig: Henschel Verlag in E.A. Seemann Henschel GmbH & Co, 1995.

Eisler, Hanns. *Gespräche mit Hans Bunge. Fragen Sie mehr über Brecht*. Leipzig: VEB Deutscher Verlag für Musik, 1975.

Follet, Diane. "Redeeming Alma: The Songs of Alma Mahler." *College Music Symposium,* vol. 44, 2004.

Haste, Cate. *Passionate Spirit: The Life of Alma Mahler*. New York: Basic Books, 2019.

Hilmes, Oliver. *Malevolent Muse: The Life of Alma Mahler*. Lebanon, N.H.: Northeastern Univ. Press, 2015.

Horowitz, Joseph. *Artists in Exile: How Refugees from Twentieth-Century War and Revolution Transformed the American Performing Arts*. New York: Harper Perennial, 2008.

Joseph, Charles M. *Stravinsky Inside Out*. New Haven: Yale Univ. Press, 2001.

Keathley, Elizabeth L. and Marilyn L. McCoy, ed. *Schoenberg's Correspondence with Alma Mahler*. Oxford: Oxford Univ. Press, 2019.

Kinderman, William. "Exploring the 'Temple of Initiation' on Thomas Mann's *Magic Mountain:* Wagnerian Affinities and 'Politically Suspect' Music." *Monatshefte,* vol. 109, no. 3, Fall 2017.

Kippenberger, Susanne. "Affentheater, Mozart, Kanonendonner." *Die Zeit,* vol. 41, 1988.

Koopman, Helmut, and Alfred Kröner Verlag, ed. "Doktor Faustus." In *Thomas-Mann-Handbuch*. Stuttgart: J.B. Metzler Verlag, 2001.

Mann, Thomas. *Doctor Faustus: The Life of the German Composer Adrian Leverkühn, as told by a Friend*. New York: Alfred A. Knopf, 1948.

——. *The Story of a Novel: The Genesis of Doctor Faustus*. New York: Alfred A. Knopf, 1961.

Monson, Karen. *Alma Mahler: Muse to Genius*. Boston: Houghton Mifflin Co., 791983.

Ross, Alex. *The Rest is Noise. Listening to the Twentieth Century*. London: Picador, 2007.

Schallert, Edwin. "Klemperer Acclaimed; New Philharmonic Orchestra Conductor Receives Ovation on Opening Night of Season." *Los Angeles Times*, Oct 21, 1933.

Schoenberg, Arnold. *Drei Satiren für Gemischten Chor. Op. 28*. Universal-Edition, 1926.

Schoenberg, E. Randol, ed. *The Doctor Faustus Dossier: Arnold Schoenberg, Thomas Mann, and Their Contemporaries, 1930–1951*. Berkeley: Univ. of California Press, 2018.

PART 6: LEISURE UNDER THE PALM TREES

"Hollywood Bowl History." Hollywood Bowl. Los Angeles Philharmonic Assoc., n.d. https://www.hollywoodbowl.com/about/the-bowl/hollywood-bowl-history.

Lesser, J. "Of Thomas Mann's Renunciation, pt. II." *Germanic Review: Literature, Culture, Theory*, vol. 26, no. 1, 1951.

Schenderlein, Anne C. "The Enemy Alien Classification, 1941–1944." *Germany on Their Minds: German Jewish Refugees in the United States and Their Relationship with Germany, 1938–1988*. New York: Berghahn Books, 2020.

PART 7: A CITY IN TRANSITION

Bahr, Erhard. *Weimar on the Pacific*. Berkeley: Univ. of California Press, 2008.

Boes, Tobias. *Thomas Mann's War*. Ithaca, N.Y.: Cornell Univ. Press, 2019.

Davis, Mike. *City of Quartz: Excavating the Future in Los Angeles*. London: Verso, 1990.

Herrick, Jessica. "Home Front: California During World War II." California State Archives, Sacramento. Digital Exhibition, 2017.

Jens, Inge, and Peter de Mendelssohn, ed. *Thomas Mann, Tagebücher in zehn Bänden*. Frankfurt: S. Fischer Verlag, 1995.

Klein, Norman. *The History of Forgetting: Los Angeles and the Erasure of Memory*. London: Verso, 1997.

Lunenfeld, Peter. *City at the Edge of Forever: Los Angeles Reimagined*. New York: Viking, 2020.

Mann, Thomas. *Das Eisenbahnunglück*. Frankfurt: S. Fischer Verlag, 1907.

McCoy, Esther. *The Second Generation*. Salt Lake City: Gibbs Smith, 1984.

Meares, Hadley. "How the Aviation Industry Shaped Los Angeles." Web log. *Curbed LA* (blog). Vox Media, Jul 8, 2019.

Parlow, Matthew J. "Unintended Consequences: Eminent Domain and Affordable Housing." *Santa Clara Law Review*, vol. 46, no. 4. 2006.

Parson, Don. "Los Angeles' Headline-Happy Public Housing War." *Southern California Quarterly* 65, no. 3, 1983.

Rothstein, Richard. "Race and Public Housing: Revisiting the Federal Role." EPI. Economic Policy Institute, Dec 17, 2012.

Schafer, Mike, and Joe Welsh. *Classic American Streamliners*. Osceola, Wisc.: MBI Publishing, 1997.

IMAGE CREDITS

All illustrations in TMLA are by Jon Stich, copyright © 2022. The photographs and ephemera are credited as follows:

Thomas Mann's Los Angeles: Stories from Exile 1940–1952
By Nikolai Blaumer and Benno Herz
Copyright © 2022 Nikolai Blaumer and Benno Herz

Design by Amy Inouye, Future Studio
Illustrations by Jon Stich © 2022 Jon Stich
All rights reserved

10 9 8 7 6 5 4 3 2 1

ISBN-13 978-1-62640-112-9

Library of Congress Cataloging-in-Publication Data is available.

Published by Angel City Press
www.angelcitypress.com

Printed in Canada

Thomas Mann House

The Manns as
Public Intellectuals

Thought and Action
Refugees, Supporters, and the New Left

Film Exile in Hollywood

Beginnings of a New Music

Leisure Under Palm Trees

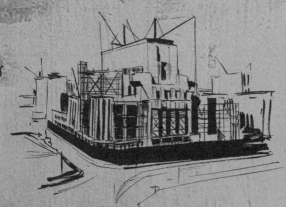

L.A.'s Literary Radiance

A City in Transition

Alfred Doblin

Alfred Neumann

Susan Sontag

Ludwig Hardt

Bruno Walter

Swiss Chalet

Theodor Adorno

Upton Sinclair House

Los Angeles Beaches

Union Station

Ernst Toch

Christopher Isherwood

Hanns Eisler